Democracy in Practice

'This book provides a balanced assessment of the various forms of democracy and the arguments for and against them. It will be valuable for students seeking a comprehensive and readable introduction to the theory and practice of democracy.'

Professor Ian Budge, *University of Essex*

This textbook provides students with a detailed look at many different aspects of democracy in practice. It is unique in clearly describing and analysing all three existing models of democracy: participatory democracy; referenda and initiatives; and representative or liberal democracy. Using numerous real-life examples from all over the world, this text explores how each is used in practice and provides discussion of the main problems with each model. It also examines the strengths and weaknesses of the main electoral systems. The book concludes by considering the merits of the three models of democracy and looks at how the level of democratic control can be increased in the future.

Two themes run through the book: the diversity of democratic practice; and the extent to which people have power over decisions that affect their lives. The challenge for democracy in the twenty-first century is not how democracy is achieved but which decisions are taken democratically and which groups of people participate.

Helena Catt is Senior Lecturer in Political Studies at the University of Auckland.

Democracy in Practice

Helena Catt

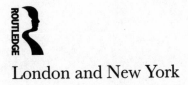

London and New York

First published 1999
by Routledge
11 New Fetter Lane, London EC4P 4EE

Simultaneously published in the USA and Canada
by Routledge
29 West 35th Street, New York, NY 10001

Typeset in Baskerville by RefineCatch Limited, Bungay, Suffolk
Printed and bound in Great Britain by
MPG Books Ltd., Bodmin, Cornwall

British Library Cataloguing in Publication Data
A catalogue record for this book is available from the British Library

Library of Congress Cataloguing in Publication Data
A catalogue record for this book has been requested

ISBN 0–415–16839–2 (hbk)
ISBN 0–415–16840–6 (pbk)

Contents

List of tables

Introduction

In its widest sense 'democracy' is interpreted as 'rule by the people' but this definition gives no indication of how to put the idea into practice. This book looks in detail at different aspects of democratic practice with the emphasis upon real procedures facilitating consideration of decision making in a wider context than national government. Using real examples, the different interpretations of 'rule by the people' are discussed to assess the extent to which people have power under different structures and in local groups, as well as in international organisations and national governments. Elected parliaments are covered along with referenda and consensual discussion: representative, direct and participatory democracy.

The first chapter provides a survey of the theoretical literature on democracy, covering the centrality of the ideas of individual autonomy and equality and the impossibility of achieving both simultaneously. It discusses the difference between democracy as a theoretical ideal and democracy as a set of decision-making procedures while emphasising that, in theory and practice, there is no single definition of democracy once you move beyond 'rule by the people'. It introduces the two themes that run through the book: the diversity of 'democracy in practice' as different groups of people have adopted specific mechanisms to fit their particular needs; and the need to question the extent to which the people have power over decisions that affect their lives. The chapter also outlines the three main types of democratic procedure that provide the focus of Chapters 3–6: participatory, direct (referendums); and representative.

The second chapter addresses the central democratic problem of how to determine which of several options a group of people prefers. This problem relates both to the people of a country electing a parliament and to a committee deciding upon a policy or how to allocate a budget surplus. Given that democracy is about a group of individuals making a decision for the collectivity, it is important to consider the procedures that may be used. The first part of the chapter describes and assesses systems designed to select one option such as plurality voting, Condorcet and approval voting. Then procedures aimed at selecting more than one option, such as single transferable vote (STV) and party lists, are described and discussed. For both, fully worked examples are provided to show the different results from the range of procedures. Finally, some of the mechanisms that have been used to ensure minority rights within a decision-making process are considered, such as the use of quotas, qualified majorities and veto. Thus, the chapter provides a (non-mathematically-dense) description of voting systems with a discussion of the debates about the desirability of majority rule and the real consequences of emphasising majority rule or minority rights.

In Chapter 3 participatory democracy is put under scrutiny. Participatory democracy refers to situations when all members of the group discuss every aspect of each decision and agree on a solution for the group. This process is used by workers' co-operatives, New England town meetings and Green parties amongst others. The first part of the chapter describes the participatory democracy processes used by a number of different groups, giving real examples. From these examples are drawn the conditions that are necessary for participatory democracy to work well and the inherent problems. The final part of the chapter discusses the extent to which the people have power when using participatory democracy.

Direct democracy is the subject of Chapter 4. While referendums are the most common form of direct democracy, this chapter also looks at other examples such as an AGM policy vote. Again the chapter starts by describing the different ways in which a direct vote is used, concentrating upon who can trigger a vote and make the final decision. The second part of the chapter considers some of the criticisms of direct democracy and seeks to determine the extent to which people have power when using these procedures.

Representative or liberal democracy is the most common form of democracy and so covers two chapters. The basic idea of representative democracy is that a few are elected to make decisions for the whole. So there are two crucial parts: the election of representatives and decision making by the representatives. The whole idea of representation is considered in Chapter 5. The different ways in which we may be represented are discussed, covering delegates who do as instructed and trustees who form a body of decision makers aiming to make good decisions. Ideas of a politics of presence, and concerns about the number of MPs who are women and from ethnic minorities, are also covered. Throughout, the impact of institutional structures such as the electoral system and form of government are discussed.

Representatives come together to form a decision-making body, a parliament, so the way in which this group operates is an important aspect of democracy in practice. Chapter 6 looks at the role of elected representatives in the policy process and assesses the extent to which representative democracy gives power to the people. In making this assessment the different players in the policy process, such as the executive, bureaucrats and pressure groups, are described along with the different parts of the process from agenda setting to the final decision. The impact of the Westminster and Madisonian systems are also covered to show how institutional arrangements affect the practice of democracy. Finally ideas of representation are tied into the discussion of the work of MPs in the policy process.

The diversity of democratic practice is one theme of the book, and Chapter 7 provides a conclusion for this discussion by asking if all variations of democracy are equally democratic. A number of schema have been produced that aim to specify a threshold for democracy, to measure the extent of democracy and to identify democratic weaknesses in existing democracies. The three types of schema are described, and problems inherent in trying to measure the extent of democracy are illustrated and discussed. The chapter concludes with a discussion of the feasibility of trying to measure democracy across participatory and direct, as well as representative, democracy.

Chapter 8 considers current areas of change in democratic practice, for instance due to developments in telecommunications and in ideas about where decisions are made. One question that is central to ideas about the future of democracy is that of which people should be included in the group making a decision. A number of current views on this subject, such as monetarism and Agenda 21, are considered. The second section examines the main factors that impede the members of a group from having full control of decisions and some of the new methods that are being used to extend popular control. The discussion pulls together ideas and themes from the earlier chapters to discuss the issues of the size of the group and the needs for experts.

1 What do we mean by democracy?

Across every continent democracy is desired but there is little agreement on exactly how to achieve it. Each country has its own set of procedures, each claiming to be democratic but based on a distinctive mix of beliefs about what is important for democracy, what is feasible and what is acceptable to the population. Looking at other groups, such as community organisations, workers' co-operatives and pressure groups, shows an even wider range of democratic practice. What all groups have in common is a need to make decisions on certain matters that affect all members, and what democratic groups share is a desire to make these decisions in a way that allows every member to participate in the decision. Democracy is now widely seen as the best method to use for national government. However, this dominance is less than a century old. The growing acceptance of democracy came with changing views on what it entailed, new suggestions about the appropriate worth and treatment of people and evolving social structures. Many strands are important to the development of democratic theory. Ideas about individuals as equal autonomous beings and the proper role of the government fuelled debate about the best way to run a country and make decisions. Changing social patterns relating to the ownership of land and wealth, industrialisation and the weakening power of elites such as the church and heredi-tary aristocracy meant that new methods had to be found. Ever-growing popula-tions and advances in communications added to the perceived need for changes in state structures. Within all aspects of democratic practice, theoretical and func-tional factors are interconnected. Most of this book examines the ways in which people have tried to practice democracy, but to do this it is important to first understand the ideas that led to the near universal acceptance of democracy as the ideal method of decision making.

Lincoln declared a commitment to 'government of the people, by the people, for the people' and so summed up what most people would recognise as demo-cracy. In linguistic terms 'democracy' is derived from the greek *demokratia* that can be broken down into *demos* meaning the people and *kratos* meaning rule. Although the translation of democracy as 'rule by the people' implies decision making, viewing democracy primarily in this way covers only some of the mean-ings often assigned to the word. As part of the widespread desire for democracy it is often used as a blanket term of approval for life in the West in relation to both institutions and cultural norms. Democracy is also used to mean a set of rights or an entire way of organising the political and economic life of a state. Concentrating upon democracy as a procedure that can be used by members of a group to reach a collective decision provides a focus for the study of democratic practice. It is easier to consider the procedures that are specified for decision making than to look at the details of a particular decision. The concentration upon institutions rather than behaviour allows for comparison across a wide range of democratic groups. However, behaviour is not totally excluded as the way in which groups actually manage to use the set procedures is an important component of the assessment of the extent of power that the people gain under the different manifestations of democracy. The next section in this chapter looks at the main aspects of theoretical debate relating to democracy. Later sections introduce ideas about why there is diversity in putting democracy into practice, and outline the rest of the book.

The fact that a nation, or any other group, needs a procedure for making collective decisions highlights the problem that a nation is both a collection of the people who live in a geographical area and an entity in itself. The idea of 'the people' as an entity is stronger in 'continental' democratic theory, deriving primarily from Rousseau's writings. In the Anglo-American tradition the entity is seen as an aggregation of individuals' views while in continental thought the entity that is 'the people' has a will of its own. So the entity, as aggregate or unit, makes decisions concerning each individual within the collectivity. For example, the government of Sweden decides how the Swedish people will receive health care and in Switzerland all the people voted to revise legislation on sickness insurance. In each case a decision is made that concerns all the people who live in the country. However, because a nation contains a great number of diverse individuals there will be a range of views that must be taken into consideration when making decisions. Obviously some issues, such as abortion, are more controversial than others, such as house-building standards. Nevertheless, on any given issue there are likely to be different groups of people with conflicting ideas about the best solution. So the decision-making process must be able to deal with conflict but produce results that all will accept. If the people whose ideas were rejected do not accept the legitimacy of the final decision then they may not follow it and thus the structure of the state will be weakened. In reaching a decision some people will not get what they wanted, which again emphasises the group aspect of democracy. So democracy is at the centre of politics because it looks at ways to deal with power conflicts in society. Problems relating to the ways in which a group can make decisions that are accepted by all are discussed in Chapter 2.

Recognition of conflicting views about what the people need is not new but the idea that the people rather than an elite should decide what to do is. Democracy contrasts with rule by a particular group, for instance aristocracy where a privileged class rule, or gynocracy (rule by women), or gerontocracy (old men), or plutocracy (the wealthy), or stratocracy (the military). In the past a monarch or aristocracy or other elite had power over decisions and such an arrangement was seen as legitimate. For instance, Plato argued for intelligent guardians while King

James of England and Scotland claimed his legitimacy came through God in the form of 'the Divine Right of Kings'. In England, France and other feudal European countries, there were assemblies who advised the monarch, but they were made up of an elite based upon hereditary title or land or the church hierarchy. During the years when absolutist rule became the norm, in the seventeenth century, such assemblies mostly disappeared. In this respect the English parliament was an exception to the general trend. In the twentieth century there have been numerous examples of individuals as leaders of their country, based most often on hereditary title (for instance Emperor Hirohito of Japan pre-1945, King Saud of Saudi Arabia) or military strength (for instance General Franco in Spain, General Abacha in Nigeria). Only very recently has democracy replaced rule by one person or an elite as the norm for a country.

In the nineteenth century to be called a 'democrat' was not taken as a compliment, but in the late twentieth century 'democracy' is a desired label, seen as conferring respectability. Democracy was the rallying call of the Allies against dictatorship in the two World Wars. In 1945 the victors ensured that the defeated Axis powers adopted democratic institutions. More recently, the USA has given aid to countries in the former communist bloc to assist with democracy. East Germany received funds to help the merger with West Germany and money given to Russia in 1991 and 1992 was tied to the elections of those years. Ideas of democracy as a good idea slowly emerged from the mid-seventeenth century, gaining momentum in the American and French Revolutions (1776 and 1787 respectively). Many different strands of thought were important in the gradual change from elite to popular rule as the favoured situation. Reformation Protestantism provided egalitarian arguments and examples of resisting traditional hierarchies (Arblaster 1987: 26). Lockean ideas about individual rights and the need for consent added another important element. Hence the importance of the American Revolution cry of 'no taxation without representation'. Ideas of individual rights, autonomy and equality are central to theoretical arguments about democracy.

There are other methods of reaching decisions that affect a group of people that are used in certain situations. In the 1980s the use of the market was advocated by many political leaders in the West and whole areas of decision making were moved from the domain of democratic government to the workings of the market, most notably aspects of welfare provision such as education and health. Lottery or random selection is also favoured for certain types of decisions, in particular if there is no rational or acceptable way to choose between the options. Conscription to the US army during the Vietnam War is a good example of the lottery in use. In this case there was no evidence that particular young men should be chosen ahead of others and all those who wished to join up had done so. The armed forces did not need all young men so they randomly selected certain dates and all with that birthday were required to enlist. With no established criteria by which to choose individuals, leaving the selection to luck is less divisive than other forms of decision making. The market, random selection, dictatorship and elite rule are all practical methods for making decisions that affect a group and could be chosen instead of democracy.

Theoretical justifications of democracy

In most theoretical writings, democracy is not valued in itself but because it provides other desirable ends. Central to the arguments for democracy and its gradual acceptance are the basic ideas of equality and individual liberty and what these concepts entail. However, both of these central ideas can be interpreted in a variety of ways and the exact nuances that are stressed affect the type of democracy that is seen as justifiable. Another problem is that individual liberty can be restricted by the implementation of equality and can also hinder equality. The ways in which tensions between the key ideas of equality and liberty are dealt with are at the centre of arguments for different types of democratic procedures. Before looking at the problems inherent in trying to use democracy to achieve liberty and equality each concept will be considered individually.

Equality is most often taken to mean that all are the same in some important respect. At the most basic we share a common humanity. However, there are and have been other ideas about what it is that is shared: citizenship; the ability to decide what is best for oneself; a capacity for rational thought; an economic stake in the country; the ability to defend one's country. The idea that all are equal is so commonplace now that few would pause to consider it, but in past centuries the belief in natural hierarchies was just as instinctive. Judaism and particularly the ideas in Protestantism whereby all are seen as equal before God was important in spreading the idea of equality as sameness. The radical group within the Parliamentarian Army known as the Levellers during the 1640s English Civil War argued for an equal say for all men because all are equal before God. The American Declaration of Independence (1776) follows the same line of argument, proclaiming that one self-evident truth is that 'all men are created equal'. However, who exactly was included within the category of 'men' and should therefore be treated equally varied. The Levellers did not include women, children or live-in servants (Wootton 1992: 75) and the Americans excluded women, children and slaves.

When all individuals are seen as equal it follows that no person is deemed to be any better or any worse than any other person. That is, all should be seen as the same as far as rights and treatment are concerned. Given this understanding of equality as treating people in the same way, two important ideas follow for the democratic making of decisions. First, if each person's view deserves equal respect and is seen as being as valid as the next, then no person should be deciding for another. Therefore, all need a say in decisions, so they need collective self-government. Second, if people should be treated in the same way then the system must be impartial in its operation. In terms of democracy this means that all must have the same chance to participate in the process. The need for self-government and equal access are seen as vital components of democracy by those who aim at achieving political equality.

In each age, the right to equal treatment has been applied to those who are deemed to be of equal status rather than to all people. In other words people who possess the key aspect(s) deemed to be shared are allowed into the democratic decision-making club. In Athens the vital characteristics were based on sex, land, age and Athenian ancestry; in nineteenth-century Britain it was sex, age and property; in present-day USA it is age and citizenship. Arguments for an extended franchise have largely been based on claims to equal rights because there is no relevant difference between those who can vote and those who think they should be allowed to. So Wollstencroft admonished women to see themselves as human beings rather than women and all that it implied (Lively and Lively 1994: 132), and in the Putney Debates one of the Levellers argued that as God gave all men reason they should all have a say in government, whether they were poor or rich (ibid.: 123). As Beetham says, the fight for an equal suffrage was to prove that all had an ability to be responsible and make decisions concerning one's life and to share the responsibility of decisions for the whole community. These capabilities were found equally in all adults and did not relate to class or gender or income or ethnicity (Beetham 1993b: 59). So it is equal ability to participate in self-governance that is important.

Equalising the franchise assumes that an equal right to take part, in this case vote, is sufficient to give impartial treatment. But some theorists on the Left ask if the crucial aspect is that all are treated in the same way or that all have an equal capacity to take part? Equal ability to participate can be interpreted as giving everyone a vote or as ensuring that inequalities in social or economic life do not affect the ability to be equal in political life. Wollstoncraft and J.S. Mill were early advocates of the need for equality between men and women in the economic and social as well as political spheres for democracy to function (Held 1987: 99). Writers on the Left argue that people who feel inferior in their income and job are not able to participate equally in the political arena with those who have more money or status (Arblaster 1987: 79; Mendus 1992: 209). In Held's advocacy of autonomy he stresses the need for equal conditions that he explains as meaning an equal access to the minimum resources needed to participate (1987: 293). Feminists argue that gender equality does not exist in modern society and therefore this is a challenge to the perception that democracy exists. Some take this argument to mean that democracy is not possible while others argue that the situation can change to recognise differences and so save democracy (Mendus 1992: 213–15). If differences rather than sameness are to be recognised then unequal treatment is called for to produce a situation of equal influence. For example, the provision of 'readers' so that the illiterate can 'read' campaign literature and the ballot paper; or the provision of childcare facilities so that parents can attend meetings.

Democratic decision making as a means of obtaining self-governance to fulfil the ideal that no person should be deciding for another is an important strand of argument in justifications for democracy. Dunn describes the enduring idea of democracy as each person being able to speak for themselves and taking a part in collective decisions (1992: 265). When all have a say in decisions this means that each person's views will be heard and respected. Here again there is a difference between the Anglo-American and continental traditions with the latter placing greater emphasis on self-government, because of its belief in the group as an entity. Rousseau saw the people as sovereign and the social contract as creating the opportunity for self-government (Held 1987: 74–75). So the people together make decisions that the government enacts as their agent.

The other strand to the argument of self-government is that all decisions should be made only after each person has had the opportunity to express their view. Only if the decision is made by all is it legitimate. In other words, why should I obey a new law when I had no part in the process that led to that decision? Of course, if I chose not to take part but had the opportunity to do so then I should accept the legitimacy of the decision. Again the ability to take part in the democratic process is an important step in attaining equality. So the arguments relating to access and the need to alleviate them are relevant to equality as self-government too. Even if all have the same access to the democratic procedures there are other conditions that need to be met, such as the availability of information. Therefore equal rights to disseminate and receive information on conflicting views are seen as a vital part of democracy. A free media plus freedom of information, association and belief are all necessary for equal participation and self-governance. The extent to which the people are informed on issues and their ability to understand them is a common theme in discussion of the success of democracy in practice.

Aristotle and Plato both listed equality as central to the Athenian idea of democracy (Held 1987: 15, 29). Modern writers agree on the importance of equality: Fishkin lists it as one of three prerequisites (1991: ch. 4); Dahl says that democracy presupposes equality (1989: ch. 22). But there is a problem of which comes first. Is democracy needed to ensure that people who are equal are treated in the same way or does the state need to ensure that people are equal in their ability to make use of democracy? While an assumption of equality between individuals within the group implies the need for democratic decision making for some writers (on the Left) the fact that the individuals are not equally able to participate necessitates intervention to create equality. Despite the centrality of equality in arguments for democracy, equality is not universally accepted as a desirable aim. Even for those who accept arguments for equality, some give a higher priority to individual liberty.

In the classic views on what was good and bad about the three types of government (monarchy, aristocracy, democracy) the 'good' aspect of democracy is liberty. Freedom, the oft-used synonym for liberty, is seen by many as central to, if not a defining part of, democracy. Farrar says that this was what marked out citizens from others in Athens (1992: 18). For J.S. Mill, democracy was the only way to ensure that individual liberties were not infringed in an arbitrary manner (Held 1987: 85). The traditional liberal ideas of individual freedom were important in the resurgence of interest in democracy in the eighteenth and nineteenth centuries. In resisting hierarchy and insisting on individual autonomy, writers such as Locke paved the way for later arguments for democracy, although he was not an advocate. More recent writers in the New Right tradition, such as Hayek and Nozick, place emphasis totally on liberty and see the only role of the state as being to safeguard the institutions that regulate the interaction of autonomous individuals (ibid.: 245).

Liberty has just as many connotations as equality and they, again, affect expectations of democracy. Miller (1991: 2–4) distinguishes three sets of ideas about
liberty: republican, liberal and idealist. In the republican view, a person is free if
they are part of a free (that is self-governing) political community. For liberals,
individuals who can do as they want without facing constraint are free. To an
idealist, autonomy is important and so are 'authentic' desires, so that a person is
free if they follow their real wants. Another, often discussed, distinction is between
negative and positive liberty. In the former the individual is free from external
constraints: the state cannot stop me eating chocolate. This idea fits with Miller's
liberal group of ideas on freedom. Positive liberty is most commonly interpreted
as meaning that individuals have the capacity to do as they want: I have money
and there is a chocolate shop nearby and open. Miller adds to this interpretation
of positive liberty the ideas of rational self-direction and control of the social
environment, in other words the republican and idealist ideas on liberty (ibid.: 10).
Running through the different interpretations of liberty is the idea of an individual deciding how to live and being able to do so without hindrance from
others.

A series of individuals living life as they wish is the central image encapsulated
in modern ideas of liberty, but when talking of democracy we are interested in
group activity. It is the ways in which the freedom of the individual interacts with
the existence of a collective group that tie liberty to democracy. One aspect of
liberty common to the different interpretations is that individuals have free choice
and should decide what is best for themselves. Therefore, democracy as self-rule is
again stressed. The other important aspect of liberty as it relates to democracy is
the need to be free from constraint, including obstacles imposed by the government. So liberty focuses attention upon the process of collective decision making
and the issues where collective decisions should be made: the institutions and
scope of the state. Despite being about the individual, liberty is concerned with
democracy primarily because of ideas about the appropriate role of the state.

Each person is the best judge of what they want, so, as was the case with
equality, self-determination is important in justifications of democracy based on a
desire for individual liberty. But self-rule does not mean that each person does as
they want because that does not imply any type of rule and does not take account
of the social context. Rather, within a group, each person should be part of the
government process that sets out rules for the group. It is the decision-making
process rather than the outcome which is of interest, so that it is better to choose
for yourself an option with a bad outcome than have a good one imposed upon
you. In ensuring that each person can take part in decision making this means that
individuals are in a position to protect both their personal interests and their
ability to live life as they want.

However, the group will, of necessity, make decisions based on the views of the
majority, so some within the group may have their interests challenged. This
ability of the majority to subjugate a minority and thus place constraints in the
way of their life choices has worried many writers from Madison to Nozick.
However, Harrison (1993: 168) argues that being in the minority and thus forced

by the collective decision to do other than what you wanted does not mean that your liberty has been lost. Rather, the fact that you had a chance to express your view and influence the decision is sufficient for ideas of self-determination. Here the distinction between freedom as an ability to express a choice and freedom as the satisfying of desires is important. When you can take part in the decision making then you can express a choice about the best outcome, but the views of others may mean that the final decision results in you not being able to do as you wanted. As individuals do not live in isolation there is a need to ensure that what one person wants to do does not arbitrarily infringe on the freedom of others. To police such rules a state is needed but the perceived role of the state varies greatly in different writings on liberty. For some liberal theorists such as Hobbes and Hayek the only acceptable function of the state is to ensure individuals do not constrain each other's choices. However, if the state is to interfere, even in this limited way, then it must do so in a fair and impartial way, which is generally taken to mean that there should be known rules to stop arbitrary action. If the state has any other functions apart from the enforcing of rules that govern individuals' interaction then liberty is in danger. Hence the state should have a minimal role. For Nozick there is no such thing as a collective entity so the only possible role for the state is to police the way in which individuals interact as autonomous beings. However, because of arguments of self-determination, the reluctantly accepted state should make decisions in a democratic manner.

In contrast, government, and therefore the possibility of democracy, is necessary for the republican view of liberty because of its stress on individual freedom within a free community. For Plato and Rousseau the state is needed to carry out the wishes of the people so the state is an agent for the collective will of the group. Again the differences between 'the people' as an aggregate of individuals or an entity is central to the argument. When it is positive rather than negative freedom that is the focus of attention then the state also has a substantial role. If constraint on free choice is taken to include economic inequality then the state is in a position to remove such obstacles and thus increase liberty. Contrary to the liberals' reluctant acceptance of what they see as a potentially dangerous state, writers wanting positive freedoms see a vital role for the state in the achievement of liberty. The arguments here are similar to those, discussed above, surrounding equality, what should be equal and whether intervention is needed.

Ideas of liberty relate to democracy primarily through views on the state. Some interpretations of liberty stress the need for self-government to protect individual wants while others concentrate on the importance of minimal constraints. At one extreme, liberal thinkers see no or little place for democracy because they do not believe in a collective community and see the sole role of the state as policing individuals' interactions. At the other extreme are those who follow the positive freedom interpretation and therefore see an interventionist role for the state. As with ideas on what equality entails, the varied nuances of the idea of liberty impact upon versions of democracy.

Individuals are seen to be free to make choices about their lives but within a social setting where they have to interact with others. Individuals have liberty but in a group context they also have equality. It is this mix of individual rights and being an equal participant in a decision-making collectivity that causes many of the tensions between liberty and equality. For instance, a system that stresses equality will make decisions based on the views of the majority and so may act against the freedom of those in the minority. The majority may vote to ban the use of mobile phones in restaurants despite the desire of a minority to use them. This dilemma of reconciling majority rule with minority rights is discussed at length in Chapter 2. When equality of access is desired then liberty may again be sacrificed. For instance if uneven income is deemed to be a problem in terms of equal access then the state may tax the rich and redistribute the proceeds to the poor, thus infringing the liberty of the rich to use their money as they wish.

At the other extreme, if liberty is given dominance then the state will not be in a position to rectify social or economic inequalities, and thus will not be able to address issues of equality of opportunity, discussed above. Stressing individual liberty may mean that no collective decisions can be made because there is no way to reconcile conflicting individual desires. In some situations and groups the tension will be minimal but in others it may be central. Mansbridge (1980) distinguishes between unitary and adversary situations: the former when there is general agreement anyway, and the latter when there is a major divide in views. It is the latter where there is a need to strike a balance between liberty and equality. In the French Revolution both liberty and equality were part of the battle cry. For some writers, such as Aristotle, J.S. Mill and Bentham, equality and liberty are interconnected so that one cannot be contemplated or achieved without the other (Held 1987: 20, 60). However, for other writers, such as Hayek, the two are inherently conflictual for the reasons outlined above. Aristotle saw the links and the tensions and recognised that the different aspects of liberty are pivotal. To the extent that liberty means taking part in ruling then equality is vital, but when liberty means doing what you want then the democratic majority may infringe upon the liberty of the individual (ibid.: 20). Different interpretations of equality do not have the same impact on relations between the two concepts.

Arguments based upon a desire for liberty and equality stress the need for self-determination but for different reasons. How self-rule is to be achieved marks the major division between different models of democracy. At one extreme is the idea of self-government whereby the people make all decisions relevant to the group (nation). Decision making that involves all in the group is seen in workers' co-operatives and is commonly called participatory democracy. At the other extreme is the idea that the people consent to be ruled by the rulers who they periodically choose. This is the common view of democracy in that most see democracy as all having the right to vote in periodic elections. This model is the common form of elected government and is known as liberal or representative democracy. In between are different shades of involvement and control such as deciding the general laws and policy or keeping the rulers accountable (Lively 1975: 30). Of particular prevalence is the practice of allowing the population to vote on an important issue in a referendum, the key form of direct democracy. As a general rule those who start from a desire for equality favour procedures on the self-government end while those who stress the protection of individual liberty tend towards the idea of people ruling by choosing leaders.

Democracy is simultaneously a set of theoretical ideas and a process that people try to implement. Just as theorists argue over the aims and details of democracy, there is equivalent variety in democratic practice. As suggested above there are three clear models of democracy: participatory, direct and representative (see Table 1.1). In participatory democracy the people rule by collectively discussing what issues need to be debated and talking about possible solutions until they agree on the best solution or option for the group. Direct democracy again involves all of the people in deciding individual issues but this time they vote on specific questions that are posed for them, most commonly in a referendum. Representative democracy, the most familiar form, entails the election of an elite who are given the task of making decisions for the people. While some writers use these three terms in slightly different ways, each is used in its broadest sense here. Within each of the models there is variation in the ways that different groups have implemented the basic pattern and these are discussed in some detail in later chapters. What all examples have in common is a desire to allow the people in the group to be self-governing in a way that ensures equality of influence for the members in making the decisions that affect the group. The choice of democratic model depends upon theoretical considerations of the balance between equality and individual liberty but also upon practical considerations related to the way in which each set of procedures works.

In implementing democratic ideas there is a tension between utopia and reality. Some aspects of the way in which democracy is put into practice are defended for reasons of functionality rather than as part of democratic theory. So alongside the justifications based upon ideas of achieving equality and liberty are ones that stress practical problems and the needs of society. In studying democracy in practice these other factors, and the tensions between them, need to be considered alongside the theoretical ideals that the procedures seek to attain. Democratic procedures have evolved to fit the historical and cultural circumstances in each place. Historically the size and composition of the group plus perceptions of the complexity of decisions in relation to the intellectual ability of the population have had a major impact on the way that democratic processes have been created. The particular combination of ideas and practical situation in place when the procedures are set up play a crucial role in the choices that are made. A small, homogeneous group of well-informed people with a strong belief in equality will

Table 1.1 Models of democracy

Model	Description
Participatory democracy	All discuss every aspect of each decision and agree on a solution for the group
Direct democracy	All vote for or against a set question
Representative or liberal democracy	A few are elected to make decisions for the group

choose a different set of democratic procedures from a large group of diverse people with a strong belief in equality.

Dahl (1989: ch. 15) describes the change of scale from city state to nation as being very important in shaping modern practices of democracy. The use of elected representatives instead of having all people meeting together was seen largely as a reaction to the reality of large populations. The Levellers wanted representatives because it was a workable way to choose rulers, and in America the framers of the constitution argued for representatives because of the geo-graphic and population size of the states (Wood 1992). The French also faced the same debate during their revolution, having to reconcile a desire for rule by assemblies of the people and the reality of a large population (Fontanna 1992). J.S. Mill accepted the same line of argument, heralding representation as the greatest modern invention because it made democracy feasible. The size of the group is an issue in each model of democracy. The composition of the group also has major implications for the form of democracy that is used. A homogeneous group will not have to deal with situations of deep conflict but a group that is deeply divided must have a way of reaching decisions that are acceptable to all. So countries with minority groups and a desire to protect individuals are likely to incorporate a Bill of Rights into their institutional set-up and thus restrict the scope of democratic decisions. Likewise countries such as Belgium which have a strong language divide introduce systems, known as consociationalism, that ensure no group can be suppressed by others. The choice of proportional repre-sentation electoral systems is also related to the composition of the people and a desire to allow distinct groups to have a say. Recognition of distinct groups within the collectivity that needs to make decisions is an important part of debates about the best form of democratic practice.

The complexity of life in the late twentieth century is seen by some writers as another major change in the reality of politics that necessitates a reappraisal of the practical aspects of democracy. Dahl asks if policy choices have become too complex for most people to understand, because if they have done so then asking the mass of voters to make an informed decision is unrealistic (1989: ch. 23). Schumpeter, Michels and Weber argue for rule by elites who understand the issues due to their education or expertise (Held 1987: 143–80). Only strong leaders, they argue, can cope with the scale and complexity of decisions in a modern state. Such views were influenced by early empirical studies of voting behaviour which showed that voters were generally not interested in politics, tended to be ill-informed on most issues and voted for reasons other than rational appraisal of policy platforms (for instance Lazarsfeld *et al.* 1948). So some models of demo-cracy are motivated by perceptions of the needs of society in a given country rather than on new interpretations of liberty or equality.

Historically 'democracy' has been discussed as both an ideal state and a prac-tical form of governance. The divide between theory and practice is not always clear as many writers who are now thought of as democratic theorists were, at the time they published, participating in real debates about the implementation of democracy. For instance, the *Federalist* papers, written by Madison and Hamilton, were part of the political debate over the ratification of the American Constitution. Hobbes and Locke were active in British politics and wished to influence their political world, while J.S. Mill was an elected MP. Some theories of democracy are prescriptive, suggesting how democracy should operate, while others are descriptive, cataloguing the way in which a recognised democracy operates. Others aim to suggest modifications to existing systems to correct a perceived defect between theory and practice. From the ratification of the American Constitution a modern democratic state came into being and so writers had a real example to discuss, whereas prior to that they were debating concepts or the ancient Athenian case. With the ability to watch and analyse democratic practice, thinking on democracy has become empirical as well as theoretical. For instance Schumpeter, prompted by the experiences of the spread of communism and the popular support for dictators in various parts of Europe, was concerned about what the masses could do if given power, and so suggested that limited popular control was desirable. Likewise pluralists took as a starting point the contention that the state was overloaded being involved in too many complex decisions and thus threatening the extent of democratic control. The practice of democracy changes due to new ideas about democracy and developments in political life. Simultaneously theories of democracy evolve in the light of experiences of democratic practice. So theory and practice continually change and affect each other. Hence the multiplicity of models of democracy in both theory and practice. Dahl (1989) argues that democracy is an unattainable ideal so to assess the procedures that are used in various countries we need to be able to decide when the practice is near enough to the ideal to be acceptable. The seemingly simple concept of 'rule by the people' can be interpreted in a multitude of ways.

Ideas of democracy are usually associated with government, whether at the local or national level. However, democracy is a procedure that can be used wherever a group of people needs to make decisions. Some theorists do not recognise the idea of a group as an entity, seeing only a series of individuals. However, there are many self-identified and constituted groups within society who do make decisions that relate to their members. Held (1987: 277) argues that as politics is about power relations then it is found wherever there are groups and is not confined to one type of activity. Therefore if democracy is desirable for government then it should also apply to all areas that matter to people. The workplace, in particular, is identified by writers on the Left as a place where many decisions affecting the lives of people are made and therefore a prime place for democracy. The need for democracy to spread into international decision-making bodies is also being increasingly discussed as such organisations become both more numerous and more powerful. Arguments about the areas in which democracy is desirable and how it could be achieved are discussed in Chapter 8. Democratic processes are used all the way from street committees to the Security Council of the United Nations. In between is a vast range of organisations that do, or could, use democratic methods. There is wide debate about the effectiveness of the democratic procedures that are used in some bodies, but the important point is that ideas of democracy pertain to a far wider range of bodies than just national governments. Many people will participate in democratic decisions at a local level and outside of government more often than they will vote in elections for their representative in the legislature. The following survey provides examples of how the three types of democracy are used by different groups at a local, national and international level (see Table 1.2). Note that 'the people' is specific to each context. So for the European Union Council of Ministers, the group of people that needs to make a decision comprises a minister from each country. Likewise in elections to a school board 'the people' are the parents of children at the school and in decisions for a Green Party Conference 'the people' are all members of the party. Later chapters will include further examples as the different types of democracy are explored in depth.

The central theme of the book is that there is great diversity in the ways in which the three models of democracy are put into practice. Running alongside is the key question of the extent to which different democratic practices give power to the people. To attempt to answer this question the whole concept of power over decisions has to be considered in more detail. Any decision is in fact a series of decisions and thus the extent of people power in each part is important. In any decision there are three parts: what is the question; what are the possible answers; and which answer will be chosen (see Table 1.3). Often the final part of the process receives the most attention but if the people cannot set the agenda or suggest alternative options then they only have partial power over the decisions that affects their life. The other important component for democracy is that the decision reached by the group is then implemented. The first three parts concern

Table 1.2 Examples of the three models of democracy

	Participatory	*Direct*	*Representative*
Description	The people discuss options then agree on a decision	The people vote on options presented to them	The people choose representatives to make the decisions for them
Local example	Workers co-operative	Local sports club voting on policy	Election of school boards
National example	Green Party conference	Referendum e.g. in Switzerland or Italy	Election of MPs or President
International example		EU Council of Ministers	Election of Members of European Parliament

Table 1.3 Component parts of a collective decision

Setting the agenda	– What is the question?
Debate	– What are the possible answers?
Choice	– Which answer is preferrred by 'the people'?
Implementation	– Putting the chosen solution into practice

Table 1.4 What does 'rule by the people' mean?

Key questions	Supplementary questions	Examples of practical implications	Chapter
Who are 'the people'?	Which group should make any given decision?	Who should be involved in local decisions? What makes someone an expert on a particular issue?	8 plus bits in 3 and 4
What do the people rule?	When is democracy the best way to make decisions?	Can democracy be used in the workplace or home? Should democracy be used in local planning matters, in the provision of health services, in determining UN policy on refugees?	8 plus bits in 3 and 4
How do we know what the collectivity wants?	How can a group of individuals have a united view?	How to aggregate the views of many people. Balancing minority and majority rule	2
How do the people rule?	Does rule mean involvement in all aspects of a decision? (participatory democracy)	How can all be involved? Are all able and willing to participate?	3
	Does rule mean giving a view on each policy option? (direct democracy)	How can all have a say? Who sets the questions?	4
	Does rule mean choosing representatives to make the decisions? (representative democracy)	How can people be represented? How can a representative be made accountable? How does the group of representatives make decisions?	5
			6
Does democracy exist?	To what extent do democratic processes deliver power to the people?	Is there a checklist of things we can use to measure democracy? Can we say that one set of procedures is more democratic than another?	7

procedure to the extent that different models and set-ups allow for varying levels of popular involvement at each stage. The implementation stage has more to do with the practice of the group and will vary from decision to decision within one group to a greater extent than do the other three components.

In looking at the way in which different procedures are created to allow a group of people to make a collective decision where all have an equal say there are a number of key questions that emerge from the theoretical literature and these form the structure of the book (see Table 1.4). First is the problem of which collective group of people are being talked about, both which groups should have a say on any given issue but also how this can effectively happen when the group is large or the issue technical and complex. These issues are addressed in Chapters 3 and 4 as part of the discussion of each model of democracy, and also in Chapter 8, which addresses the extent to which the people can have power over different types of decisions. The other framing question is which decisions are to be made democratically, which refers both to which types of groups and to which types of decisions. These questions are covered in the discussion of the different models. Having determined which group of people is to make the decision and the types of issues they are to look at then there are a number of questions about the way in which those democratic decisions are reached. Given that the group is a collection of individuals there must be a way to determine what the group as a whole prefers and there are a number of mechanisms that are used to find this, as discussed in Chapter 2. This process relates only to the choice component of the decision but there are wider questions of how the group is to set the agenda, debate options and make the choice. The answers to these questions form the basis of the three models of democracy: participatory, direct and representative. Each of these is covered in depth in a separate chapter. Finally, the overriding question is the extent to which these different practical permutations of democracy actually deliver the theoretical ideas of all having an equal say in self-governance. Questions of the extent to which it is possible to compare different manifestations of democracy are covered in Chapter 7. The aim of the book is to describe the different ways in which groups make democratic decisions, to understand why the different processes are used and to discuss the issues related to the different models.

2 How can a group make collective decisions?

The people are to rule, according to democratic theory, but how do we know what they want? Democracy is used by people who need to make decisions that concern them as a group. So 'the people' may mean 'all citizens of USA' or it may mean 'government representatives at the International Whaling Commission', or even 'members of the Alice Springs Autumn Fair Organising Committee'. However the group is created it contains a number of individuals who must reach a collective decision. Having identified the group of individuals, the big problem is how they are to agree on a collective choice. In choosing the preferred options for the group there will be differences of opinion between individuals but the group as a whole must reach a decision. If all are to have a say, a part in ruling, then each voice must have equal weight. Were a group in society to have their views count for more than other groups then it would be an oligarchy masquerading as democracy. As democracy is about choice democratic decision making involves people expressing a preference for one option over the others and the final decision reflecting those preferences. So, for the people to rule they must all have their preferences weighed equally when a final decision is made. The big question then is how to determine the opinion of the group as a whole. This chapter will consider the different ways that are used to reach a collective decision. The first section looks at methods of aggregating votes when one option must be chosen and so covers different ideas about ascertaining which option is the favourite. The second section considers the ways in which a group can select a number of options, for instance electing three representatives. The last section considers the question of individual or group rights, particularly when they are in the minority, and looks at processes such as the veto and qualified majority that are used to stop the tyranny of the majority.

Choosing a single option

In most policy decisions a single option must be chosen. For instance those living in a British electorate must choose an MP; a school board of trustees must decide how it wants to spend a budget surplus. Likewise a government may have to decide on the appropriate sentence for aggravated robbery or the UN on which proposed 'solution' for a war-torn country should be followed. In each case there are a number of options but agreement needs to be reached on the one that will be followed. The basic question is: how to decide which option the people who make up the group prefer? Each individual has a view but how should these be aggregated so that we know the collective will? In some forms of democracy the aim is to have long discussion until the option agreeable to all is found (see Chapter 3), but in most decision making situations a vote will be taken as the best way to find the winner. As with many aspects of democracy in practice, there is no simple answer because there is no universally accepted method of counting votes and determining the option that is most preferred. The different methods are based on diverse ideas about what makes a winner and how much information is needed about the preferences of the group members.

Details of six ways to determine which option is preferred by the group as a whole will be discussed in this section. Using an example will make this process much easier to follow so we will imagine a parliament that has to decide among four schemes for providing students with money on which to live (see Table 2.1). The decision-making method that many people instinctively use is for each to vote for their favourite and the option backed by the most people wins. This is called a plurality or simple-majority result. For the sake of argument, there are 150 people in our parliament, 50 of whom want full state-funding, 40 want a graduate tax and the same number want a commercially run loan scheme with the remaining 20 favouring a state-run low-interest loan scheme. So in a plurality vote the state-funding is seen as the group's favourite because it got the most votes. This is the way in which many decisions are made including which candidate will represent the constituency (become MP or congressperson, etc.) in Britain, Canada, India and the USA. When this process is used for electing a representative it is commonly called the first-past-the-post (FPP) system. The plurality system is criticised by many writers because it can pick a winner that most people did not want. For instance in our example, while 50 people wanted state-funding, 100 people preferred another option, so only a third of those involved backed the winning option. The second major criticism is that plurality voting only asks about which option is preferred and not how the other options are viewed.

The most common way to meet these criticisms is to use a process that ensures that the winning option is preferred by over half of the people, that is the majority. Although in FPP elections, the winner is often described as having a majority, of for instance 2,000 votes, this is not an accurate use of the term. Strictly speaking a majority means more than half, while having more votes than all others but less than half is a plurality. So in looking at voting systems talk of a majority always means when a candidate or option wins over half of the votes cast. To be able to find the majority winner, we need to know which option would be the second and

Table 2.1 Parliamentary voting example – plurality

	Full state funding	*Low-interest loans*	*Commercial loans*	*Graduate tax*
Votes	50	20	40	40

third choices of each person. In looking at different ways of aggregating the views of a group of people it is assumed that everyone can put the options in a rank order. For instance, the 50 people in our example who favoured full state funding see low-interest loans as the next best option, followed by having a graduate tax, and commercial loans is their worst option (see first row of values in Table 2.2). Likewise, the 20 people in the Rural Party (see third row of values) think graduate tax is the best option and state funding the worst, in between they prefer commercial loans to low-interest state-run ones.

Given ranked information, or a preference ordering for each person, then it is possible to find the option that over half of the group like (see Table 2.3). First, everyone votes for their favourite, exactly the same as in the plurality system, and if one option receives half the votes it wins. In our example, state-funding has the most votes but 50 is less than the 76 needed for a majority. So the least popular option, low-interest loans, is removed from the contest and everyone votes again. Most groups can still vote for their favourite option but the Liberals have to move to their second option, which is commercial loans, so those 20 votes are added and commercial loans now has 60 votes. Still no option has half of the votes so the

Table 2.2 Parliamentary voting example – full preferences of 150 members

	Full state funding	Low-interest loans	Commercial loans	Graduate tax
Socialists 50 people	1st	2nd	4th	3rd
Christian Democrats 40 people	4th	3rd	1st	2nd
Rural Party 20 people	4th	3rd	2nd	1st
Greens 20 people	4th	2nd	3rd	1st
Liberals 20 people	4th	1st	2nd	3rd

Table 2.3 Parliamentary voting example – majoritarian

	Full state funding	Low-interest loans	Commercial loans	Graduate tax
1st vote/preference	50	20	40	40
Transfer	50	cut, to commercial loans	60	40
2nd transfer	50	–	100	out, to commercial loans
		winner – commercial loans		

option now with the fewest votes, graduate tax, is eliminated and everyone votes again for one of the two remaining options: full state-funding or commercial loans. Both the Greens and the Rural Party wanted a graduate tax so they have to go with their next preference. The Rural Party's second preference is commercial loans so they vote for that option, but for the Greens, their second preference of low-interest loans has been eliminated so they go to their third preference, commercial loans. So in the final round the full state funding has 50 votes from the Socialists and commercial loans has the backing of all other groups and with 100 votes is the winner. If those making the decision are all in one place then a series of votes can be taken in this way, and it is commonly called an exhaustive ballot.

However, for the election of candidates it is usually not possible to have all voters in one place so a paper version is used. Preference voting (PV), also known as the alternative vote (AV), asks voters to rank the candidates or options by writing '1' next to their favourite, '2' next to the second favourite and so on across the options. First, each 1st preference is counted, just like a plurality vote, and if one option has the backing of half the people then it wins. If no option has majority backing then the option with the fewest votes is eliminated and those ballot papers re-allocated according to the second preference. Again, if one candidate has half the votes they win, if not the lowest-polling candidate is eliminated and those ballot papers re-allocated to the next preference. This process continues until one candidate or option has half of the votes cast. This paper majoritarian system is used in Australia to elect members of parliament. In France the same general idea is used with each person voting for their favourite on the first Sunday of elections and if no candidate gets half the votes then the people vote amongst the most popular candidates the following week. This system is also used, through a series of votes, in both the USA Senate and House of Representatives to elect the 'majority leader'. Trade unions tend to use this system too. In Britain, in the past, votes were commonly taken at a meeting so a series of votes was used, but now they must, by law, be conducted by post so the preferential system is used. All of these systems aim to find an option that is backed by over half of those in the group, but recognises that for some this will be enthusiastic support and for others lukewarm backing of the 'lesser of two evils'.

The fact that some people have their second or third preferences considered but others do not is seen by some as a defect of the majoritarian method. For instance, in the parliament example, the Socialists and Christian Democrats only expressed a first preference while the Greens were down to their third preference. Related to this is another set of criticisms based on the idea that the 'winner' is everyone's second best rather than many people's favourite option. In our example, 40 people saw the winning option of commercial loans as the best and for another 40 it was their second preference. This distinction between one large group's favourite and the majority's second best is central to the plurality-versus-majoritarian debate.

In a committee situation, another common method of making decisions is to vote for or against a series of options. Normal standing orders for committees in the UK and the USA state that a meeting can only look at proposals one at a time.

If there are a number of proposals relating to the decision, as in the parliament spending decision example being used here, the decision may be divided into general and specific parts. In our example the four options could be grouped into two general categories of loans versus government schemes (full funding and graduate tax). The first stage of the vote would pit these two groupings (see Table 2.4) and in the example loans lose. Now the more specific options within the winning category of 'government schemes' are pitted against each other and the graduate tax beats full funding by 100 votes to 50. When several amendments to a resolution have been tabled then they must also be taken in order and again each is accepted or rejected.

This resolution-acceptance or binary method has been criticised because it does not allow people to compare different options. For instance, in the decisions illustrated in Table 2.4 the members of parliament are not asked to compare the graduate tax option with either of the two loan schemes. It is also possible for the person chairing the meeting to affect the outcome due to the way in which options are grouped or the order in which votes are taken. For instance, if the first vote was on whether or not to have a graduate tax (see Table 2.5) then it loses with 40 to 110 votes. The next step is to vote yes or no on loans and loans wins 100 to 50. Finally the vote is between the two types of loans and the low-interest one wins over the commercial loans. There are other possible ways of ordering the vote, each perfectly logical, but each leading to a different 'winner'.

Another set of counting procedures addresses the argument about not using all the information about voting preferences, and not pitting each option against the

Table 2.4 Parliamentary voting example – resolution process: loans versus others

	Commercial loans	Low-interest loans	Full state funding	Graduate tax
General round	loan – 60		government schemes –	90
Loans loses, so specific round	–	–	50	100
		winner – graduate tax		

Table 2.5 Parliamentary voting example – resolution process: graduate tax versus others

	Graduate tax	Commercial loans	Low-interest loans	Full state funding
General round	40	other options – 110		
Tax loses so specific round 1 – loans versus funding		loans – 100		50
Funding loses so specific round 2 – type of loans		60	90	
		winner – low-interest loans		

others. Borda, Condorcet and Approval voting, the other three ways in which to determine which of several options the group prefers, are less frequently used. However, most academics who study voting systems prefer them. McLean (1987) and Merrill (1988) both use Condorcet as a criterion to assess systems and Black (1958: 66) proposes it be used. Both the Borda count and the Condorcet idea of a winner involve looking at the full preference listing of each person, that means that all of the information given in Table 2.2 for our example would be used.

Using the Borda count, which was invented by Borda then rediscovered by Lewis Carroll, each person gives each option a number of points. The worst option gets zero points and the favourite option gets one less point than the total number of options. In our example there are four options so the favoured one gets three points. So each of the Greens would give three points to graduate tax, two points to low-interest loans, one point to commercial loans and zero points to full funding. The total number of points given to each option are then added and the winner is the one with the most points, in our example this is graduate tax (see Table 2.6). So again this is a method that looks for the option that has the widest backing, even if at a low preference. Few groups use this method for decision making but it is common in choosing teams or individuals for sporting honours in the USA. The main problem with this system is that it would be easy for a group of voters to change the results through strategic point allocation (see below).

Count Condorcet, whilst imprisoned during the French Revolution, came up with the method of aggregating votes that bears his name. As with the Borda count, information about the full preference lists is used. In this process each option is compared with each other option to see which one wins against all of the others. For instance, pitting low-interest loans against graduate tax, the Socialists and Liberals prefer low-interest loans to a tax, and for the other parties the reverse is true so graduate tax wins by 80 votes to 70 (see Table 2.7). However, low-interest loans wins when pitted against full state funding as only the Socialists prefer full funding to low-interest loans. When each option has been pitted against each other it is possible to see if one option wins against all others. In our example the idea of a graduate tax beats each other option and the idea of full state

Table 2.6 Parliamentary voting example – Borda count

	Fund state funding	Low-interest loans	Commercial loans	Graduate tax
Socialists	$50 \times 3 = 150$	$50 \times 2 = 100$	$50 \times 0 = 0$	$50 \times 1 = 50$
Christian Democrats	$40 \times 0 = 0$	$40 \times 1 = 40$	$40 \times 3 = 120$	$40 \times 2 = 80$
Rural Party	$20 \times 0 = 0$	$20 \times 1 = 20$	$20 \times 2 = 40$	$20 \times 3 = 60$
Greens	$20 \times 0 = 0$	$20 \times 2 = 40$	$20 \times 1 = 20$	$20 \times 3 = 60$
Liberals	$20 \times 0 = 0$	$20 \times 3 = 60$	$20 \times 2 = 40$	$20 \times 1 = 20$
Total	150	260	220	270

winner – graduate tax

Table 2.7 Parliamentary voting example – Condorcet count

State funding vs low-interest loans		State funding vs commercial loans		State funding vs graduate tax	
50	100	50	100	50	100
		Low-interest loans vs commercial loans		Low-interest loans vs graduate tax	
		90	60	70	80
				Commercial loans vs graduate tax	
				60	90

Number of times each option wins	State funding	Low-interest loans	Commercial loans	Graduate tax
	0	2	1	3

winner – graduate tax

funding loses to each other option. Note that the option that loses the Condorcet count was the one that won in the plurality vote, a common situation and another argument against using plurality. The Condorcet system aims to give maximum satisfaction to a majority as compared to Borda, which aims to give the greatest overall satisfaction to all who are voting. Again there is this subtle but fundamental difference between ideas of what is the option that collectively the group likes best.

The major problem with using Condorcet in a practical sense is that there is not always a Condorcet winner (see McLean, 1987: 162–64). It is quite possible that no option beats all of the others. For instance, if the Rural Party changed their ordering so that commercial loans was their first preference and graduate tax their second then commercial loans would beat graduate tax in a Condorcet contest. So the final score would be state funding zero, low-interest loans two, commercial loans two and graduate tax two, giving no Condorcet winner. However, if a body recognised the possibility of no Condorcet winner and chose a method to use in that particular circumstance then the system would be feasible for decision making. Another reason for this process not being used more widely seems to be mechanical. If a large number of people are voting then the counting of the result would take a long time if done manually. The increasing use of computers may encourage more organisations to utilise this form of voting when one option has to be chosen from many.

In approval voting each person marks as many options as they like and the option with the highest number of approval marks wins. A voter may mark approval of just one option or all or some of the options. Members of the UN Security Council use this method to choose the Secretary General of the UN. Several professional associations in the USA use approval voting, for instance the Institute of Electrical and Electronics Engineers (Brams and Nagel 1991). An alternative, and possibly a more psychologically satisfying one, is to score out all disliked options and the winner is the one that has been scored out the fewest times. Voters who were given a choice between candidates in former communist countries were, in effect, working this system. It is not easy to illustrate this system using the parliament example because we cannot tell if an option seen as 'worst' is in fact approved of or not and, likewise, some voters may disapprove of all but one option but can still rank them according to a scale of relative disapproval. However, making some assumptions about how far down their preference order their 'approval' goes we can simulate a possible approval vote (see Table 2.8). In this case the Christian Democrats and Liberals approve of their first, second and third preferences while the Socialists and the Rural Party will only vote for their first two options and the Greens just their first option. Here the low-interest loans win with a score of 110, mostly because they had a low, but still approving, score from the Socialists and Christian Democrats. As with alternative vote, an option that is accepted but not a strong favourite wins. One criticism of approval voting is that each voter can cast a different number of votes.

Using these different voting methods, the parliament in our example could have chosen each of the four options (see Table 2.9). Clearly, there are alternatives in the ways that the views of individuals in a group can be aggregated and each is based on a different idea of how the 'favourite' is determined and they can reach different conclusions. Unfortunately, academics have not been able to unanimously declare one system better than all others. In fact, theoretical work has

Table 2.8 Parliamentary voting example – approval voting

	Full state funding	Low-interest loans	Commercial loans	Graduate tax
Socialists	50	50	0	0
Christian Democrats	0	40	40	40
Rural Party	0	0	20	20
Greens	0	0	0	20
Liberals	0	20	20	20
Total	50	110	80	100
	winner – low-interest loans			

Note: Voting assumes Christian Democrats and Liberals approve of preferences 1, 2 and 3; Socialists and Rural Party approve of preferences 1 and 2; Greens approve of preference 1

Table 2.9 Parliamentary voting example – winner in each system

System	Winner
plurality	state funding
majoritarian	commercial loans
committee – resolution	graduate tax or low-interest loans
Borda	graduate tax
Condorcet	graduate tax
Approval	low-interest loans

shown that it is impossible to have a perfect system (see McLean 1987: ch. 8 for one of the easier-to-follow explanations).

In particular, any system can be manipulated by strategically minded voters. What this means is that a voter can alter the result by casting their vote in an order other than their preferred rank order. For instance, voting for your second preference rather than your first preference because you think that this will produce a less-bad result, for instance your second preference winning rather than your last preference. Some systems are easier to be strategic in than others, and plurality is probably the easiest. When a person voting in a plurality election votes for their second-best option because they think their favourite option will lose, this is a tactical vote and an example of a strategic vote (Catt 1989). During the 1997 general election in Britain there was much talk of tactical voting and some newspapers advised voters on how to vote tactically to defeat the Conservatives by indicating whether the Liberal Democrats or Labour was most likely to be able to beat them. Using the parliament voting example (see Table 2.1), if the Liberals voted for their second choice, low-interest loans, it would gain 60 votes and so beat state funding, which was the worst option for the Liberals. To be successful in a strategic vote it is important to know how others are likely to vote, but with opinion polling this is often the case in elections. In the case of a committee taking a vote the prior discussion may have provided enough information about the views of others to make a strategic vote worth a try.

Arguments about the different forms of majoritarian voting relate to this question of having the information needed to cast a strategic vote. In the Australian system, where all preferences are marked at one go, then voters have to make assumptions about the views of others if they want to be strategic. But in France or the USA Senate everyone knows the result of the first vote before they make their second choice so they can then use this information for a strategy to prevent their worst option winning. If voters know how others are voting then this may provide them with information and stimulus to vote for a candidate who is not their favourite to avoid the election of their worst candidate. For instance if after the first vote and debate the Socialists realised that their favourite was not liked by any other party and thus would lose, they might decide to back graduate tax on the second vote because they prefer that option to commercial loans (refer to Tables 2.2 and 2.3). In this situation on the second vote commercial loans would have received 60 votes and graduate tax 90, making the tax the winner. The Socialists then gain their third rather than fourth preference.

One of the major criticisms of a Borda count is that it is easy to manipulate. A group can enhance the chances of their favourite by giving zero points to the option they think is most likely to beat their favourite, even if it is not their worst option. For instance, if the 20 Liberals each gave 'graduate tax' zero points and 'state funding' one point rather than the other way around then low-interest loans would win instead of graduate tax (refer to Tables 2.2 and 2.6). In reversing their third and last preferences, the Liberals manage to ensure that the option they like best wins. This is another example of strategic voting. In each case voters choose to vote other than according to normal preferences in order to help the chances of their favourite or to stop their worst option from winning. This means that a group of voters who understand the system can alter the result and thus it may not be a real measure of the collective views of the group. The extent to which the possibility of strategic voting mars the outcome will vary according to the group and will be affected by the extent of information and the strategic skill of specific groups of voters.

Choosing several options

Sometimes a group needs to choose more than one of the options on offer. For instance, a committee deciding which five capital projects to fund in the coming year or a pressure group determining which policies to highlight in their campaign literature. However, the most common time this sort of decision occurs is during elections in countries that have multi-member constituencies. In the Netherlands, the whole country is one constituency with 150 representatives. Most of continental Europe and much of South America work with large constituencies, each of which has a number of legislators. Most countries are divided into geographical regions, each with a number of representatives; for instance in Norway there are between four and 15 members per area and Japan has three, four or five. In multi-member situations the point of aggregating individual views is not to find the favourite but rather the combination of options that best represents the views of the group. Again there are differences in approach. If three places are to be filled should they be three individuals who are each the favourite of a sizeable group in the area or a team of three that together satisfy most people or the three individuals who are collectively liked by most voters? Five different methods will be described.

The most straightforward method is to divide the available seats between competitors according to the number of people who voted for their party. For instance, in the Netherlands, in 1994 the Labour Party received 24 per cent of the votes and 24.6 per cent of the seats while the State Reform Party won 1.3 per cent of both votes and seats. Such a party-list system depends upon the existence of political parties but this is the case in most elections. A proportional representation (PR) system, such as this, is the most common method of election; however, countries vary greatly in the details of their systems. Some ensure proportionality for the entire country while others, such as Germany, give PR within regions. New Zealand now uses a system that allocates MPs in parliament on a proportional basis for the whole country, but also has plurality elections to choose local MPs. This is an example of a 'top-up' system where voters are allowed to select an individual to represent them locally (see Chapter 6) while still ensuring proportionality in parliament. Some countries have a threshold so that only parties of a certain size gain MPs, for instance 4 per cent in Sweden and 1.5 per cent in Israel. Another way in which PR systems vary is in how they determine the number of seats each party is entitled to, because it is impossible to make an exact allocation. For instance, if there were 100 seats and a party won 12.5 per cent of the vote, strict proportionality would give them 12 and a half MPs, but it is difficult to obtain half an MP. Therefore one party must get an extra fraction of an MP and others lose a fraction. The different allocation systems vary as to whether they give the spare fractions to a large or small party (for details see Gallagher 1991).

Regardless of the details of the allocation system used, the idea behind a proportional allocation of seats in a situation where a number of candidates are needed is simple. Each group of voters has a group of representatives of equal magnitude to its size in the population. Equality is provided by letting each person participate in choosing one of the options. This system does not work where there are no parties or factions and therefore is not feasible for most small-scale committees. Again it is easier to follow the different systems by using an example. We are in an electorate with 15,000 voters who elect three people. The Socialists, Conservatives and Greens each stand three candidates. On a party vote the results are Conservatives 7,300 votes, Socialists 4,300 votes and Greens 3,400 votes (see Table 2.10). This means that the Conservatives gain two seats and the Socialists one. If we were electing five MPs then on the same vote there would be a different result depending upon the allocation method used. Under the D'hondt rule and the Droop rule the Conservatives would have three, and the other two parties one MP each, while using the St Lague system the Conservatives and Socialists would each have two MPs and the Greens one. If seven MPs were being elected then again there are different results with the Conservatives benefiting from D'hondt and Droop but the Greens benefiting from St Lague. This example illustrates the way different systems treat large, medium and small parties. The party-list system allocates seats to the parties with no indication of which people will fill the seats. Countries using the party-list electoral system specify how those places are filled by the parties. In the closed-list system the party publishes a ranked list of candidates before the election and places are filled using that while in the open-list system the voters can express preferences for people within the list that was proposed by the party they vote for (see Chapter 5).

A common way for committees to choose a number of members is to use the plurality method with each person voting for their one favoured candidate. If five people are needed then the five with the highest numbers of votes win. This method is also used for national elections. In some cases, such as Japan pre-1994, each voter could vote for one candidate and those with the greatest number of votes won; this was called the 'single non-transferable vote'. The idea here is that

Table 2.10 Election example – PR results (15,000 votes in total)

	Socialists	Conservatives	Greens	Allocation method
Votes	4,300	7,300	3,400	
%	28.6	48.6	22.6	
3 MPs	1	2	0	D'hondt, Droop, St Lague
5 MPs	1	3	1	D'hondt, Droop
	2	2	1	St Lague
7 MPs	2	4	1	D'hondt, Droop
	2	3	2	St Lague

each successful candidate is backed by a sizeable group of voters, so like PR, each different group is given a representative. In our example the voters can be broken into 11 groups according to their first three preferences (see Table 2.11). For the single non-transferable vote only the first preferences are needed and the three with the highest vote are David and Ella from the Conservatives and Ahmed from the Socialists (see Table 2.12).

In elections for the Tunisian parliament, Russian upper house and Spanish Senate, many 'at large' State legislature elections in the USA, and some local council elections in Britain, voters can cast as many votes as there are seats. For instance in London, each area elects three councillors and so each voter can put a cross beside three names. When all the votes have been totalled, the three candidates with the highest votes win. Here the intent is quite different as the same large group of voters can elect all of the winners. In our example, each voting block gives the three votes to their top three preferences (see Table 2.13) and the winners are again David and Ella for the Conservatives but Betty wins amongst the Social-ists because she gains some votes from otherwise Conservative voters. However, if all voters had voted just for the three candidates from their favourite party then the Conservatives would have won all three seats with 7,300 votes for each of those candidates, 4,300 votes for each Socialist and 3,400 for each Green.

Two variations are used in parts of the USA. With the limited vote, used in

Table 2.11 Election example – top three preferences

		Socialists			Conservatives			Greens		
Voter blocs		Ahmed	Betty	Chris	David	Ella	Fran	Grant	Hal	Imogen
A	2,300	1	2	3						
B	1,400	2	1		3					
C	600		2	1	3					
D	2,800				1	2	3			
E	2,300		3		2	1				
F	1,600		3		2	1				
G	600				3	1				2
H	800				3			1		2
I	1,200							3	1	2
J	900		3					2		1
K	500				3				2	1

Table 2.12 Election example – single non-transferable vote – one vote

Socialists			Conservatives			Greens		
Ahmed	Betty	Chris	David	Ella	Fran	Grant	Hall	Imogen
2,300	1,400	600	2,800	2,300	2,200	800	1,200	1,400

Winners – David (Conservative), Ahmed (Socialist), Ella (Conservative)

Philadelphia, voters have more than one vote but fewer than the number of seats being filled. In Alamogordo, New Mexico, voters have as many votes as seats to be filled but they can give some or all of them to one candidate. If we assume that the Green voters campaign to concentrate all votes on one candidate who is seen as having the best chance and that the other groups of voters give two votes to their first preference and one to their second then we can see how a small group can gain a seat (see Table 2.14). This process of cumulative voting is championed by some African-American groups in the USA. These hybrid versions still allow the largest group in the area to dominate the election but smaller groups can gain a representative if they concentrate all of their votes on one candidate. Indeed one criticism of these methods of plurality voting in multi-member or 'at large' districts is that a large faction may be able to determine all of the winners. For instance, in 'at large' elections in the USA, African-Americans have often found it hard to be elected despite forming a sizeable proportion of the population (Welch 1990). If all of the whites vote for white candidates they can win all of the seats. Another criticism is again the idea that preference ordering should be used in determining the views of a group.

Preference information is used in the single transferable vote (STV), a commonly used way of electing a committee in Britain. Voters write a '1' beside their favourite candidate, a '2' beside the next favourite and so on. A quota is used to determine how many votes are needed to gain a seat (usually the number of votes divided by one more than the number of seats to be filled, that is one sixth if five people are to be elected). In our example three people are to be elected so the quota is one quarter of the votes cast, which is 3,751. First preferences are counted and any candidate reaching the quota is elected; in the example no candidate reaches quota so Chris, who has the fewest votes, is eliminated and those votes are

Table 2.13 Election example – at-large voting – three votes each

		Socialists			Conservatives			Greens		
		Ahmed	Betty	Chris	David	Ella	Fran	Grant	Hal	Imogen
A	2,300	2,300	2,300	2,300						
B	1,400	1,400	1,400		1,400					
C	600		600	600	600					
D	2,800				2,800	2,800	2,800			
E	2,300		2,300		2,300	2,300				
F	1,600		1,600			1,600	1,600			
G	600				600		600			600
H	800				800			800		800
I	1,200							1,200	1,200	1,200
J	900		900					900		900
K	500				500				500	500
		3,700	9,100	2,900	9,000	6,700	5,000	2,900	1,700	4,000

Winners – Betty (Socialist), David (Conservative), Ella (Conservative)

Table 2.14 Election example – cumulative voting – three votes each

		Socialists			Conservatives			Greens		
		Ahmed	Betty	Chris	David	Ella	Fran	Grant	Hal	Imogen
A	2,300	*4,600	2,300							
B	1,400	1,400	*2,800							
C	600		600	*1,200						
D	2,800				*5,600	2,800				
E	2,300				2,300	*4,600				
F	1,600					1,600	*3,200			
G	600						*1,200			600
H	800							800		*1,600
I	1,200								1,200	*2,400
J	900									*2,700
K	500									*1,500
		6,000	5,700	1,200	7,900	9,000	4,400	800	1,200	8,500

Winners – Ella (Conservative), Imogen (Green), David (Conservative)

Note: * Signifies that two or three votes were cumulated. Allocation based on the assumption that Socialist and Conservative voters gave 2 votes to their 1st preference and one vote to their 2nd. Green voters concentrated on Imogen as she was seen as having the best chance of success.

given to the second preference, Betty (see Table 2.15). Still no candidate has 3,751 votes so Grant, with the fewest votes, is eliminated and the votes transferred to the second preference, Imogen. Still no one has reached quota so Hal is eliminated and the votes again go to Imogen. With no one at quota Betty is eliminated. Her 1,400 original votes go to the second preference, Ahmed, and the 600 that were transferred from Chris now go to David, the third preference. Still no candidate is elected so Fran is eliminated with all votes going to the second preference, which is Ella for 1,600 of them and Imogen for the other 600. Now Imogen and Ella have reached the quota and are elected. To find the third person to be elected, David is eliminated as he has fewer votes so Ahmed is elected. So each voter has one vote that is moved from one candidate to another until it is used to help elect someone. Imogen was elected with first preference votes from groups J and K plus second preferences from H, I and G. Again each person helps to elect one person so each sizeable group in society should have someone who talks for them. STV is used in Australian senate elections, Malta and the Republic of Ireland as well as New York community school boards and council elections in Cambridge, Massachusetts.

Choosing several options relates to elections of committees or legislatures rather than to policy decision making although STV or plurality voting could be used to decide which three proposals were to share available funding or which 17 hospitals were to receive new intensive care units. As was the case with different systems for choosing one option, there is no agreement on the best way. Each system aims to give people a say in different ways and so may appeal to different groups or be appropriate for different situations. One fundamental difference is whether each person has the chance to elect one of the team of people or if each

Table 2.15 Election example – STV vote

	Socialists			Conservatives			Greens		
Stage	Ahmed	Betty	Chris	David	Ella	Fran	Grant	Hal	Imogen
1	2,300	1,400	600	2,800	2,300	2,200	800	1,200	1,400
2	2,300	2,000	Out	2,800	2,300	2,200	800	1,200	1,400
3	2,300	2,000	/	2,800	2,300	2,200	Out	1,200	2,200
4	2,300	2,000	/	2,800	2,300	2,200	/	Out	3,400
5	3,700	Out	/	3,400	2,300	2,200	/	/	3,400
6	3,700	/	/	3,400	3,900	Out	/	/	4,000
7	3,700	/	/	3,400	Elected	/	/	/	Elected

Stage	What happens	Situation
1	1st preferences counted (same as total vote in SNTV count). Quota is calculated : (15,000/ 4) + 1 = 3,751	No candidate crosses
2	eliminate Chris, votes go to Betty	No one at quota
3	eliminate Grant, votes go to Imogen	No one at quota
4	eliminate Hal, votes go to Imogen	No one at quota
5	eliminate Betty, initial 1,400 votes go to Ahmed, later 600 votes go to David (3rd preference)	No one at quota
6	eliminate Fran, 1,600 to Ella, 600 to Imogen	Imogen and Ella have reached quota so are elected
7	David eliminated	Ahmed left so gets the third seat

Winners – Imogen (Green), Ella (Conservative), Ahmed (Socialist)

has a say on all who are to be elected. The difference has a great impact on the position of small groups such as ethnic minorities who may be able to elect one person if each voter has one vote but will not gain a representative if all elect all. Where there is a clear majority and minority each of which wants a particular type of candidate and will generally all vote the same way then the choice of system will affect the outcome. The impact of a large group voting the same way is not limited to those situations when there is an organised vote but also covers the many instances when those people who comprise the majority all tend to vote for the same type of candidate. When each person has one vote then a minority group can gain a representative in a multi-member electorate providing that the minority is large enough. But the same minority group would not be able to elect a representative when each voter has a number of votes. The use of single or multi-member electorates also has an impact on the success of certain candidates. Women are more likely to be chosen as candidates and to be elected when there are multi-member electorates. Candidates from ethnic minorities also benefit from multi-member electorates if voters from that group are geographically dispersed, but if the community lives in a compact area then a single-member electorate may be advantageous (Darcy *et al.* 1994: 169–71).

Given that 'the people' are a group of individuals (and therefore a collective decision needs to aggregate their views), and that democratic theory demands all have an equal say, some process is needed. In looking at different methods that are used to decide what the people want there are three clear messages. First, there are a wide variety of ideas about what the winner is, for instance the biggest group's favourite or the one the vast majority will accept (see Table 2.16). Second, there is no perfect system. In particular, every system can be prone to voters altering the result through strategic voting. Some systems are more easily manipulated than others, but those choosing a process should be aware of the possible ways in which strategies could be used. Third, no system is effect-neutral. So, when choosing a system, the effects it will have on final decisions should be understood and matched to the situation.

Unanimity, veto and qualified majority

So far the voting systems covered have aimed at finding the option or options that are acceptable to a large part of the group, defined in a number of ways. But some decision-making bodies want a higher approval level and so will aim for consensus or use a veto or require a two-thirds vote for a major change. Sometimes consensus is needed as a means of ensuring compliance because those who voted against cannot be forced to go along with the majority decision and therefore the group needs to find a solution acceptable to all. Decisions of the UN Security Council are a good example as the UN cannot force any country to do something. In other cases unanimity or a qualified majority is used to ensure that each sizeable group has a say or because of a theoretical desire to seek agreement rather than have one part of the group force views on the others. Unanimity may also be used because it is seen as important that the 'right' decision is made and therefore it is important to err on the side of caution, for instance with a jury dealing with a case where the death penalty could be applied. These methods of reaching a decision show up some of the problems within democracy of trying to achieve equality while at the same time protecting individuals or minority groups.

Aside from the problem of ascertaining what the majority wants, there are theoretical arguments about the legitimacy of the ideal of majority rule. In particular writers such as de Tocqueville and J.S. Mill (1859) worried about the 'tyranny of the majority'. The majority is seen as having power because it has the right to make the decisions. As the view of the majority prevails this can lead to the assumption that the majority is right and always knows best. In this situation those with a minority view may feel that they must be wrong and so will not express opinions. If equal voting and decision making using some sort of majority rule are employed, then the majority may impose its will upon the minority. Further the minority may be oppressed by the majority in terms of what it can do or the extent to which it can participate in the democratic process. Not only did Mill fear that the majority would oppress the rights of a minority by passing laws but he also warned of the imposition of societal norms. Worse, in his eyes, this would lead to mediocrity and the lowest common denominator in taste and cultural norms. In this he foreshadowed many arguments about television programming! Mill and de Tocqueville thought the situation could worsen further. Because the views of the masses prevail then a demagogue who can influence or control the views of the mass, through advertising, rabble rousing or great oratory, can gain great power. Instead of individual liberty there is a strong pressure to conform and a large group can restrict the behaviour of a small one. In other words, just because the greatest numbers of people want something it does not mean that it is the right answer for all covered by the law. The majority may well make decisions in terms of self-interest rather than for the common good.

In a country with few social divisions worries about majority rule are small. However, in deeply divided societies the minorities may well fear the power of the majority. In particular, if the groups are rigid so that the same people are always in the majority then minorities may be oppressed. If there are fluctuating majorities, made up of different groups for different issues, then one group is unlikely to be routinely oppressed. If a group believes it has a good chance of being the minority some of the time then it is likely to treat other minorities carefully. Therefore, in much discussion of democratic procedures, the need to protect individual or group freedom is stressed along with ideas of equality. As mentioned in Chapter 1, the two principles of equality and liberty produce a tension that necessitates value choices when implementing democratic practice. In this section a number of techniques that are used to protect minority rights against the possible tyranny of the majority are considered.

In choosing one option, the idea of equality specifies that each vote counts for the same. But concerns for minority rights and the possibility that the majority may vote to hurt the minority have led to some restrictions on the way votes are used to make decisions. Most commonly, a two-third or three-quarter vote in favour of an option is required before it can be implemented. For instance the 1994 International Whaling Commission's decision to establish a whale sanctuary in the southern oceans needed a three-quarter vote to pass. Normal standing orders used in meetings specify a qualified majority for censuring elected members or changing the organisation's constitution. In Finland all legislation that is not voted for by two-thirds of the legislators will be deferred until after the subsequent election. For an amendment to be made to the US constitution, three-quarters of the State legislatures have to pass the measure. On the European Council of Ministers, routine decisions are also taken using a qualified majority with the added complication that each minister's vote is weighted according to the size of the country. So the German minister has 10 votes, Belgium five and Luxembourg two. For a motion to pass, 54 of the possible 76 votes must be cast in favour. In practice this means that at least seven countries must vote together to pass a motion and it needs at least a bloc of three to defeat a motion.

If the qualified majority requires a two-third vote then any minority whose members comprise more than a third of the decision-making group will have an influence upon the outcome. If the minority group is smaller then there may be the need for a unanimous vote to ensure the minority cannot be outvoted. In effect this means that any member has a veto and so can stop any decision. An

Table 2.16 Details of different voting systems

System (common names)	Principle behind it	Example of where used	Common criticism
CHOOSING ONE OPTION			
Plurality (first-past-the-post)	Option favoured by the largest group wins	Elect MPs Britain, Canada, USA, India	More people opposed winner than voted for it Strategic voting likely
Majoritarian (preference or alternative vote, exhaustive ballot)	Winner needs backing of at least half the voters	Elect MPs Australia and France Trade-union decisions in Britain	Most people's 2nd best wins May use or 3rd or 4th preference as same weight as 1st
Resolution – amendment (committee or AGM method; binary voting)	Always look at just two options. Can accept or reject each, can be general then specific	Most meetings where normal standing orders are used	Result easily changed by putting options in different order
Borda count	Options scored, 0 for worst, 1 for 2nd worst, etc. (e.g. if 4 options, favourite gets 3 points), then all points added	Choose 'most valuable player' in the USA	Strategic voting easy and likely Time consuming
Condorcet	Each option pitted against each other, winner can beat all others		There may not be a winner
Approval	Vote for all approve of, as many as like. Winner has greatest overall approval	Some profession associations in the USA	May get strategic voting Some people get more votes than others

CHOOSING SEVERAL OPTIONS
Examples based on filling three places

List votes	Each party or faction gets same proportion of seats as won votes. Each voter helps elect one person	Most elections in Europe and S. America	Need parties
Plurality with one vote (single non-transferable vote)	The 3 candidates who each have the biggest followings win. 3 winners each have a large personal following. Each voter elects 1 person	Elect legislators in Japan pre-1994	Based on personality votes
'At large'	The team of 3 liked by the largest group of voters wins. 3 winners all liked by the same group. Each voter elects 3 people	USA local elections, British council elections	Hard for minorities to gain a representative
Cumulative voting	Voters have as many votes as seats but can give them all to one person. Each voter may elect 1, 2 or 3 people	Some places in the USA	Strategic voting is easy
Single Transferable Vote (STV)	Each sizeable group gains a representative. Each voter elects 1 person	Elections Malta, Eire and Australian Senate	Some people's later preferences used but others not

important difference between a veto and qualified majority is that in a veto you know that you can stop any decision but under a qualified majority you need to work with others to stop a decision. International organisations are particularly keen on unanimous votes, so that the sovereignty of each member state is not compromised. In both the Security Council of the UN and the European Council of Ministers when initiating new policy, if one country votes against an option then it cannot be implemented. As any one member of the decision-making body can stop a decision this gives them greater power than all of the other members combined. Here the desire to protect individual or group rights is seen as far more important than the idea of equality. Although unanimity and consensus are frequently used as synonyms there is a subtle difference. With unanimity all have actually voted in agreement or chosen to abstain. With consensus no one has said that they disagree but there probably was not a vote, rather it was agreed that the feeling of the meeting was to do whatever. So if I am not entirely happy with what the rest of the group wants, if working under consensus I have to choose between protesting and keeping quiet but if working under veto I choose between voting against or abstaining. The two procedures may lead to the same result but the subtle difference can be important and there is a difference between taking a series of votes and in talking until all stop disagreeing (see Chapter 3).

Voting, either in an election or on an issue, is what many people associate with democracy. For most citizens the election of representatives is the main way that they take part in democratic structures. But few people think about the method of voting or the impact that the system could be having on the outcome. Each method of aggregating votes is based on a specific idea of what constitutes a winner. When choosing several candidates then the system will have a marked effect on the proportion of women and members of ethnic minorities who are elected. Treatment of minorities is also a strong component in the decision to have a veto or qualified majority rule. For a group to make decisions they need a method to decide what the group wants but the way in which the views of individuals are aggregated will have an impact on the result. As no system is effect-neutral, groups should know the ways in which their method works.

3   Participatory democracy

In many small groups decisions are arrived at collectively by all members after some discussion of the alternatives and without recourse to a vote. When such methods are adopted by a more formal group this is known as participatory democracy. This distinct form of decision making should not be confused with a desire to increase the level of participation in the political system: some who write about participatory democracy are primarily concerned with encouraging more people to vote, take an interest in politics and join political groups (Morgan 1970). Other writers concentrate on the workplace and seek to encourage greater participation by workers in the decisions of the firm through the inclusion of workers on the management board or a greater role for trade unions (Bachrach and Botwinick 1992). While participatory democracy leads to a higher level of participation in politics because people are directly involved in the decision making, this is not its sole defining aspect.

Participatory democracy is not used as part of the national government process in any country but there are a wide range of smaller groups who routinely use these methods. There was a resurgence of interest in the idea of participatory democracy in the late 1960s and early 1970s as part of the radical politics of the 'counter culture' or 'new Left', seen in student movements, women's groups and environmental groups. All were interested in changing 'the system' and saw process as important and so in their own organisations wanted to practise equality, change the traditional hierarchical structures and encourage wider participation in decision making. However, the use of participatory democracy is not confined to such groups nor to the later part of the twentieth century. The classic Athenian forum was a form of participatory democracy and the early town meetings in the New England states of the USA also followed this model. Workers' co-operatives, around since the late nineteenth century, also stressed equality and collective decision making. The Quakers and Israeli kibbutzim have also followed these norms for a long time as part of their respective emphasis upon equality. Some indigenous peoples, most notably the Maori of New Zealand, also use participatory democracy methods. What these diverse groups have in common is a desire to be inclusive and to discuss all aspects of decisions in a way that stresses equality of participants.

With such a wide range of groups using forms of participatory democracy there are no hard-and-fast rules as to how it operates. However, there are key aspects that distinguish participatory democracy from other forms of decision making (see Table 3.1). The necessary conditions for participatory democracy are face-to-face meetings where possible solutions are proposed and discussed until agreement on the best solution emerges. As equality is the primary motivation behind participatory democracy, the involvement of all members of the group in each step of the decision-making process is vital. The normal structure is to have face-to-face discussion where all have the opportunity to suggest the issues that need to be raised and possible solutions, express their views and take part in the final decision. From this structure come other important aspects. As decisions are made by those involved, this is a form of grassroots politics and therefore there is no expectation that those who are involved have any political experience. The emphasis on discussion also means that there is a tendency to strive for a consensus decision rather than using a vote. For participatory democracy to work well there are necessary practical requirements such as the size and nature of the group. Such facilitating components are discussed in the second section. First, some real examples of participatory democracy are outlined, concentrating on the reasons that these groups choose a participatory democracy structure; the ways in which group members take part in decision making; and the ways in which decisions are made. The examples are followed by a discussion of the commonalties across participatory democracy. The conclusion asks if participatory democracy gives the people power over decisions and discusses the problems inherent in this decision-making structure.

Participatory democracy in practice

In the US there is a long tradition of local government where 'all' take part in a town meeting that decides important issues. There has been variation as to who was included by 'all', as in the past women, non-freeman and 'undesirables' were excluded in some places. Now elected councils are the dominant form of local government but there is a move to build in greater consultation with the public and so there has been a spread of consultative town meetings of various sorts. These encompass some aspects of participatory democracy, most particularly the importance of deliberation.

For towns in the New England states of the USA 'form of government' is usually specified as 'selectmen, town meeting, board of finance'. Town meetings as the central form of government were first used in the Massachusetts Bay Colony in the 1620s and then spread to New Hampshire, Connecticut, Rhode

Table 3.1 Necessary components of participatory democracy

- All can raise an issue, suggest solutions, take part in final decision
- Face-to-face meetings
- Much discussion – all who want to can contribute
- Tendency to want consensus

Island, Vermont and Maine (Zimmerman 1986: 17). They survived the creation of the Union of states and the introduction of representative democracy for federal matters. De Tocqueville (1948: 68) praised the practice of town meetings because it was government coming directly from those affected by the decisions and so, even if the decisions were not the best ones, the way in which they were arrived at made up for the problems. Town meetings were held in each town and males over 24 years old who had property and were regular churchgoers could attend but in some cases only the freemen could vote. The meetings elected a range of officials to carry out specific duties such as constable, treasurer and checking weights and measures. Meetings were also needed whenever a new policy or expenditure was required and could be called as the need arose. Attendance was compulsory in most places with fines for those who did not participate. Each man was also expected to take on one of the official posts at some point and these jobs were paid so as to facilitate the participation of the poor as well as the rich. Zuckerman estimates that in 1710 there were about 60,000 adult males in Massachusetts but less than 100 in the average town. As there were no feudal or aristocratic families to assume authority, order in each town had to come from the community through the decisions in town meetings. However, these meetings had no way to compel compliance, hence consensus became important (Zuckerman 1970: ch. 2). Even the numbers of votes cast for each candidate were not recorded, and may even not have been reported at the time, all as part of the drive for accord not division (ibid.: ch. 5). Zuckerman further suggests that the need for a homogeneous group and unanimity played a crucial role in the approval of new settlers and that when there was a major conflict the creation of a new settlement was common so that two new homogeneous communities were created to replace the divided one.

Although most larger towns now have elected government, the town meeting remains as the main decision-making body in other places. Town meetings are used to decide local matters such as hiring and firing teachers, curriculum content, town celebrations, the order in which roads are to be snow-ploughed, fire and police protection and how to raise taxes to cover these things. In some places there are special committees to advise on financial matters or schooling decisions, but the ultimate decision is with the town meeting. Typically a meeting takes a whole day and the agenda is published beforehand. While some issues are passed with little debate others are hotly contested. The normal practice is to allow discussion for as long as anyone wants to say something. Once someone has the floor they are free to speak as long as they stay on the subject and follow normal parliamentary procedures (such as not calling other people liars). The aim is for unanimous decisions but secret ballots and majority systems are used on some occasions. After her detailed report of one town meeting Mansbridge sums it up as an event where the people had debated and made decisions, covering practical and ideological aspects of each issue, and so were able to have an input into areas that would affect their lives (Mansbridge 1980: 59).

US citizens outside of New England also have opportunities to participate directly in local decisions although not with so much power. In the 1960s,

President Johnson incorporated citizen participation into federal legislation when he set up an anti-poverty scheme that was supposed to provide local solutions for local situations with 'maximum feasible participation'. Since then public involvement programmes have been included in the management scheme in many federal laws across a range of services (Berry *et al.* 1993: ch. 2). Typically local groups are involved in monitoring the activity of specific agencies. Some city governments have also sought to include citizens in detailed decisions. Such programmes run alongside elected government and are usually based upon neighbourhood groups. In *The Rebirth of Urban Democracy* (Berry *et al.* 1993) the successful city-wide neighbourhood programmes in the US cities of Birmingham, Dayton, Portland and St Paul are studied. In these cities face-to-face neighbourhood meetings make the final decisions on some local matters such as land use and planning. In other policy areas they tell the elected councillors the views of the neighbourhood. All in the area are encouraged to attend meetings, with much time, money and staff employed in disseminating detailed information on issues to be discussed.

Many works on participatory democracy use workplace democracy, in particular workers' co-operatives, as a prime example (Pateman 1970; Mansbridge 1980). While workers' co-operatives are commonly stereotyped as being in the 'alternative' sector, for instance a wholefood shop, a radical newspaper or a paper-recycling centre, many are in more traditional areas, for instance in manufacturing and publishing. Many major orchestras are workers' co-operatives as are groups providing services such as housing, healthcare or women's refuges. In each case basic co-operative principles, including equality and democracy, underpin the organisational structure. Italy and the Basque region of Spain have a high concentration of workers' co-operatives while interest in the UK and the USA is low but has grown in recent decades.

The Rochdale Pioneers who set up a workers' co-operative in 1844 are now seen as the founders of the co-operative movement. Their principles, since adopted and adapted by the International Co-operation Alliance (ICA) state, amongst other things, that there should be democratic control of each co-operative organisation, based on one member, one vote. In other words all decisions relating to the work and future of the co-operative are to be made by the members, either directly or through their chosen representatives. Other principles set out the philosophy of participation, equality and concern for the community showing that the co-operative movement is concerned with economic and social matters. At the heart of ICA principles is the idea that the workers are all equal 'owners' of the business and therefore all take a part in making decisions relating to work. Workers' co-operatives come in many shapes and sizes but there are important commonalties in terms of decision-making structures. Equality of all members is central to the co-operative ideal so in decision making all can raise an issue, express a view and take part in the final decision. In all co-operatives the sovereignty of the collective is important as is the idea that all come together to make a decision, rather than, for instance, using a postal vote.

A classic workers' co-operative is a wholefood shop with six workers/owners who have an interest in organic and wholefoods, a desire for a non-hierarchical workplace and a wish to act for the benefit of the community. Jobs such as advertising, routine administration, stocktaking, and serving in the shop are rotated between the members. All members take part in a weekly meeting to make policy decisions about the running of the shop but routine job-related decisions are taken by individuals in line with previous policy decisions. Issues to be discussed at the meetings can be raised by any member and all can express their views, with discussion continuing until a decision is reached. Meetings are deemed to be part of the work time and attendance is expected. For descriptions of real workers' co-operatives see Cornforth *et al.* (1988: 138–42), Cornforth (1995: 497–504) or Rothschild and Whitt (1986).

At the other extreme, the commonly used example of a large, successful workers' co-operative is the Mondragon Co-operatives Group in the Basque region of Spain. Created in 1956, in 1996 it comprises 100 different co-operatives with over 26,000 workers. Most of the co-operatives are industrial but others provide distribution, training, finance and research services. In each co-operative the workers are members, and management decisions are taken by all on an equal vote basis. All members are part of the General Assembly that meets at least once a year; elects the Governing Council; votes on all major policy changes; and has the ultimate power over all decisions. The elected Governing Council, made up of workers rather than managers, takes on-going decisions. There is also a Social Council that takes workers' concerns to the board. The assumption is that all members will take a turn on the Social Council, will attend the General Council and will take an interest in the decisions being made. There is a monthly newsletter and work time is set aside for information sessions so that all will know the details of impending decisions (Whyte 1995: 226). The corollary of a worker's right to participate is an obligation to be informed and to use all opportunities to participate in decision making. New workers have a trial period where the extent to which they fit into the co-operative environment is assessed and there are regular seminars to reinforce the ideals of co-operatives amongst the existing workers. In between the small shop and Mondragon is a range of workers' co-operatives that run on the ideal of equality, democracy and participation (see Cornforth *et al.* 1988: 142–46; Cornforth 1995: 504–14; Mansbridge 1980: ch. 12 or Rothschild and Whitt 1986: 29–42, for case study descriptions).

A number of 'new Left' or 'counter culture' or 'post-materialist' organisations have espoused the use of greater participation and equality in their internal practices. Of all the radical groups of the 1960s and 1970s, women's groups were the most widespread users of collective face-to-face decision-making processes. In the 1990s many feminist groups still use these structures as do environmentalist groups, including most Green Parties.

In the vast number of small women's groups that emerged in the 1960s and 1970s, across the Western world, there was a strong tendency to use collective decision making. Many feminist groups were started by women who had left other new-Left groups due to feelings of discrimination because many of the men assumed they should have the power and the women were there to provide secretarial assistance, food and sex. As women's groups were reacting against the traditional hierarchical structures of other radical political groups they paid great attention to how they organised. Stressing equality they worked to eliminate hierarchy based on experience, socio-economic status or personal characteristics. From this stress came the collective, face-to-face discussion decision-making process and the strict rotation of jobs. The interest in new forms of organisation was philosophical as well as a reaction to experiences in other groups.

The organisation of THE FEMINISTS, a New York group of the 1960s, provides an illustration of the procedures used. Their constitution states that they have a political aim of an equal society and so within the organisation there are no officers but instead jobs are shared between members each time they need to be done. Further, in seeking equality they emphasised the need for members to share experience, information and knowledge with other members and not to hoard it as a source of power. At each meeting the chair and secretary were chosen by lot and all other jobs such as writing a pamphlet, washing the teacups or putting up posters were drawn by lot as required. If a member drew a task she did not know how to do then she could ask for help from members with experience so that all would learn the necessary skills for political activity. Meetings to discuss the activities of the group were frequent, allowed for all to have a say and involved long discussion. Attendance at meetings was stressed because each member was deemed to have a responsibility to the other members and because only through regular attendance would all acquire the necessary skills and knowledge needed to help the political cause. A member missing more than a quarter of meetings in a month was not allowed to vote again until the third consecutive meeting she attended, and if anyone was penalised three times over three months then their membership lapsed (Koedt *et al.* 1973: 374). The group was very serious about its structures and so imposed tough rules to ensure equality.

Environmentalist groups also stress non-hierarchical structures and equal participation as part of their wider political philosophy. Decentralised decision making and inclusion are seen as vital parts of the move to a better society. In general, Green Parties stress discussion and aim for consensus on a decision. There is no universal set of procedures used by Green Parties, so the example of one, the Green Party of Ontario, Canada, is used here. Their statutes state a belief that ecological problems have social causes and so the solution is a society with an emphasis on equity and decentralisation. Therefore, the organisation is run in a non-hierarchical way with power in the localities not the centre. When a new issue is to be discussed the resolution is put to the meeting. The facilitator will then call for a minute's reflection and ask if any clarification of the resolution is needed. Members sit in a circle and each member takes turns to give their view. If there are disagreements then discussion will continue to try to find a position acceptable to all. The facilitator decides the length of time needed for discussion. The aim is for consensus but if there is none the resolution may be sent to another group for more discussion or they may hold a vote, needing 60 per cent to pass. The standing orders state that, wherever possible, the aim is to find a solution which all can accept and that this process of amendment creates a better final outcome. Any decision that becomes part of the party's policy at the Annual Policy

Conference will have been discussed in this way in a number of different meetings, published in the newsletter and probably amended by this process.

Both the feminist and environmentalist philosophies oppose hierarchy and seek a decentralised and inclusive form of decision making. Thus the groups are seeking to practise what they preach and are prepared to put in the necessary time to make the system work. The basic participatory democracy structure is used in a very similar way across the range of organisations. Rothschild uses eight criteria to differentiate the 'collectivist-democratic' from the 'bureaucratic' organisational ideal type (Rothschild-Whyte 1979: 519; Rothschild and Whitt 1986: 62–63, 50–62). Not all of these differences relate to the decision-making structure but some do: authority; compliance; minimal stipulated rules; the ideal of community. Vitally the authority for decisions 'resides in the collectivity as a whole' so all decisions must be made or endorsed by the group. In reaching a decision compliance is to the consensus of the collective. The structure is as informal and non-hierarchical as possible, to enhance equality and participation. To ensure as little hierarchy as possible knowledge is shared and jobs are rotated. The ideal of community as an important entity worth working for binds the whole enterprise together. Some aspects relate to how the organisation operates and others to the norms and values of the group.

These different examples illustrate the range of ways in which the aims of participatory democracy can be put into practice. Across the examples there are also commonalties of experience in likely problems and components that tend to make the procedures work better. With participatory democracy emphasis is upon giving each member a full and equal say in that decision: in taking part at each step of the process, from deciding what is an issue through suggesting alternative solutions to determining the final outcome. For a participatory democracy group a desirable decision is one that all in the group feel happy with and one that is owned by the group as a decision to follow. This necessitates consensus, defined as a solution all in the group agree to and are sufficiently committed to that they will implement it. So discussion amongst the group members is needed and such discussion is most effective when it happens face-to-face. Also, to ensure the interests of each member are addressed and that all have an input into each part of the process it is important that there is some equality between members: at minimum that each is given equal respect for their views and each feels able to take part, not only that they have the chance to do so. Giving respect to each person and finding a solution all are happy with is much more likely to happen if the people in the group share key values and beliefs and are not unequal in terms of socio-economic status. So a homogeneous group will find it easy to talk out a consensus. The talking and the chances of finding consensus are made much easier if the group is small as hearing each person's view takes less time, all can hear and understand the needs of others, and there are fewer possible differences between people, even if each has a distinct view. To achieve the four parts of participatory democracy listed above (see Table 3.1), the group has to operate in certain ways (see Table 3.2).

Table 3.2 What contributes to participatory democracy working?

Component	What makes it easier?	
All can raise an issue, suggest solutions, take part in the final decision	• Equality between group members • Feeling comfortable together	
Face-to-face meetings	• Small groups • Homogeneity	Underlying all components
Much discussion – all who want to can contribute	• No time limits • Small groups • Equality between group members • Feeling comfortable together • Etiquette of conflict	is a need for those in the group to believe in the process and to have a desire to make the process work
Tendency to want consensus	• Homogeneity • Equality between group members • Feeling comfortable together	

Making participatory democracy work

Clearly participatory democracy is not easy: it needs time and a homogeneous group willing to debate issues face-to-face and strive for a solution acceptable to all. Such a group is most likely to comprise people with a belief that it is worth it, that the decisions are better because they recognise the needs of all or allowed each to have an equal say; or that the process is intrinsically preferable because it improves people. Those who use participatory democracy have distinct requirements and so it should be assessed in terms of these rather than the needs of those who want fast decisions. In assessing participatory democracy the following aspects need to be examined: the degree of equality between members; consensus; homogeneity; the size of the group; a belief in the system. The remainder of this chapter examines each of these aspects looking at reasons for it, the extent to which it is present and inherent problems.

For all to have power, the vital component is to maintain equality between all members. It is not necessarily the case that the people need to be equal in terms of 'status' in the outside world but rather that they are treated equally inside the collectivity and that any inequalities, such as in education level or time commitments, are nullified within the collective. There should be an equality of respect (Mansbridge 1980: 28) and members must trust each other (Fisher and Ellis 1990: 28). Note that participatory democracy stresses an equality of taking part, not that each person needs a voice of equal weight to protect their own interests (Mansbridge 1980: ch. 17). Equality demands that all can bring up an issue, propose solutions and express their views on any issue and that the decisions of the collectivity are followed. If this is the case then the people have power over the decisions of the group. Studies of groups that use participatory democracy show that inequalities have to be confronted. Some inequalities relate to structure and others to the actual people. Can each member find the time to attend all of the meetings and stay as long as the meeting lasts? Does sitting in one part of the meeting room increase your chance of being heard? Do some people feel unsure of their ability to express their views and so hold back? Do all have the necessary information to follow the issues under discussion? Are those who express a contrary view treated with hostility by the collectivity? Do some members have more influence than others?

Do practicalities of the meeting time and venue lead to inequalities? Meetings can take a long time so outside constraints on the time people have available can be a problem. Some members may have responsibilities, such as children, which mean they cannot attend all meetings. Some may have work commitments or feel uneasy travelling across town to the meeting room at night. In workers' co-operatives there is a tendency to treat the meeting as part of the work day to eliminate these types of inequalities. If members have other demands on their time then the group will have to deal with a tension between long discussions and the need to watch the clock; between curtailing debate or accepting inequalities. Does the set-up of the room allow all to participate in the same way? Is it possible for each person in the room to speak and be heard and to hear and see the reaction of others? In a small group it is easy for all to sit in a circle so each person can hear and be heard and see the reaction of all other members. However, as the group gets bigger, a circle becomes impractical and so it is hard for any one person to gauge the reaction of others. As the group gets bigger it becomes harder to speak, in part because a larger group is more daunting, in part because of making oneself heard. When a group needs to use a microphone then the whole ambience of the discussion changes (Mansbridge 1980: 286). Such seemingly minor decisions as the time and venue for the meeting can affect the equality of those involved.

Individuals within a group will have differing oratory skills and varying levels of confidence. To participate fully, and thus have power, a person must be able to speak before others, to use language well, to grasp an argument, and in some cases to be heard in a large room. Some people's jobs enhance these skills and those with greater experience in groups will feel more comfortable speaking. People do have different skills so the group has to ensure these differences are negated as much as possible within the group. An individual's greater skills will only lead to greater influence if the person chooses to use them and some with the ability to dominate may be self-aware and act to guard against undue authority within the group (Cornforth 1995: 504). However, commitment to the group and a feeling that participation is worthwhile will encourage even the most shy member to speak (Fisher and Ellis 1990: 184). Rather than relying on such impulses, some groups formalise processes to equalise speaking time. For example, THE FEMIN-ISTS, in New York distributed a number of disks to each member at the start of the meeting. To speak a member had to redeem a disk, thus ensuring an equality in the number of times each person spoke (Morgan 1970: xxviii). Such a system encourages all to speak but does not address the advantage held by those with a good grasp of the language and an ability to persuade others with their arguments. Differences in oratory skills may mirror differences in education, income or ethnicity and there are cultural differences in the interpretation of shouting or gesturing and the ability to deal with verbal conflict (Riger 1994: 294). Long discussion and disagreement is emotionally hard for some but exhilarating for others. Because discussion is such a vital part of participatory democracy, if the group wants equality of input it has to ensure that all members are empowered to speak and do not feel intimidated.

Another aspect of equal participation in discussion is equal knowledge about relevant issues. Dissemination of information is important so that all know the details, sometimes very technical, of what will be discussed (Rothschild and Whitt 1986: 104–15). Not only must information be spread but people must be given time to absorb it and ask questions if necessary. When mastery of much detailed information is needed in order to be able to participate in discussion then it is easy for an interested and technically competent elite to emerge (Holmstrom 1989: 16). In the USA the commitment to good information flow was one of the reasons given for the success of neighbourhood groups (Berry *et al.* 1993: 50, 60–61). At Mondragon a great deal of time, energy and money is spent on the dissemination of information. Details of the business plan and any proposed changes are presented to the members by trained people, during work time. As well as the presentations, members can ask questions, and discussion of the issues is encouraged (Whyte and Whyte 1991: 226–27). When those in the group do not have detailed information relating to the issues then it is common for the recommendations of those perceived to be knowledgeable to be followed with little discussion.

The other vital piece of information for all to have is the way in which decisions are made, for without this some will be at a great disadvantage in participating equally in the final decision (Freeman 1973: 287). For the sake of equality it is important that all, new members as well as old ones, understand how decisions are made, so teaching newcomers the process is important. However, for a fluid group with the potential for new members at every meeting, the need for constant induction can be time consuming (Landry *et al.* 1985: 38). Having history and rules written down makes it easier and enables new members to participate equally at an earlier stage (Rothschild and Whitt 1986: 53). THE FEMINISTS specified that all new members, as well as being familiar with and believing in ideas of feminism, had to attend two induction sessions (Koedt *et al.* 1973: 373).

The final important aspect for ensuring equality is the lack of hierarchy amongst group members. Central to the participatory democracy ideal is that all are equal and hierarchies are removed, hence job rotation and minimal pay differentials (Rothschild and Whitt 1986: 59–61). Many co-operatives give everyone the same pay or determine differences based upon need, or if there is a pay scale then it is as flat as possible. When pay is low, respect and feeling part of the group may be the only reason to stay working in a co-operative. Cook and Morgan characterise participatory democracy as the inclusion of amateurs in decision making, based on a desire to say that experts are not needed and that information, tasks and knowledge can be shared (Cook and Morgan 1971: 4). So as well as disseminating technical information, it is important that jobs and knowledge about the process are shared so no one has an advantage. Rothschild and Whitt (1986: 138) list widespread skills, information and technology as one of the conditions that helps co-operatives work. It is important that all members can do most of the jobs undertaken within the co-operative because otherwise there will be a hierarchy of skills. Rotation of jobs so that knowledge is shared is a common practice, for instance the lot system used by THE FEMINISTS or the rotation practised in a small co-operative. However there are problems attached with this philosophy: job rotation can diminish the quality of the work; teaching others a skill takes time; and those with a skill may want to have their ability recognised (Rothschild and Whitt 1986: 71). There is also an assumption that anyone can learn any skill rather than the conventional belief of individual aptitude for certain types of tasks. Job sharing and the attempt to avoid skill hierarchies works best when members start with similar skills, for instance in a lawyers' co-operative. The other way to ensure an equality of skills is when there are no jobs requiring great specialist or technical skills.

If there are specialised roles, or the same three people always start debate or set the agenda or have the last word or claim to be the only ones to understand key operational issues or how to publish a newsletter, then there is not real equality. Within the literature on workers' co-operatives the 'degeneration thesis' is widespread (Cornforth *et al.* 1988: ch. 6; Cornforth 1995; Riger 1994: 283–91; and Rothschild and Whitt 1986: 179–82). This argument follows Michels' 'iron law of oligarchy', which states that an elite will always take over an organisation because of the need for efficient, fast and unpopular decisions. As a group grows, the time taken to spread information and reach decisions will increase to the point where the process leads to inefficiencies. The need for fast, authoritative decisions is especially important for a group that provides a service, produces something or in some way has deadlines and targets to meet. The ever-present problem of dealing with personnel issues may also lead to the desire for someone in authority to discipline others, choose who to hire and generally give orders. Approaching the issue from another angle, Freeman talks of the 'tyranny of structurelessness' (Freeman 1973). Basing her ideas on experiences within student and women's movements she argued that all groups have a structure, it is just that some are formally recognised and others are not. The informal structure, is known to only a few and thus there is a self-perpetuating hierarchy based on knowledge that the members divulge only to those they choose to include within the power elite. As decisions become harder, and the amount of information that has to be absorbed increases, a small group will come to dominate decisions (Cornforth *et al.* 1988: 140–42). As the group grows and so has to deal with more people and a greater demand for the work of the group then there are pressures to formalise procedures, to use memos instead of discussion, to set up a committee to master some technical information, all of which can lead a participatory democracy group towards a bureaucratic, representative democracy structure (Riger 1994: 283–85).

Given that there are times when an individual or small group is necessary for fast decisions, or to act as spokesperson or to master very detailed material, how can a group that practises participatory democracy cope? While authority may need to be delegated, it comes from the collective and can be removed by the collective. This emphasis on the collective as the source of all authority is a defining aspect of a co-operative (Rothschild and Whitt 1986: 62). Holmstrom emphasises the need for a circular structure so that, even when managers are brought in, the people who must do as the manager says are also the ones who make policy in the meetings (Holmstrom 1989: 16, 53). Mondragon has managers who are answerable to the members of the collective because they are selected for four years by the governing council and a council can remove them during that time (Whyte and Whyte 1991: 235–37). Having people with specified authority does not mean there is a hierarchy as long as those people know the limits of their authority and are accountable to the collective (Freeman 1973: 298; Landry *et al.* 1985: 41). Rotating these jobs also helps to lessen the chances of a hardened hierarchy because of the sharing of skills and knowledge. In accepting the need for some positions of authority, there is a recognition of the needs of efficiency and some difference in skills but there is the assumption that those in positions of authority will change and that others in the group know enough about the issues to be able to question their actions and thus ensure accountability to the group. Only when those in authority have a monopoly on information and the members tend to unquestioningly follow their suggestion has a hierarchy replaced the equality of participatory democracy.

The acid test for equality would be to ask a member at random if, upon hearing a report at a meeting that 'x' had happened, they knew enough about the issue to feel comfortable asking a question, were able to interrupt and put the question and felt comfortable in expressing disagreement with what had happened, regardless of who had made the initial report.

The aspect of decision making that is most marked in participatory democracy is the tendency to aim for consensus. This practice again increases the time needed to make decisions so why is it prized so highly? Consensual decisions foster solidarity because of the assumption that it is possible to find a solution acceptable to all, but consensus also means that when there is conflict, everyone's interest is safeguarded because anyone can veto a decision (Mansbridge 1980: ch. 18). Because a minority's views cannot be ignored by the majority, consensus fits with ideals of equality and caring about the whole group. A consensual decision also helps reinforce the idea of a unified group as in seeking consensus the commonalties are stressed. To find common ground people have to listen to others and try to understand their view. This also means friendship bonds are stronger, as each trusts the others not to make decisions harmful to themselves. In striving for a mutually acceptable solution, it matters more to each person that the harmony of the group is maintained than that they get exactly what they wanted on a particular issue.

Another more practical reason for favouring consensus is that a decision will only be wholeheartedly followed if all accept it. Due to the time taken over decisions and the emotional input from all involved there is an idea that group decisions are owned by the members and therefore likely to be followed (Mason 1982: 38; Rothschild and Whitt 1986: 65). This aspect is important for many groups as collective agreement is the only force that leads members to comply. For instance, in the New England towns there was no external force to compel compliance so agreement by all was necessary (Zuckerman 1970). Only consensus decisions have the 'weight of moral authority' and so are 'binding and legitimate' (Rothschild and Whitt 1986: 51). The UN Security Council has to work on unanimity because it has no means to force dissenting members to comply with a majority decision. As discussed in Chapter 2, consensus is not the same as unanimity because as well as all agreeing to the decision, a consensus implies some commitment to the decision by all in the group (Fisher and Ellis 1990: 142–43, 153).

Despite the theoretical and practical reasons for using consensus, a pressure for consensus can be problematic, with some feeling a strong social pressure to keep quiet when they disagree (Cook and Morgan 1971: 32; Cornforth *et al.* 1988: 162) and so a 'false consensus' is reached (Mansbridge 1980: 33–34). The nature of many groups using participatory democracy increases the likelihood of pressure to conform. In women's groups, disagreeing could be labelled 'anti-feminist' because of the central message of 'unity of sisterhood' (Riger 1994: 291). Likewise, in New England town politics, keeping the peace was a vital aim and so discussion and compromise were important tools of political debate (Zuckerman 1970: 125). Also the nature of the group, with face-to-face discussion and an emphasis on caring for the group, means that many may find it hard to argue with other members, particularly if disagreement is seen as criticism (Mansbridge 1980: 34, 273). Consensus gives power to a minority (as discussed in Chapter 2) but if there is strong pressure to conform then the danger is that a minority will be silenced. When the group agrees out of a desire for conformity, rather than through discussion of the issues, then the decision is likely to be ill thought out. Lots of discussion means that each idea is tested and debated but if all agree without discussion then the solution will have missed this refining process that is so central to the whole idea of participatory democracy (Fisher and Ellis 1990: 218–20). It is the deliberation and striving for a common solution that distinguishes participatory democracy, so false consensus and fear of conflict are real problems.

However, the group aspect may also mean that people are willing to modify their views for the sake of the group. Consensus works best when the group is comfortable with the idea of argument and disagreement and sees the process of amendment as positive (see Ontario Green Party above). A committed and cohesive group should be a comfortable place where people feel safe to disagree (Fisher and Ellis 1990: 185). There is a fine line between modifying one's views through discussion to create a solution beneficial to all and refraining from argument within the group to protect unanimity. Berry's team found that, contrary to the expectations of detractors, the local meetings could reconcile the wishes of different groups in the community and reach a commonly agreed view on the best solution (Berry *et al.* 1993: 202). While conflict can be emotionally draining for some people, any group needs to determine how to deal with contentious issues:

an 'etiquette of conflict' (Cornforth *et al.* 1988: 157–63; Riger 1994: 295). If only the easy decisions are made then the group may not be making the important decisions. If hard issues are side-stepped then the problem is just deferred until it reaches crisis point (Landry *et al.* 1985: 39) when real discussion is unlikely to be possible. Of particular difficulty in workers' co-operatives are personnel issues, for instance telling someone they are not doing their job well enough (Morgen 1994: 679–81). Long-standing groups tend to build in processes that make conflict easier to contain. For instance, some workers' co-operatives specify that every decision must be ratified a week after the original decision, to allow time for reflection and thought away from the pressures of the group discussion, others may bring in a facilitator. Another method for dealing with conflict and alleviating the pressure to conform is the use of secret ballots, but this is anathema to some as it seems like a process that institutionalises division. To ensure equality the group must find a way to ensure all can have a say, even if this means consensus is hard to reach on some issues. The tyranny of the group can be just as pernicious as the tyranny of the minority. So whilst consensus helps to build collectivity there are inherent problems of enforced agreement and avoiding contentious issues.

Consensus, discussion and equity are all easier in a homogeneous group (Mansbridge 1980: ix–x, 8–9; Mason 1982: 32; Morgen 1994: 669–70; Rothschild and Whitt 1986: 138). Mansbridge's central argument is that participatory democracy (she calls it unitary democracy) is taking the norms of friendship into a formal political setting (Mansbridge 1980: 8). One characteristic of a collective organisation is the ideal of community (Rothschild and Whitt 1986: 62). While participatory democracy is based upon ideas of solidarity and commitment to the group, these conditions likewise enhance the chances of a successful group. In a study of town meetings Zimmerman (1986: 31) found that meetings in homogeneous towns had a very different atmosphere from those where there were clear divides amongst townspeople. Homogeneity helps consensus as there are no inbuilt cleavages (Rothschild and Whitt 1986: 95–97). A New England town with a major divide in views was likely to split and create two new homogeneous towns because decisions needed consensus. Feeling comfortable together, sharing knowledge, feeling equal respect and being able to criticise each other are all made easier if there is a strong community feeling, or friendship. If all feel part of the whole then there is likely to be mutual respect that is vital for real equality of participation. Friends are also likely to empathise with each other, to care about the views of others and be willing to compromise to find a solution acceptable to all. A cohesive group feeling comes from mutual liking between members (Fisher and Ellis 1990: 34).

People tend to like those they perceive as sharing key values and beliefs (ibid. 1990: 41). Many of the groups who use participatory democracy have shared values (women and environmentalist groups) or see other members in day-to-day life (small towns, workplaces). The more successful neighbourhood meeting structures used existing neighbourhood boundaries so as to tap into the existing feelings of identity (Berry *et al.* 1993: 49). The practices of collective decision making can reinforce this intimacy. Face-to-face discussion and the sheer amount of time spent together can build feelings of solidarity even in a group that initially has little in common. Time and emotion spent together leads to solidarity and commitment (Fisher and Ellis 1990: 42; Morgen 1994: 669; Rothschild and Whitt 1986: 65). The emphasis on consensus, and thus the need to empathise with others, helps feelings of intimacy and means that members tend to know a lot about each other, more than workmates would normally know. In many groups the sharing of personal matters is common. The group can become the centre of social life so that time is spent with other members of the group outside the workplace or political group. Knowing you will see other members again, especially if not just in meetings, helps the feeling of community (Berry *et al.* 1993: 10–11; Mansbridge 1980) but may also increase the pressure to conform and not criticise others (see above). Also the extent of time spent together and shared emotional discussion can become stifling and give the feeling that the group is taking over and each is living in the others' pockets (Cornforth *et al.* 1988: 105).

So as to ensure the continued harmony of the group, recruitment and induction of new members are important. Each new member must fit into the group and feel equal to those with longer membership, they must also believe in the system and share other common values. A group needs to grow and thus absorb new members but this process cannot be allowed to harm the workings of the group. Each new addition adds potential for disagreement and conflict so vetting can be vital. Therefore, many workers' co-operatives have a probation period for new members (Cornforth *et al.* 1988: 168–69; Whyte and Whyte 1991) and seek to recruit others who share the homogeneous elements of the group (Riger 1994: 282; Rothschild and Whitt 1986: 54–56). Employment is based on friendship and shared values rather than on the recruiting norm of job skills and experience. As described above, THE FEMINISTS expelled those who were seen as not participating enough. Some New England towns enforced homogeneity by hounding out those who did not fit the profile in terms of religion, background or values (Zuckerman 1970: ch. 2).

Participatory democracy works best when members have common interests: they will trust others to make good decisions because usually all want the same thing. But if this commonality is over stressed there will be pressures to conform and conflict may be stifled, as discussed above. Another potential problem arises if the bonds of friendship are strong amongst only a sub-set of the group. If this happens, then the friends can become an elite who work as a group, not necessarily through a desire to control decisions, but because friends discuss issues, tend to back each other and feel more at ease when airing their views (Freeman 1973: 288). Like consensus, homogeneity is necessary but carries inherent problems.

The three components discussed so far, equality, consensus and homogeneity, are intrinsic parts of the participatory democratic ideal and practice. The following two important components are purely practical. An ideal group for participatory democracy is a group where members have common values, behave like friends and believe in the system enough to work at preserving equality. Such a group is likely to be small. Throughout the literature size is seen as a factor in the success of participatory democracy (Cook and Morgan 1971: 25–27; Holmstrom

1989: 16; Mansbridge 1980: ch. 20; Riger 1994: 282; Rothschild and Whitt 1986: 91–95, 138). The fewer the number of people, the less chance for difference and the easier it is to maintain bonds of friendship. When there are differences, a small group is more likely to work towards a mutually acceptable solution and individuals are more likely to empathise. Within a small group it is easier for each to have the time to explain their position and so, with better information, it is easier to find common ground. A small group is likely to emphasise harmony and avoid conflict and to put energy into maintaining this situation. When part of a small group, individuals are more likely to take responsibility for the decisions of the group, to feel they are a part of the process. Communicating to a small group is less daunting and proximity is important for non-verbal communication, such as emotion, which is important for increasing empathy and bonds of friendship.

But there are no hard-and-fast rules on how big 'small' can be. Because of the advantages of having a friendly group that cares about other members the group must be small enough for each to know the other members. As the group gets bigger chances of democracy being eroded increase. But a group of 40 confident, articulate people may manage to ensure power for all members better than a group of seven where one member is a powerful orator, and another claims an expertise in accountancy. To ensure equality a small homogeneous group works best but the organisation may need to grow to achieve their reason for existing, such as running a wholefood shop, producing a newspaper or organising a political protest action. Because equal respect is important, one way to look at size may be that the group should only be as big as is needed to do the job, if there are 'spare' people whose time or skills are not vital to the enterprise, then equality of respect may be jeopardised. To address the tension between needing to be big to do the job but small to aid participatory democracy, some larger workplaces have split into section groups for much decision making, allowing for small groups with a common interest or area of expertise. Or a whole new co-operative will be created for a new venture, for instance a wholefood shop developing a bakery. In Mondragon the different co-operative enterprises support each other and work together in areas such as banking, distribution, education and research, thus staying small but benefiting from economies of scale.

But, because small groups are needed, this limits the situations in which participatory democracy can be used. There is also the suggestion that small groups decide small problems but cannot address such things as poverty, foreign relations or the education budget. So you can have much control over local, small-scale decisions. When norms are to equate big with power and influence, staying small may hinder participatory democracy groups in their ability to spread their message and be taken seriously.

A final, helpful component is a strong belief in participatory democracy so that all will put effort into ensuring that the system works, even if it takes time, is emotionally tense and sometimes means sacrificing efficiency (Holmstrom 1989: 17; Riger 1994: 281; Rothschild and Whitt 1986: 56; Whyte and Whyte 1991: 233). Some co-operative workers will stay on lower pay for longer hours because they like being part of the decision-making process. Indeed, belief in the process may become the crucial shared common value that helps to create harmony and a feeling of community. One of the reasons for the success of certain neighbour-hood meeting schemes was a strong personal commitment to make it work amongst those setting them up (Berry *et al.* 1993: 48). Those who have a commit-ment to the group and think the process worthwhile will put in time and energy, but those who are not committed will hinder the chance of consensus because they do not have that desire to help the process (Fisher and Ellis 1990: 184, 195).

However, a belief in the system will be a problem if this means the process is deemed to be perfect in every aspect. One reason for the continuing success of Mondragon, despite its size, is that the members are always willing to discuss how the process is working and how to deal with any problems (Whyte and Whyte 1991: 234). Cornforth also emphasises the need for regular self-audits of how the organisation is working and in particular the desired balance between collective decision making and efficiency (Cornforth *et al.* 1988: 145, 158–59, 170–71). But there is a problem if all the time is spent discussing how decisions are made so that no time is left for making real decisions or doing whatever it is that the group does. The process of collective decision making cannot become the sole purpose of the group: as with all democracy, it is a means to an end.

Summary

Central to participatory democracy is full involvement of all in all stages of the decision-making process, using face-to-face meetings with unrestricted discussion so as to reach a consensus. To achieve these aims it helps if the group is a small, homogeneous collection of equals who believe in the process and have established a means of dealing with conflict. However, these conditions mean that participa-tory democracy is not appropriate for all groups and may hinder inclusivity. There are also worries that hard problems will be avoided and that fast solutions are impossible thus causing inefficiencies and adding to a tendency towards elite take-over. Furthermore the process may become all important, meaning that the activity for which the group was established will take second place to the means of decision making (see Table 3.3).

However, there are strong advocates of participatory democracy who argue that the benefits of this procedure are worth the time and energy that is needed. In particular there is the feeling that experience of participatory democracy helps the individual to develop into a better citizen. There is a recognition that partici-pation in decision making has to be learned and small groups where the people feel they are making a difference are a good training ground. In particular, the workplace is seen as a good place to learn about politics and so develop citizens for a greater involvement in the wider political world (Pateman 1970: 105). By taking part, people practise the process of democracy but also see that they can have an influence and some control over what happens to them. This feeling of political efficacy then carries over into the wider political community so people will feel less alienation from the political structures, more interested in politics and willing to take a more active part. Another psychological change valued by many advocates

Table 3.3 Problems with making participatory democracy work

Helpful condition	Potential problems
Equality between group members	• Hard to remove inequalities • Job rotation and non-delegation take time and energy • May be inefficient
Etiquette of conflict	• Have to deal with conflict • Emotionally hard
Homogeneity and feeling comfortable	• Not inclusive • Pressure to conform • Lack of skill diversity
Small group	• Not inclusive • Limits what the group can achieve • Can a small group make big decisions?
Belief in the process	• Not inclusive • Will not apply to all groups • Process can become all important

of participatory democracy is the acquisition of a feeling for the community as group discussion encourages individuals to think about the needs of the group rather than themselves. Because of the extent of discussion, listening to the views of others, striving for a solution acceptable to all, the participatory democracy process leads to a group of people who act like citizens in that they care about the general good and are used to thinking about political matters (Barber 1984: 197).

In assessing participatory democracy it is important to bear in mind that those who use it have different values to others. Making decisions acceptable to all and maintaining equality are seen as important while quick efficient decisions are of lesser importance. However there are some important problems. Can participatory democracy be used for a divided group or a large group or one that does not have a belief in the system? In other words can it only be used for the type of organisations that use it now. Can it only be used for small decisions?

4 Initiatives and referendums

The people may exercise decision-making power by voting on specific issues. As this process is usually used alongside representative democracy the voters are not asked to decide all issues. Most countries have used this type of democracy, often on questions relating to the constitution. Indeed, since 1945, Costa Rica, Germany, India, Israel, Japan, the Netherlands, Mexico and the USA are the only democracies to have not held a national vote on a specific issue. However, Switzerland and various states within the USA are the only polities to have regular popular votes.

Those who advocate issue votes stress the desirability of involving all people in important decisions and the need to lessen the power of elite groups, to give people a direct say rather than one mediated through representatives. It is for the people to decide which issues are important and where new policy is needed because they are sovereign. When the people can raise an issue then the political elite cannot ignore certain areas because they are difficult or divisive or trivial. So direct democracy gives the people control over setting the agenda and making the final decision.

Putting issues to the people

As with other aspects of democracy, there are a variety of ways in which issues are put to the people (see Table 4.1). Each method provides a different degree of popular control, each of which will be discussed in some detail. The method used to put issues to the popular vote is commonly called a referendum. However, in places that use several of the above methods 'referendum' is used in a more specific way. The literature varies in the use of specific terms and some are country related (see Table 4.2). When looking at examples of direct democracy in

Table 4.1 Types of popular votes

- A group of people raises an issue and the wider population votes on it.
- Voters demand that a law passed in the legislature is put to the people for ratification.
- The government asks the people to approve of political structures.
- Voters are consulted on their views on an issue.

Table 4.2 Definitions of terms for a vote on an issue

Initiative	A group of people propose a new issue that is put to the popular vote
Referendum	General term for any popular issue vote in the USA when the people challenge legislation
Facultative	Swiss version of USA referendum
Plebiscite	General term for any popular vote Sometimes used to signify that the result was not binding on the government

practice, it is important to remember that the whole point of such proceedings is to give power to the people. Therefore, the extent to which the people, rather than the government, control each part of the process is important. Relating to the parts of a decision discussed in Chapter 1, three areas are of particular import-ance when looking at popular votes. First, who decides that there will be a vote on a particular issue, that is sets the agenda. Second, in terms of providing different options, who actually writes the question for the vote, and third, are the wishes of the people implemented?

The greatest popular control comes when the people put issues onto the agenda. In Switzerland, Italy and 24 states within the USA a group of voters can raise a particular issue and have it decided in a popular vote. To start the process, a group must register its intent and then demonstrate that there is popular support for the measure by collecting the signatures of a specified number of registered electors. In Switzerland and Italy the number is static at 100,000 and 500,000 respectively (1.5 and 1.1 per cent of population). In the different states of the USA the number of signatures needed on a petition is a percentage of those involved in the previous election and this can vary from under 15,000 in South Dakota to over 600,000 in Illinois (Schmidt 1989: 296). Once a petition has been verified as having sufficient valid signatures, the government in each polity is required to put the question to the voters.

The wording of the proposed new legislation is provided by the group that initiated the process in Switzerland and states of the USA. Voters are then asked to accept or reject the full proposition. In Switzerland only one issue can be addressed but the legislation can cover many details. The Swiss government can propose an alternative amendment that the people also vote to accept or reject. A voter can accept both the original and the counter proposal then the one with the highest vote wins. In the USA, other groups, if they fulfil the petition require-ments, can suggest another detailed proposal on the same issue. A 1988 prop-osition in California concerning automobile insurance was countered by four other proposals but the original was the only one to succeed. In Italy, all a group can do is ask for part or all of an existing piece of legislation to be repealed. If the vote is in favour of repeal then the parliament must write new legislation within 150 days: the preferred replacement wording is usually made clear during the campaign.

The final decision is, in theory, made by the majority vote; however, there are some qualifications. A simple majority will win a vote in each state in the USA but the courts can rule that the proposed legislation is unconstitutional. For instance, a successful 1974 initiative in California to limit campaign spending was squashed as it was deemed to breach freedom of speech. The majority of successful initiatives in California have been altered or nullified by the state court. However, once an initiative becomes law it has a higher status than other legislation because it can only be repealed or amended by another popular vote. In Switzerland, a double majority is needed but if that hurdle is passed then the result is sovereign. A double majority means that at least half of those voting must accept it plus there must be a majority vote in half the cantons (regions). The court cannot strike it out unless it was conducted wrongly. For a valid vote in Italy, turnout must be over 50 per cent.

Direct democracy is used at the sub-national level too. The annual general meeting (AGM) of an organisation is a common venue for a series of policy votes by those attending. The annual conferences of many political parties, trade unions and pressure groups vote on policy matters. In most organisations any member can suggest an issue to be discussed and the proposer writes the details of the question, although most meetings allow for amendments to be suggested from the floor and then voted upon. Some organisations have membership votes on key policy issues where all members are allowed to participate. In 1994 the National Trust in England decided to hold a vote of all members on the question of allowing stag hunting on the land that is owned by the Trust. This issue was originally raised at the AGM of the organisation but the executive committee decided that such a contentious issue needed to be put to all members.

In Switzerland the initiative must suggest a constitutional amendment, but as the constitution covers many issues of a policy nature, this rarely hinders the initiators (Kobach 1993: ch. 3). For instance, the right to work (1946), abortion (1977, 1985), and the building of nuclear power plants (1979, 1984, 1990) have all been put to the vote through a constitutional amendment. Issues more commonly associated with the constitution have only been raised in relation to the electoral system (1900, 1910, 1918, 1942) and the use of direct democracy (1921, 1938, 1949, 1961, 1977, 1987). Initiatives in Switzerland have often failed to win a majority of votes. In the first 20 years of constitutional initiatives, nine collected enough signatures, of which two were passed: method of cattle slaughter in 1893 and a ban on selling the strong liquor absinthe in 1908. In more recent times failure has also been common. The 1987 initiative to stop the building of a military base on scenic moors was only the second to succeed since 1949, although 53 had been put to the vote in that time. The next success was in 1990 with a 10-year moratorium on nuclear-plant construction. Recently there has been more success: in 1993 voters agreed to make the National Day a public holiday and the next year a move to protect the alpine region by moving freight transportation from road to rail was narrowly passed. The number of issues being put to the vote has been increasing: eight in the period 1980–84; 15 between 1985 and 1989; 18 from 1990 to 1994.

Within the USA initiatives can propose a new law or a constitutional amendment and states vary as to which they allow (Magleby 1994: 226). Between 1989 and 1994 there were nearly 2,000 initiatives on ballots and just over a third have been accepted. Use of the initiative is increasing with nearly 150 questions put to voters in 1994 compared to 128 in 1992. That was over double the 61 in 1982, itself a 50-year high. Since the 1970s, three-fifths of initiatives have been about government spending, moral issues or political reform (ibid.: 237). In 1994 the three most common issues were term limits for elected officials, tax restrictions and criminal-sentencing guidelines. In the late 1980s, abortion and gay rights were common topics, while environmental issues predominated in the early part of that decade. A range of measures to restrict tax levels were proposed in the late 1970s. Other issues have ranged across moral, monetary and political matters. Several states have voted for the use of the death penalty while other popular subjects have been the introduction of a state lottery and disclosure of campaign funding.

Italian initiatives must ask for the repeal of legislation, but this relates to old laws as well as new ones so any issue can be raised. For instance, the abortion questions in 1981 related to a 1930 law. Suggested changes to old laws have been used to bring up a range of new issues such as restricting advertising during films (1995), changing the electoral system (1993), making hunting illegal (1990) and holding judges accountable for wrong verdicts (1987) (Kobach 1993: 229). Use of this device is growing, with 12 questions in June 1995 compared to 10 over the preceding five years. Of the 26 initiative votes in Italy between 1974 and 1994, 14 were successful, five in 1987, one in 1991 and eight in 1993. In 1995, turnout was just high enough for the results to be valid but the results were mixed with five being passed and two narrowly losing.

Demanding that new legislation be referred to the voters for approval allows the people to keep a constant check on those they elected. Only Switzerland, Uruguay and 24 states in the USA give voters the right to challenge the implementation of a new law. If a challenge is signalled then the law is suspended until it has been approved by the voters. While Italians can challenge a law, there is no time limit so the underlying democratic process is different.

In Switzerland voters have 90 days after legislation is passed by parliament to lodge the intention to challenge and then to collect 50,000 signatures. Twenty-five per cent of voters are needed on a petition in Uruguay, while numbers in the USA vary. If sufficient signatures are collected then voters are asked to accept or reject the new legislation. There is no need for a double majority in Switzerland so in all places where this procedure is used the majority prevails. As an existing piece of legislation is being challenged, all of the details are known and have been written by legislators. Some legislation is detailed and covers several issues so the matter can be more complex than an initiative. For instance, in 1992 a Swiss law that covered the decriminalisation of homosexuality and sex between minors plus a definition of rape within marriage was unsuccessfully challenged in a popular vote.

In Switzerland challenges to legislation, called *facultative* are common and frequently successful. There were 112 challenges between 1848 and 1992 (Kobach 1993: 87) but this constitutes less than a tenth of all legislation passed. The types of legislation that are challenged in Switzerland range widely. The first challenge in 1875 related to civil status and marriage and the next two were about voting rights and the issue of banknotes. In 1992 there were 10 challenges, a high number compared with previous years: there were 10 across the preceding six years. The topics ranged from the level of water in reservoirs, to regulation of genetic technology, farmers' inheritance regulation and an increase in MPs' salaries (ibid.: 78). In 1994, five pieces of legislation were challenged: modifying air-traffic laws; changing the criminal code to (amongst other things) make racial discrimination illegal; changes to sickness insurance; changes to the treatment of foreign nationals and allowing Swiss troops to join UN peace-keeping missions. Only the last was rejected by the voters. This level of success for the government when challenged follows the trend of previous years (they won all three in 1993 and eight of 12 in 1992) but in the preceding 10 years they lost as many as they won.

In contrast, this procedure has not been used in California since 1952, because of the large number of signatures that must be collected in a short time. In 1990 370,000 signatures would have been needed, compared to the 50,000 in Switzerland. People in other states do use this procedure occasionally. In 1988 there were five challenges to legislation: sales tax on cable TV was challenged in North Dakota; the sale of cheap handguns was stopped in Maryland; an increase in state legislature pay was rejected in Massachusetts; a ban on the state funding of abortions was approved in Michigan; and deregulation of intra-state phone services was upheld in South Dakota. Two challenges have occurred in Uruguay: in 1989 over an amnesty law; and in 1992 on privatisation (Butler and Ranney 1994: 7).

In the vast majority of countries constitutional matters are the only issues to have been put to a popular vote. Usually it is the sole preserve of the government to launch such a vote. A popular vote to accept a new set of rules has a strong legitimising component both internally and in the eyes of the international community. This legitimising function has been sought by some regimes that would not be considered democratic, but that have held popular votes in an attempt to show general acceptance of the government. The series of votes held by Hitler in the 1930s to approve of his leadership and the Nazi government are prime examples, but the practice was also followed in Haiti when Duvalier held a vote in 1964 to make him President for life and in the Philippines when Marcos held one vote on the introduction of martial law in 1973 and one to sanction its continuance in 1975. The practice continues: Hussein held a referendum in Iraq in 1995 where over 95 per cent of voters endorsed a further seven years of his presidency.

In many places a government will choose to hold a vote on suggested changes in the regime structure to acquire a popular seal of approval. Three types of amendments are particularly likely to be put to a vote: territorial sovereignty, the constitution and treaties. In each case the people are being asked to approve new rules for the way in which they exercise power over the government, so the vote is being used to show that the people accept the details of representative democracy.

Of the 15 countries to emerge from the former Soviet Union, nine held a ballot on independence from the Soviet Union (Brady and Kaplan 1994: 193). Direct democracy has been used a great deal in Eastern Europe since 1989 but votes for independence are not confined to emerging democracies. For instance, Iceland voted to separate from Denmark in 1944, and in 1979 Greenland followed suit then three years later voted itself out of the EEC too. Various regions of Spain have voted for increased autonomy. Voters in the Canadian Northwest Territories voted in favour of the creation of an Inuit homeland, Nunavut, in 1992. The Inuit later voted to accept the land claim that had been negotiated with the government (Fenge 1993). In 1997, voters in Scotland voted for a Scottish parliament and the Welsh voted for their own assembly in Wales. Self-determination is a widely accepted aspect of nation building so a popular vote to settle territorial questions helps to give the new entity legitimacy in the eyes of the world community. However, as the series of independence votes in the former Yugoslavia prior to the outbreak of hostilities illustrate (Brady and Kaplan 1994: 207–10), votes on regional or ethnic self-determination can also be destructive as they emphasise differences rather than unity.

In using a popular vote to legitimise the creation of a new sovereign body, the issue of who should be asked is relevant. Usually only those people in the area that wants autonomy are eligible. In 1979 and 1997 the voters in Scotland and Wales were asked if they wanted devolved powers from the UK parliament but those voters living in England had no voice. Likewise, the 1980 and 1995 votes on Quebec's independence from the rest of Canada was only put to those registered to vote in that province. The vote in the Canadian Northwest is one of the few examples where voters in the area being left as well as those seeking independence were polled and the endorsement of the whole community was seen as vital in giving the new territory legitimacy.

Moves to unite separated countries, although less common, can also benefit from the legitimacy derived from a popular vote. The two Somalias voted to unite in 1961 and East and West Cameroon voted to join together in 1972. The 1998 Northern Ireland Agreement was put to separate referendums in Northern Ireland and Eire and only progressed when it was backed in both votes. It is notable that the unification of Germany was not put to a vote, a sign of the lasting mistrust of direct democracy in that country after Hitler's use of popular votes to acquire an aura of legitimacy.

Amongst the many newly democratic states to emerge in the 1990s, a vote to adopt the new constitution was common in Eastern Europe and Africa. For instance Burundi and Romania in 1991; Ghana and Lithuania in 1992; Malawi and Russia in 1993. In each case the new arrangements were accepted by the vast majority of those who voted, thus giving the new regime authority and a legitimacy boost. A popular vote on a new constitution has also been used in the past although success is not guaranteed. Massachusetts, the first state in America to put its constitution to the vote, had it defeated in 1778 due to the absence of a Bill of Rights. The revised constitution was ratified in 1780.

Changes to constitutional details may also be put to the people for ratification. Indeed in Australia, Ireland, Switzerland and all states of USA except for Delaware, a vote on a constitutional change is mandatory, whether initiated by a petition or the government. This requirement can make changes very difficult. For instance, in Australia only eight of the 40 proposed constitutional amendments have been accepted, largely due to the qualified majority used and the partisan stance taken by the political parties on the votes (Kobach 1993: 222). The government in other countries may choose to gain the backing of the people before making major changes to the constitution. For instance, direct democracy was used to give some stability to a potentially volatile situation in South Africa during the move from apartheid. In 1992 the 'whites' voted to continue the reform process and thus gave the government support in the battle against white supremacist groups. But in Canada, the Meech Lake Accord, a negotiated agreement on relations between provinces, designed to ease the question of Quebec's sovereignty, was defeated in a vote in 1982 (Butler and Ranney 1994: 8–9).

The way in which elections are held is the most common subject of a popular vote on a constitutional amendment. In Switzerland a change to a proportional representation (PR) system was attempted in 1900 and 1910 before succeeding in 1918. The Irish rejected plans to change their single transferable vote (STV) system in 1959 and 1968. In Italy, the method of marking the ballot paper was changed by popular vote in 1991, and the system of Senate elections was changed away from PR in 1993. The same year the voters of New Zealand voted to adopt a PR system. In Guyana in 1978 voters ratified a proposal to abolish the need for referendums on constitutional change. In each case the voters are determining details of the way in which they exercise democratic power in national politics.

The Irish constitution, like the Swiss one, covers issues not normally considered constitutional, such as abortion and divorce, but changes to any part of the constitution need to be endorsed in a national vote (Manning 1978). The allowing of divorce was defeated in 1986 but narrowly accepted in 1995. Abortion has been voted on several times. A constitutional ban was accepted in 1983 but provisions for free movement of people and information within the European Union, as part of the Maastricht Treaty, meant that elements of the law had to be reconsidered in 1992. Voters approved of changes that would allow people to obtain details of abortion services in other countries and to travel to use them. A wider question that would have legalised some abortions in Ireland was rejected. Although these issues have been voted on in other countries as popular initiatives, the form of the Irish constitution, with its original inclusion of Catholic principles, means that such issues are constitutional ones. The people cannot demand a vote on such issues but if the government wants to change any part of the constitution then they need to put it to the people. The new regulations concerning divorce and abortion are also part of the constitution so any future changes will need to be put to the people.

Standard standing orders specify that a change to the constitution of an organisation must be ratified by the membership so this form of popular vote also has its parallel in meetings. Some other issues that are central to the working of the organisation may also need a vote amongst the members. British trade unions must, by law, have a postal vote of all members before taking any kind of industrial action such as a strike. Every ten years unions must also hold a postal ballot on the issue of having a fund that is used for political purposes, such as supporting the Labour Party.

Relations with other states in international organisations can affect the power that the people have over government decisions. For instance, member countries of the European Union are bound by decisions taken at the collective level. Therefore, the governments in some countries put the issue of membership to a popular vote. The Norwegians have twice rejected the idea of joining (1972 and 1992) but voters in Austria (1994), Denmark (1972), Finland (1994), Ireland (1972) and Sweden (1994) endorsed proposals to join the European community. The Maastricht Treaty, setting out closer union between members, was ratified in a national vote in Ireland, France and Denmark (on the second attempt). In all other member countries, the treaty was ratified by the legislative assembly. In Switzerland all treaties must be voted upon and in 1986 the people rejected the government's move to join the UN. Holding a popular vote on membership of international organisations is still the exception rather than the norm but this may change as power moves from national to international decision-making bodies.

The government may hold a popular vote to ascertain the views of the people but not be legally obliged to follow the majority view. In the countries that have used such consultative votes there are no rules about when a government should put an issue to the vote, rather they tend to be used for political expediency. Often the vote is used on issues that split the political parties, for instance the 1975 British vote on staying in the EEC. Both Labour and the Conservatives were split internally over British membership of the EEC and so the Labour government put the question to the people (Bogdanor 1994: 38–40). Australia has had three consultative votes. The most interesting was in 1977 to choose a new national song from a choice of four (Hughes 1994: 169). The 1991 all-union referendum held in most regions of the Soviet Union was not legally binding but was designed as a test of popular support for the continuation of the union. Votes for independence in some of the states that broke from the Soviet Union were also not binding but the overwhelming votes in favour of independence were acted upon.

New Zealand is unique in allowing the people to call for a non-binding vote on any issue if they collect the signatures of 10 per cent of the electorate. This legislation was passed in 1993 and the first vote, held in 1995, was on the level of staffing in the fire service. Other early petitions sought to ban the sale of eggs from battery hens, make a party's manifesto legally binding and provide comprehensive state-funded health and education (Catt 1996a). There were no successful petitions in 1996 or 1997. In 1998 petition issues called for a reduction in the number of MPs, the introduction of a written constitution and an increase in the percentage of gross domestic product (GDP) spent on health services.

A consultative vote is similar to a very large opinion poll with the two advantages of a public debate and the chance for everyone to express their view. However, it is also an expensive way for the government to gauge the opinion of the people. George Gallup, an early founder of opinion polling in the USA believed that opinion polls played an important democratic role. He was a strong populist who thought that politicians needed to heed the public view and that polling provided a scientific measure of public opinion. He argued that opinion polls were the 'pulse of democracy' because they allowed for the voices of ordinary people to be heard above organised interest groups (Crespi 1988: 3–12). In contrast to the optimistic views of polling pioneers, opinion polls are now generally treated with suspicion and they clearly do not have the same legitimacy as popular votes, even though they are more efficient.

There have been attempts to mix the debate offered in a popular vote with the speed and ease of an opinion poll. In a *televote* a random sample of people is sent unbiased information on certain issues and then asked to phone in their responses to a set of questions. Participants are encouraged to think about the issues and discuss them with others before reaching a decision. This procedure avoids the problem of opinion polls asking for responses on issues the person has not thought about and includes some of the benefits of discussion outlined in Chapter 3. Academics in Hawaii have conducted several *televotes* on both constitutional and legislative issues (Slaton 1992).

McLean (1989: 132) has suggested that these discussion-enhanced opinion polls could regularly be used by legislators. With a sample that is statistically representative of the population the results of the poll should be similar to the results if there was a popular vote. If the poll showed a narrow margin for one option then acting on the 'vote' of a sample would not be safe. However, if the enhanced poll showed a clear majority in favour of one option then the government would be safe in assuming such a view would be held by the majority of the population if given the same information. Using enhanced opinion polls would be more valid than making policy decisions on normal opinion polls and both quicker and cheaper than holding a consultative vote on the matter. Budge favours putting about 50 issues to the popular vote each year but using political parties as mediators to process information and assist voters in understanding the issues and reaching a decision. He also envisages the use of telecommunications systems to allow a wide spread of information and debate (Budge 1996: ch. 7).

Do the people have power?

There are two important areas to be considered in looking at the amount of people power provided by different manifestations of direct democracy: who determines that there will be a vote on a given issue; and must the government heed a majority vote. At one extreme is where the people can raise an issue and the vote is binding and at the other extreme is government-sponsored votes that are non-binding (see Table 4.3). In the table, the top left corner is where the people have the most power and the bottom right where they have the least. Interestingly, the former cell is empty but the latter contains many examples. Few places allow the people to raise an issue for consideration, so elected representatives generally control the agenda. In terms of the people being sovereign, qualified majorities or judicial review (both controlled by the elected government) are common restrictions. Although direct democracy gives the people more power than they would have without it, that power is restricted and operates mainly in relation to elected representatives.

In the literature on popular votes a number of questions are raised about how well they work (see Table 4.4). These cover all stages in the process, from initiation to result, and touch on both the feasibility of the system and the extent to which the people have power. One theme in the perceived problems for popular votes is the extent to which the people can and will take part, in raising issues, in becoming informed before a vote and in voting. Then there are questions about how reliable the result of the vote is as an indication of popular views, due in particular to the influence of well-funded campaigns and the tendency for conservative reactions to an issue but also to the problems of a very close result. Each perceived problem is discussed below.

The idea behind using a petition to trigger a vote is that the people can

Table 4.3 The power of voters to raise and decide issues

People raise issue		Initiatives in Switzerland, Italy and states within the USA	New Zealand initiative
People react to issue	Swiss *facultative*, Uruguay and USA state referendum		
Government raises issue	French 1946 constitution; Congo, Malawi constitution; Irish divorce vote *	Swiss and Australian constitutional amendment	British EEC; Australia national song; Lithuania independence; Soviet Union 'all-union' *
	Majority vote fully binding	Threshold needed or court challenge allowed	Purely consultative

Note: * Just some examples, not an exhaustive list

Table 4.4 Questions about popular votes

1 Do the people raise issues?
2 Can a suitable question be set?
3 How much do voters know about the issues?
4 Does money 'buy' a result?
5 Who votes?
6 Are voters generally 'conservative' or 'radical'?
7 Do votes provide a clear decision?
8 How does a popular vote fit with representative democracy?

influence politics at grass-roots level. However, the mechanisms of collecting sig-natures, writing a proposal and running an effective campaign need organisation and money. Therefore established interest or pressure groups are in the best position to take advantage of such procedures. Some groups successfully organise a vote without professional assistance but it takes lots of people with time and commitment. In the 1980s only two-fifths of Swiss initiatives came from newly formed groups. California has seen new groups gain sufficient signatures, for instance on coastal zoning or decriminalising marijuana, but the very process of running such a campaign created a well organised pressure group that went on to lobby in other ways for the desired legislation.

It is not uncommon for those involved in party politics to use the initiative process. Following their opposition to the Catholics' push to have the divorce laws repealed, the Italian Radical Party won seats in parliament and, even after their two 1978 initiatives were defeated, their vote increased in the 1979 election (Kobach 1993: 230). In Switzerland the same is true of the Greens and the Auto Party. The near success of the Swiss anti-foreigner proposals led to the formation of a new party and a shift in Swiss party politics (ibid.: 47). Larger parties have also used the process to advance their agenda, for instance the five questions put to the Italian voters in 1987 were sponsored by the opposition Socialist party. In Australia the parties take sides, with the opposition trying to see the government humiliated by voter rejection of their proposal. Candidates for governor in the states of the USA often associate themselves with a particular initiative as a way of establishing a profile and legislators may use a popular vote to avoid having to debate a contentious issue in the elected assembly.

Even in places where it is the people rather than the government who can bring an issue to the vote, it tends to be organised political groups that make use of the procedure. To steer an issue from petition to successful vote takes a great deal of organisation so existing groups will have an advantage. Those people with time and education, that is the middle classes, are the most likely to take part in the initiative process, just as they are the most likely to participate in all other political activity. Some groups within society are less able to mount a campaign, for instance the homeless, those living on state welfare or single parents. As with arguments surrounding participatory democracy discussed in the previous chap-ter, equal access to a democratic procedure does not mean that all can equally make use of that opportunity.

Votes often relate to complex issues yet must be put to the people as a simple choice. Usually the voters are asked to agree or disagree with a detailed prop-osition or even an entire constitution. When presented with an issue the voters can either accept or reject it, they cannot pick and choose on the details. For instance, in April 1993 the Russian people were asked if they approved of the socio-economic policies that the government had passed since 1992 and had to vote 'yes' or 'no' to the whole package. Likewise, in each country that has a vote on the new constitution, the voters cannot comment on each clause but must pass judgement on the entire document. While the rules in most countries specify that only one issue can be addressed in a vote, there are often many details in the way the issue is presented. For instance the proposed constitutional change in Ireland in 1995 specified that divorce would be allowed after four years of separation and covered details of how separation was defined and the process to be followed to obtain a divorce.

The way that a question is presented to voters may also cause problems as full details of the issue are rarely on the ballot paper. When a new piece of legislation is proposed only its name or description will be used. For instance the Quebec question on sovereignty refers to a bill that contained a preamble, 27 clauses and the text of a negotiated agreement. Any voter wanting full details would have to find a copy of the bill. In Italy, where a vote removes part of existing legislation the words appearing on the ballot paper are again a description of the main aspect of the issue. Here there is the problem that when voting on a challenge to a law a 'yes' vote means you oppose the law, that is you agree with the challenge. In most cases voters need to have done their homework to know what each vote is about and what a 'yes' vote means. In the USA the need for other information on the meaning of each proposition is not helped by the practice of referring to each issue by its number so posters may say 'vote yes on proposition 13' with no explanation of the issue involved. When the details of a piece of legislation are complex or the name ambiguous then voters may not be sure if it is a yes or a no vote that corresponds with their view. Even when the full question is supplied it may be phrased in a way that does not highlight the main consequence of the proposal. For instance the three Irish questions relating to the availability of abortion did not actually contain the word 'abortion' in their texts.

Levels of voter information about the issues on the ballot have been measured in surveys (see Linder 1994: 111–12; Magleby 1984: 151–53). For voters who want information there is plenty provided by those on each side of the argument, the state and the media. In American states each voter is sent a pamphlet that summarises the issues, giving the wording of the question and a brief statement from each side. However, especially on technical issues, most voters do not avail themselves of the information. The majority in a USA survey said they did not use more than one source of information and, indeed, many were voting without access to information on the wording or details of the debate (Magleby 1984: 152). Even on contentious issues and those that affect most voters, levels of information were low and interest in the campaign minimal.

There is obviously a difference between voters faced with one issue and those having to make decisions on many. In California voters may need to decide on over 20 issues and so need to do their homework and have prepared a list of how they wish to vote on each numbered proposition. The Swiss also tend to face a series of unrelated matters on one ballot: in March 1993 they had to vote on petrol tax, legalising casinos and a ban on animal experimentation. In most years Swiss voters are called to the polling booth several times and are likely to be asked to vote on between two and four issues on each occasion. In 1994 the conscientious Swiss voter needed to become informed on 13 separate issues.

When the vote is on a new constitution, general interest is also likely to be higher than for an issue that is seen as less fundamental. However, detailed knowledge of the document and surrounding debate may not be widespread. When voters are asked to accept or reject a large document there seems little reason for them to be acquainted with the details but rather to have an understanding of the underlying sentiment of the piece of legislation or new constitution. In Denmark, copies of the full Maastricht Treaty were made available to voters but most of the debate centred on general issues of European union rather than clauses of the treaty. Voters cannot accept parts of the proposed constitution and reject other bits so all they need is an overall appreciation of the type of regime that is being proposed.

In California there is a large industry geared to help with an initiative: a group can pay to have signatures collected, to write the proposition, overcome legal challenges and manage the campaign. The same thing now happens in Switzerland. Unlike election campaigns, restrictions on spending during the campaign over a popular vote are rare and it is not uncommon for one side to vastly outspend the other. There is a widespread view that the side with the most money will win.

Linder (1994: 144) states that, all else being equal, money is the most important factor in determining the result. He reports on studies showing that the side with the largest budget wins more often than not in Switzerland and the USA (ibid.: 112–14). Propaganda is particularly effective on issues that are complex or abstract. People tend to have views on such matters as abortion but are unlikely to have thought about the detailed workings of government. Magleby's data (1984: 147) shows that out-spending your opponent cannot guarantee success but does increase the chances of winning, especially if opposing an initiative. If you have money the best chance of using it effectively is to oppose an initiative on which few people hold a view. However, there are examples of the poor side winning. In the New Zealand votes on the electoral system (1992 and 1993) the successful campaign in favour of a change was heavily out-spent. In California, proposers of an initiative to liberalise marijuana laws were defeated despite spending over 42 times as much as their opponents.

An imbalance in the money spent is usually most noticeable in the quality and quantity of the media campaign. Campaigning can be crucial on complex issues because voters must make a decision on a matter that is unfamiliar to them. Many issues are decided by voters who do not comprehend the written description and obtained information from only one source, usually television. As emotive slogans used in advertising are the most commonly used source of information, voters are susceptible to propaganda. Partisan adverts may be their only source of information, unlike elections where there are party cues or name recognition to help. Again there is the question of unequal ability to buy advertising time and professionals to write campaign slogans. If voters are primarily moved by slogans then the unequal access to this medium seems likely to have an effect on the success of popular votes. In the US the vast majority of money comes from corporate bodies or a few rich individuals so there is again the question of who has power in the process (Magleby 1994: 243).

Swiss surveys of voters have found that there are three distinct groups (Linder

1994: 93–96). About a third of citizens always vote on issues and see it as a duty while at the other end of the spectrum about a fifth never vote. The remaining half pick and choose, voting sometimes and abstaining at other times, depending upon the issue. The consistent voters tend to be from the higher socio-economic group and the abstainers in lower groups. Those who are members of a political party or have a party identification are more likely to vote so they are all-round politically active. With turnout usually lower in a popular-issue vote than at an election, there is evidence that those who participate are not a cross section of the electorate. Studies in the USA and Switzerland show that those who vote on propositions tend to be disproportionately well educated, affluent and white. In reality a small unrepresentative group decides an issue because turnout is often low.

Apathy towards the process or issue is most commonly measured by looking at turnout levels (see Table 4.5). However, such an exercise is complicated by the fact that in the USA and Australia the vote is held at the same time as an election. In

Table 4.5 Turnout on single-issue popular votes held separately from elections

		Voter turnout	*Difference election-issue*
New Zealand	Election 1993	83	28
	Vote on electoral system 1992	55	
Ireland	Election 1982	74	
	Vote on banning abortion 1983	55	19
Switzerland	Election 10/1991	46	
	Vote on transport funding and voting age 3/1991	31	15
Ireland	Election 1987	76	
	Vote on permitting divorce 1986	63	13
Ireland	Election 11/1992	68	
	Vote on Maastricht Treaty 6/1992	57	11
Britain	Election 1974	73	
	Vote on staying in EEC 1975	65	8
Sweden	Election 1995	86	
	Vote on joining EU 1994	82	4
Philippines	Election 5/1987	90	
	Vote on new constitution 6/1987	87	3
Russia	Election 12/1993	50	
	Vote on draft constitution 12/1993	55	−5
Burundi	Election 1993	91	
	Vote on new constitution 1992	97	−6
Norway	Election 9/1994	76	
	Vote on joining EU 11/1994	89	−13

Sources: Butler and Ranney (1994), Appendix A, Keesing's *Record of World Events*

the majority of cases more people vote in the election than on the issue, regardless of subject matter, suggesting that choosing representatives is more important than deciding issues. The few cases where turnout at the election was lower than for the popular vote are where the issue related to the rules of the game: a new constitution in Burundi and Russia; joining EU in Norway. On the plus side, the novelty of a direct vote and the importance of the issue in countries that rarely use such a device can help raise turnout. The highest votes are for countries that are ratifying a newly democratic constitution.

Progressives tended to be in the forefront of pushes for the use of direct democracy, viewing it as a way of bringing their ideas to fruition. However, conservative groups have also made use of popular votes, most notably Catholics in Switzerland and Italy. Some conservative groups fear the use of popular votes because they believe that it will usher in radical change while many radicals fear the use of a popular vote as it would 'bring back hanging' or other such 'reactionary measures'. Worries that voters will make the 'wrong' decision are central to many fears about putting an issue to the voters. Given such apprehension about the ability of voters to use the popular vote, what does the experience of this procedure show about the type of initiatives that are accepted?

The general tendency of the people to vote a given way can be assessed by studying the results of non-constitutional votes (see Table 4.6). It is not always easy to determine which is the conservative and which the radical option so instead it is easier to look at status quo versus change. Of course some initiatives aim to make conservative changes and others radical ones: for instance limiting the number of foreigners and decriminalising homosexual acts. As there are not many issues that have been addressed across several countries comparisons are difficult. On those issues that can be compared, patterns vary across the subjects. Votes on abortion are overwhelmingly opposed to it, be that a vote for change or status quo. Decisions on the building of nuclear plants show no clear pattern in terms of wanting change. Votes on tax changes are also balanced between having them or not but there does seem to be a tendency to approve specific rather than general taxes. On the issues where there have been votes in several countries there is no evidence that voters generally favour change, the status quo, the conservative or the radical option. Countries vary too. In Switzerland the vast majority of initiatives fail and Australians rarely agree to a constitutional change. However, voters in the US, especially California, approve about one third of initiatives.

Apathy rather than a conservative disposition is often blamed for the tendency of some to back the status quo: those who know little about the issue may see 'no' as the safest vote. In Australia, the combination of a compulsory vote and a short campaign no doubt increases the number of voters who vote 'no' through disinterest or lack of information. In California the complexity of some questions is blamed for the large 'no' vote, again because it is seen as the safest option. However, in Switzerland there is no evidence of any difference in the tendency to vote 'no' on complex rather than simple questions. A propensity to deny the government what it wants has been suggested as occurring in some votes. If the people are generally displeased with the government then they may see a direct

Table 4.6 Patterns of change versus status quo

	Proposition put	Introduced by	Change wins?
ABORTION			
Switzerland 1977, 1978	Allow it	People	No
Italy 1981	Repeal restrictions	People	No
	Repeal law allowing it	People	No
Ireland 1983	Ban it	Government	Yes
	Allow in some cases	Government	No
Arkansas & Michigan 1988	Ban it	People	Yes
Colorado 1988	Repeal ban	People	No
NUCLEAR POWER CONSTRUCTION			
Italy 1987	Stop making it easy	People	Yes
Maine 1987	Ban it	People	No
Massachusetts 1988	Ban it	People	No
Switzerland 1990	Moratorium	People	Yes
TAX CHANGES			
Switzerland			
1977, 1979, 1991	Introduce sales tax	Government	No
1983	Introduce petrol tax	Government	Yes
1993	Increase petrol tax	Government	Yes
1993	Increase sales tax	Government	Yes
California 1976	Cut property tax	People	Yes
Idaho 1978	Cut property tax	People	Yes
Massachusetts 1980	Cut property tax	People	Yes
N. Dakota 1976	Cut sales tax	People	Yes
California 1988	Increase cigarette tax	People	Yes
Colorado 1988	Limit tax rates	People	No
Nevada 1988	Prohibit state tax	People	Yes
S. Dakota and Utah 1988	Limit property tax	People	No

Sources: Butler and Ranney (1994) Appendix A; Kobach (1993) Table 3.1; Schmidt (1989) Appendix I; information supplied by the Ambassador of Switzerland in New Zealand

vote as a way of expressing such feelings. In Switzerland such nay-sayers are estimated to comprise between 10 and 25 per cent of voters (Kobach 1994: 48). This expression of alienation from the system is, again, assumed to favour the status quo in that it tends towards a 'no' vote.

There is also the question of minority rights and the ability of the majority to be oppressive. In places without constitutional safeguards that override a popular vote, minorities have not always been respected. The first successful initiative in Switzerland was anti-Semitic. Some American initiatives have hurt minority groups, for instance limiting the bussing of schoolchildren; making English the official language; refusing education for illegal immigrants; or rejecting laws designed to stop discrimination against gays. The backing of the status quo can also be detrimental to minorities because it continues the rights enjoyed by the 'haves' and denies the extension of rights to more recently recognised groups. Any push for rights to be extended to a group such as a specific ethnic community or homosexuals needs the wider community to grant this change rather than falling back on the status quo. Even more open to the potential of oppression are those who cannot vote: it took until 1972 for the men of Switzerland to vote to allow women the vote. However, in the western states of the USA women gained the vote earlier than in many other states, through initiatives, so 'out' groups are not always excluded by voters. Minority oppression through popular votes is uncommon, probably because they are generally used in homogeneous societies, or where minorities have constitutional protection.

The norm is for voters to be asked to agree or disagree with the proposal so there will be a majority decision. However, sometimes the result is less than clear. In 1995 four votes had very close results: divorce was accepted by 50.3 per cent of Irish voters; 50.6 per cent of those in Quebec rejected independence; Italians voted by 50.027 against weakening large trade unions, and changes to the election of mayors lost on 50.6 per cent. In 1997 the Welsh vote on an assembly was carried by 50.3 per cent. Such close results, while giving a majority, do not confer legitimacy. The victors cannot claim widespread support and the losers were so close to victory that they are unlikely to easily accept defeat. However, as discussed in Chapter 2, there are problems associated with the idea of imposing a higher threshold such as 75 per cent of voters.

Even when there is a large margin between the 'yes' and 'no' votes, there can be problems of interpretation. In particular there is some ambiguity about the meaning of rejection. A 'no' vote may occur because the voters think that the proposal either is wrong, or did not go far enough, or is good but need not be enshrined in the constitution. A large 'no' vote may be taken by legislators as a signal that voters do not want change in that area. However, if voters are actually rejecting certain details, such an interpretation may mean that legislators ignore issues that the majority of voters want action on. There is also argument about the value to be placed on abstention. Does a low turnout mean most people were not interested or that most opposed the change or most accepted the change?

Some places allow more than two options on a question but then the government must decide how to determine the winner. In 1957 Sweden held a referendum on pension schemes that contained three alternatives. None of the options received a majority vote so the government was left with an unresolved problem and organised blocks backing the different positions. The same thing happened in 1980 over nuclear energy. In Australia the use of a vote to choose one of four options as the national song led to the choice of what even the composer describes as a banal song. As each voter could mark two preferences the song that was most people's second choice won.

In Britain and other countries with a strong tradition of parliamentary democracy, the decision to hold a referendum has been portrayed as the legislators opting out of a tough decision or running away from a divisive issue. Elections are supposed to be the mechanisms by which the government answers to the people but the use of popular votes confuses that accountability. As will be discussed in Chapter 6, voters must be able to hold the government accountable if representative democracy is to give power to the people. But if major decisions are taken directly by voters rather than by elected representatives then who can be blamed for a mistake? If voters elect a government whose policy favours a reduction in state provision of healthcare and at the same time vote on an initiative that calls for an increase in state spending on primary health provision then it is not clear what the people want.

If direct democracy is widely used then elections will be less important as a means of determining the policy direction desired by the people and so elected representatives may be restrained in their actions. Swiss governments have problems raising revenue because the voters are loath to allow tax increases and have never approved an income tax. State legislators in California have also been limited in financial areas because initiatives have stipulated how portions of the budget are to be spent. For instance a 1988 vote specified that 40 per cent of the state's general fund was to be spent on basic education. As legislation brought into being by an initiative can only be changed by another popular vote, the legislators must work within these parameters until the people want a change and introduce a new initiative.

When a popular vote is needed, innovation tends to be slow and incremental as each step must be approved by the majority of the people. This point is seen as a definite plus to those who think the people are sovereign but is anathema to those who think government needs to make tough decisions and force reform. The speed of change under new Right governments such as the one in Britain in the 1980s would not have been possible if the voters had been able to challenge legislation. In Switzerland there is a widespread belief that the *facultative* provision makes legislators think about the popular reaction to legislation before they pass it because they know that unpopular laws will be challenged. In this sense the use of the referendum mechanism has more to do with the workings of representative democracy than direct democracy. The publication of regular opinion polls on current issues can fulfil the same role of alerting legislators to the views of the voters, but in a more easily dismissible way. Keeping legislators aware of the views of the voters is deemed by some to be an important part of democracy but others argue that elected rulers do not need backseat drivers. The ways in which elected representatives respond to the views of voters are discussed in Chapters 5 and 6.

Even those who accept the use of popular votes tend to exclude some types of decisions as being the proper preserve of the legislature. For instance, Italian legislation excludes popular votes on financial legislation, pardons and treaty ratification. In the USA votes are not held nationally, only within a state, so foreign policy cannot be an issue in a popular vote. Swiss voters, on the other hand, can determine foreign policy because there is a mandatory popular vote on all treaties. The problem of government in a time of crisis is recognised, however, with an urgency clause that allows laws to be passed without referral to a vote, in times of emergency (Linder 1994: 121).

Moral issues are often raised in popular votes, but there are arguments that representatives are more level headed and so better able to make such emotive decisions. On controversial issues those who prefer legislators to make decisions do so because MPs are able to look at a range of views and negotiate to find a solution that is acceptable to as many people as possible. Further in the same vein, the issues that face a country are many and inter-related so decisions on any one issue should be taken in light of the others. By asking voters to pass judgement on a single issue such context is lost but legislators are making decisions on all issues and can therefore look at the implications. Likewise, with complex issues, the argument is that legislators have more time to devote to understanding the issue plus the interest to do so. Thus they are better able to make decisions on such issues.

The debate in the legislature plus the normal process of submissions from outside groups provides the discussion aspect of decision making that was stressed as important in Chapter 3. Direct democracy invites conflict rather than consensus. Because the vote is to either accept or reject the whole piece of legislation, campaigning will also be dichotomised. So on an issue where debate might have led to a negotiated position that both sides found acceptable, a popular vote will entrench polarised adversarial views. Across a wide range of issues that are raised about popular votes, some see legislators as superior because of their interest, level headedness, community view and participation in debate. In other words this is one aspect of the general elite-versus-masses argument.

Summary

Assessment of direct democracy depends very much upon the standpoint of the accuser. Throughout the debate the tension between populist and elite decision making is pervasive. For those who want the people to be sovereign and have as much say as possible, the main arguments of interest are those relating to the extent of power the people exercise using these procedures. Here details about the kind of people who control each part of the process are important, especially when they suggest inequalities of access. Direct democracy is seen as a feasible way to let all have a say and so improves on participatory democracy, but some critics worry that too much people power is lost. For those interested primarily in good government, arguments about the ability of voters to make decisions and the effects on representative government are vital. At the basic level there is the argument that representatives will make better decisions than the people as a whole. Questions of individual liberty are also important here. Direct democracy is the bastion of majority rule and hence there are worries about the position of minorities. Allowing the people to raise any issue also means that there can be no control on the limits of government action, another worry for some liberal thinkers.

While an elite argue about theoretical aspects, people are making greater use of direct democracy. In those countries where a popular initiative is possible there are growing numbers of successful petitions. But turnout levels are still lower for popular votes than for elections. In other countries, the use of a popular vote on matters relating to the rules of democracy is increasingly becoming the norm. As self-determination continues as one of the buzzwords of the times then votes on matters of territory and independence are likely to proliferate.

5   Representation

The third form of democracy, representative or liberal democracy, is character-
ised by the people choosing a few who make decisions for them and are accountable to the people for those decisions. As this is the form of democracy used by
national governments there are two chapters covering representative democracy.
Here ideas of representation are considered while the next chapter looks at the
role representatives play in governmental decision making. In representative
democracy decisions are taken on behalf of everyone by a sub-group of the whole
but the results are seen as democratic because the people have some influence
over those decisions (see Table 5.1). In other words, rather than choosing the sub-
group by lot, hereditary status or military prowess, all of the people play a part in
choosing the representatives and those chosen must account for their actions to
those they represent. Choice for voters and accountability of representatives are
the key aspects and are provided through regular elections. The extent to which
there is a relationship between voters and elected representatives between elections is more debatable: the theoretical literature divides into those who think the
elected people are there to follow the instructions of the voters and those who
think the elected people were chosen as a body of decision makers. Within each
school of thought there are further divides on how such representation can occur.

Voter choice is structured by three important institutional aspects: the electoral
system; the geographic electoral units; and the party system. Each shapes the type
of decision open to voters and therefore the kind of representation that is possible.
Electoral systems are a crucial aspect of the institutional structuring of voters'
choice of representative. Each is designed to give the voters a different choice (see

Table 5.1 Types of representation

Model of representation	Role of MP	Basis of voters' choice
Delegate	To act on behalf of voters	Promises of future actions Willingness to follow wishes of voters
Trustee	To make good decisions for everyone	MP's past record Personal qualities

Chapter 2). The simplest task for voters is provided by closed party lists, as used in Chile, Spain, Israel and Italy, to name just four. Here voters are asked to select one of the parties on offer, each party receives a proportion of seats that matches the proportion of votes they received and the seats are filled by candidates from a pre-published ranked list. In an open-list system, as used in Belgium, Denmark, Italy and the Netherlands, amongst others, the principle is the same except that voters can indicate a preference between candidates from that party and such prefer-ences are used to allocate seats to candidates within the parties. So voters can choose by party and then select between candidates from that party. Both systems work with large electoral districts, sometimes the whole country, so each area has a number of elected representatives. Under single transferable vote (STV) there are also multi-member districts but smaller than with party lists (see Chapter 2). Each party puts up a number of candidates and voters list their preferences for all of the candidates. Therefore the voters are being asked to choose between people. This system is widely used to elect committees and other bodies where parties are not relevant because, unlike the party-list systems, STV does not need the pres-ence of parties. However, when used to elect a legislature, parties do stand candi-dates and voters tend to follow party lines. In Australia, the vast majority take the option of following a party's preferences rather than marking their own prefer-ences across parties. In Eire voters tend to stick to one party for their first three preferences, which are the ones that determine the winners in most elections (Bowler and Farrell 1991: 314).

In the plurality system, used in Britain, Canada, the USA, Argentina and India, voters elect a single representative for their local constituency so combining the choice of party and person. It is widely accepted that the party label is more important than the person when voters make their decision (Curtice and Steed 1992: 340). Under plurality the strength of each party in parliament depends upon each party's ability to gain the most votes in each local area. The majoritar-ian system works in much the same way except that the winner must receive half the votes and so voters mark preferences between candidates (see Chapter 2). Again the principle choice is between parties and there is no voter choice amongst candidates from the same party. Uniquely, in the USA, the voters play a part in choosing the person who stands for each party through the use of primaries. In a primary the voters from one party are asked to choose which candidate will contest the election for that party. There are other systems and combinations but the above six are the most common types and cover the key ideas on electoral systems. Obviously these different systems have an impact upon the type of repre-sentation a voter can choose and details of this will be discussed as each type of representation is covered.

The geographic organisation of elections also has an important impact. In the Netherlands, Israel and Paraguay there are no divisions into constituencies but in all other countries some kind of smaller units are created. In the multi-member systems the constituencies are large, often covering a whole city or a region while in single-member systems the areas are small. Elections of the upper house are often conducted on a regional basis, in particular for federal countries where the

Senate is the body that gives equal voice to each state. For instance, in the USA each state elects two senators even though California has 52 members of Congress to Wyoming's one because the idea is to allow each state an equal say in decisions. Non-federal countries may also see the upper house as providing regional representation: each Polish province sends three representatives to the Senate. Use of geographic electorates means that the groups of voters who share a representative are organised on a spatial basis. In single-member district systems it is assumed that all those who live in a given area share certain views or can at least be represented by one person. Where multi-member districts are used the assumption is that the group of representatives for that area can between them act for the range of voters. In a single-member district all are represented by the one person, whether they voted for that person or not, while in a multi-member electorate there are a number of representatives so each could be seen as talking for their own voters.

To some extent all countries seek to equalise the population covered by one MP; therefore, as the population changes, so must the allocation of MPs across the country. As the population grows some countries increase the number of MPs and others maintain a specified size of parliament. Israel always has 120 MPs as that number is in the Torah, the USA Congress has remained at 435 since 1911 to alleviate worries that if it grew any larger it would not allow for debate and would be easier for elites to dominate. Since 1945 the number of British MPs has increased from 635 to 659, in Australia it has almost doubled from 75 to 147, in Italy it rose from 556 to 630 and in the Netherlands from 100 to 150. As the population distribution across areas changes then MPs need to be re-allocated. In multi-member areas, rather than change the boundaries, the number of MPs elected for each area can change (McLean and Butler 1996: 11). However in the single-member systems the boundaries must be redrawn. Equal population is a factor in all countries but the toleration of variation differs markedly from less than 1 per cent in the USA to 25 per cent in Canada (ibid. 1996: 13). In Britain there is an expectation of equal population but only within the constituent countries because the number of MPs for Scotland and Wales is static regardless of how their population size changes in relation to England. So in 1996 the average population size for a Scottish electorate was 54,569 compared with 69,281 for England and 58,525 for Wales. Likewise, in Canada no province will face a decrease in the number of representatives they had in 1974. Despite the widespread desire for equal electoral population there is no international agreement on the optimum size of an electorate: at the extremes of English-speaking countries are New Zealand on 52,000 and India on one million (ibid. 1996: 13). Again these variations impact on the extent to which a group will feel that the person they elected represents them. Whether round single- or multi-member electorates, the drawing of boundaries can have a profound impact upon the election outcome. Redrawing has potential for political controversy because parties may try to have boundaries drawn that will assist their election by bringing together people who are likely to vote for them, a process known as 'gerrymandering'.

Political parties provide the range of options available for the voters both in terms of which policy packages are on offer and which people are standing. In most countries all candidates are standing for a political party and thus adhere to the party's manifesto and campaigning strategy. This is particularly true in closed-list systems where the voters choose a party not a candidate. Therefore the range of policy packages available to the voters is limited by the range of parties that contest the election. The type of people who stand for election is also affected by political parties. To be a candidate a person must be chosen by the party so the candidate selection process used by political parties determines the people the voters are allowed to choose between (Norris 1997). The number of parties standing candidates, the chance each has of being part of the government, and the ease with which new parties can gain election all shape the choice that voters can make at an election.

A representative acts on my behalf

The most obvious way in which representatives act for me is when they do as I ask, they follow my instructions and thus are delegates. Personal characteristics of the representative are not important as they are nothing more than a conduit for the demands of the larger group. Pitkin describes this as 'representation as activity' (1967: 112–15). A delegated representative may not always have instructions to follow but the central idea is that if the constituency sends instructions they will be followed regardless of the personal views of the representative. In looking at representation as delegation there are two important questions: for whom is the representative talking, and how can the representative know what those people want on each issue? (see Table 5.2). In national elections the most common ideas of who constitutes the group for which the representative is a spokesperson are: the locality; those who voted for the representative; and those who sponsor the MP. In some places an MP may be sponsored by a particular group and will be

Table 5.2 How can a representative be a delegate?

Key questions	Main answers	Practical implications
Who is the MP spokesperson for?	The locality	Local MP working for the area, may lead to pork-barrel politics
	Those who voted for the MP	Ideological or group-based representation
How does the MP know what the people want?	Listens to their views via opinion polls or correspondence	Difficulties in gaining good information and finding out what the majority rather than the vocal want
	Assumes voters want the election promises fulfilled	May mean following the party line May mean following a specific-issue stance May mean following group interests such as class or ethnicity

seen as that organisation's spokesperson in parliament. For instance in the 1992–97 British parliament, 143 MPs were sponsored by a trade union.

The idea that the representative is a spokesperson for the local area is particularly associated with single-member districts because each district has just one representative. As the representative of the constituency the MP is expected to put local interests above any others and to secure benefits for the local area (Bogdanor 1985: 48, 66; Hauss 1994: 30). The USA Founding Fathers expected representatives to be delegates for their local community: the directly elected executive was to look after the national interest and Congress was a voice for local interests (Birch, 1971: 42). This idea of acting on behalf of the local people is also strong in some multi-member systems, such as Ireland, Italy, Japan, Belgium and Tasmania. It is no coincidence that all have an electoral system where voters express preferences between candidates from the same party and thus each MP will seek to win local votes. In Japan, Italy and Ireland 'clientelism' or delivering goods to the locality in the expectation of votes is an important part of how politics works (Bogdanor 1985: 162–63, 238–39; Hauss 1994: 202–03). In the USA this idea is referred to as 'pork-barrel' politics and again the member of Congress is expected to secure rewards for the locality such as government contracts, new schools or favourable terms for the dominant industry. Members of Congress seek to service the constituency and will use evidence of the money and contracts they have acquired in seeking re-election (Davidson 1994: 137). Although in each case the MP is meant to be acting for the locality, the role is really closer to that of ambassador than delegate as MPs act for the good of the area rather than following local instructions.

In contrast, the strong tie between representative and locality is missing in most multi-member district systems. Because a voter living in a district can choose between a number of MPs for that area there is a tendency to go to one from the preferred party. So we get delegation, where MPs act according to the wishes of those who elected them. MPs are seen as talking for those who voted for their party in that area. Even though there is no formal way in which MPs are deemed to speak for those who elected them, the desire for re-election fosters this approach. Especially in systems where voters are choosing a person, not just a party, the MP will seek to please those people in anticipation of a vote at the next election. As much voting is on party lines the idea that representatives are delegates for those who elected them ties closely to ideas of party discipline, discussed later.

So how are MPs to determine the views of those they are deemed to represent? In eighteenth-century debate in Britain, Thomas Paine and the Chartists saw frequent elections as the way voters could keep control by giving frequent mandates. However, no country uses annual elections so other means of communication are needed. Opinion polls play an important role because they are a commonly available source of information on what voters are thinking, plus their statistical nature gives them an aura of scientific certainty. Many opinion polls are conducted by the media as part of their agenda-setting role (see Chapter 6) but opinion polls are also used by MPs, the government, parties and pressure groups.

As MPs are meant to be acting for the people, such evidence of popular views can be given great moral weight. MPs may also react to the views expressed in letters sent to them by local voters. In the USA, each representative has a large staff whose sole job is to determine the views of local voters through analysis of communications to the representative, local opinion polls and media comment (Hauss 1994: 30). Another important aspect, although impossible to measure, is the 'anticipated reaction' of voters at the next election as MPs will not go against their perception of the will of their voters because they want to be re-elected.

The other way in which MPs can be delegated is when there are mechanisms to allow voters to have some control over the actions of their MP between elections. The clearest example of this is the re-call. Fifteen states within the USA have provisions for voters to demand that the incumbent face a special election if they collect sufficient signatures on a petition. The re-call provision, which applies to state positions and not members of Congress or Senate, has been used to remove mayors, governors and members of local legislatures who have been accused of extravagance, corruption, incompetence and lack of responsiveness. The re-call device is championed as a means of ensuring that elected representatives are servants for the voters (Cronin 1989: ch. 6). However, detractors see it as a cumbersome tool that can easily be swayed by campaigning rhetoric and distorted by partisan arguments. There is a big question over the extent to which the voters know what their representative is, or should be, doing. Such questions strike at the heart of representation. Mutual ignorance means that representatives do not know what constituents want on many issues and electors do not know what the representative is doing much of the time and so cannot express a view (Budge 1996: 49).

If voters do not instruct MPs how to behave, then they must look for other means of assuring their representative acts on their behalf. The easiest method is to choose a candidate who you believe will vote as you would if you were in parliament. Voters may choose the candidate who shares their concerns on key issues; or choose the candidate whose party ideology coincides with their own worldview; or choose a person they see as being like themselves. These three options cover the main models in voting behaviour: issue, party and socio-economic voting. In terms of representation the idea is that the MP voices the views of the voters because they share the same views. There are many similarities between issue and party voting: both are based on voters assessing the programmes of the candidate or party and selecting the best package. Socio-economic voting does not relate to the views of the candidates and so will be dealt with separately from the other two.

Issue stance as an explanation of voting behaviour gained popularity in the late 1970s and early 1980s (Franklin *et al.* 1992: 399–403). Prior to this, the general view amongst psephologists was that voters knew little about the policy stance of the parties and did not hold consistent views on specific issues. The issue-voting model draws on Downs' ideas of the rational voter (Downs 1957: ch. 3), which looks at the cost and benefits of different candidates winning and so creates a balance sheet for each party. If one likens the voter to a consumer, the parties or candidates are seen as representing different groups of policy packages and each voter will select the package with most in common with their own 'shopping list' of policy interests (Himmelweit *et al.* 1981: 8–12). Using survey data voters' views on a range of issues can be added together, as on a balance sheet, and used as a good predictor of the party they voted for (Sarlvik and Crewe 1983: 264–69). Studies in the USA have shown evidence that voters are aware of the issues and hold stable views (Abramson 1986: ch. 15; Nie *et al.* 1976: ch. 10, ch. 8). Another strong strand in writing on voting behaviour contends that voters assess the policy stance or general direction of the different parties and choose the package that most closely resembles their own views. This model considers the underlying principles and approaches rather than specific issues. Studies of the British election of 1983 found that political values were the greatest single influence (Rose and McAllister 1990: 183) with nine distinct groups of values, distinguished by voters' position on Left–Right economic issues, the environment and international relations (Heath *et al.* 1985: 107; Rose and McAllister 1990: 10).

When views are consistent and organised they constitute an ideology. In most democracies the prevailing ideological divide is along the economic Left–Right spectrum. Sometimes another dimension is needed to adequately place all parties, for instance an authoritarian–liberal dimension. Recently studies have concentrated on a materialist–post-materialist dimension based on placing emphasis upon the state of the economy and law and order as opposed to the environment and human rights (Inglehart 1990). If voters have a perception of their own views as being a consistent worldview and also see the parties in the same way then the choice will be based upon a comparison of ideologies. Parties offer a set of policies that lies within this issue space and thus voters are presented with a number of policy packages or ideologies to choose between. There is some debate over the extent to which voters hold a consistent set of views that would constitute an ideology. Scarborough found that over half of her sample had an ordered set of beliefs (Scarbrough 1984: 169) but 10 per cent of them did not vote for the party that matched their ideology (ibid.: 191). Most election surveys ask voters to place themselves on the Left–Right spectrum and also ask where they would place each political party, thus allowing researchers to measure the distance between each voter and the party they voted for. In a study of the European Parliament elections of 1983, such a measure was found to have the largest impact on vote choice (Oppenhuis 1995: 132).

While both issue and ideological voting can apply to individual candidates, these ideas are more often associated with political parties. In the USA incumbent candidates are assessed in terms of their voting record, with a number of groups, such as Americans for Conservative Action and Americans for Democratic Action, publishing roll-call details and measures of how conservative or liberal each member is. In all other democracies, candidates are members of a disciplined political party and thus the record and intent of the party is of greater relevance. Obviously in the closed party-list systems the voter is only given a choice between parties. But even in other electoral systems where voters are choosing between candidates, surveys of voters indicate that party is more important to the voter than are the personal traits of the candidates. If voters are selecting a party because of their policy in the manifesto or based on perceived ideology then the voter is expecting the representatives to follow those policies or ideology. The voter chooses a candidate in the expectation that the representative will behave as the voter would if faced by the same decision, this assumption is based on knowledge of shared views on specific issues or an ideology. So the voters are choosing the party that best fits their own views in the expectation that the party will follow its manifesto. This is often taken as giving the party an electoral mandate to implement its professed policies. So the party that wins is obliged to follow the measures outlined at the election and to do this the MPs must be disciplined into voting along those lines, regardless of their personal views. This line of argument is known as the 'responsible party model'. So MPs are 'lobby fodder' for the views of the party and their own views are irrelevant, a view in stark contrast to the idea of a trustee discussed below.

The third method I may use to identify a representative who will behave as I would is to choose someone who is like me in some way, based on the idea that a person like me will share my concerns. Such a group consciousness has several important aspects. First is recognition of group membership and that the way one is treated by the political world is in part a consequence of being female, black, working class and so on. Then comes a belief that political action is needed for the group because of this treatment. If a group has a shared perception that actions of the state are putting the group at risk, making it hard for them to live as they wish, then members of the group will react in a political way. Once one feels that one's political treatment and behaviour is shaped by group membership then the next step is feeling that others from the group will also act in the interests of the group, and thus in your interests (Rinehart 1992: 14).

The groups are not ones that people join but rather the large divides across society based on race, class, gender, religion, ethnicity and so on. All societies have a number of divides, although the type will vary. Some of these divides will have a political aspect because members of the group feel that group membership has a social and a political impact. These political divides, called cleavages, are import-ant in studies of political parties and voting behaviour. Cleavages are those per-sistent divides between social groups which impact on attitudes and behaviour and some lead to the formation of distinct political parties while others do not. Patterns differ across countries and even those with a similar cleavage do not follow the same pattern of party system. In Belgium there is a socialist party for Dutch speakers and one for French speakers and the same is true of the Christian Democratic and Green parties. But in Switzerland, a country with an equivalent language mix within the population, there are no language-based parties. There is a party for Swedes inside Finland but no German party for the Germans inside Denmark. Just as not all social cleavages are also political cleavages there are political divides that are not defined by cleavage but instead relate to views on a specific issue, for instance environmentalist parties.

So, there are divides within society: people see themselves or are seen by others as being part of certain groups. Some of these groups are politicised and feel they are treated differently in the political system and that group membership will have an impact on political views. There is an assumption that others of the group will have the same agenda, policy preferences and political views and so group members may wish their elected representatives to also be from that group. Some of these politicised groups create political parties to ensure a voice within the system while others do not. These two types of political groups will be considered separately as they have different connotations for representation. Again the party system plays an important role in structuring the choices that voters make when choosing their representatives. So if you identify as working class then in most countries there is a party that expresses the views of the working class but if you identify as a woman then there is not a party that speaks for women. However, for the working-class voters there is the complication that although there is a socialist party that claims to talk for the working class it may be that few of the candidates have a working-class background. For instance, in the 1992 British election only 14 per cent of Labour candidates had held a manual job. Here there is a distinction between what the party says and who the candidates are. Likewise all the black community in a country may vote for a given party but that does not mean that the party has black candidates or that the party claims to be a voice for the concerns of black voters. At this stage we are dealing just with the aspect of choosing a representative whereby a person votes for a candidate because of a shared group membership.

So which groups are important in politics in that members tend to want elected representatives from their own group? Some characteristics have greater importance than others. Lipset and Rokkan talk of four major cleavages: centre–periphery; state–church; land–industry; and owner–worker (Lipset and Rokkan 1967: 47). Lijphart, in his study of 22 democracies found traces of seven issue dimensions, of which four relate to social cleavages: socio-economic (class); religious; cultural-ethnicity; urban–rural (Lijphart 1984: 128). Derived from these cleavages, the most common group-based parties in Western democracies are working class, Christian, rural, regional, and cultural-ethnic. Class and religion are the most common in Western democracies: all but the USA have a working-class party and most of those in continental Europe also have a Christian party. The other cleavages are evident in some places. In Finland, Iceland and Sweden there is a rural party but not in the more southern European countries. Canada, Spain, Britain and Italy have regional-based parties while Belgium's parties are language-based. Note there are not always parties on both sides of the divide: there are Catholic parties but not distinctly secular ones, there are rural parties but not urban ones. It is those groups who feel threatened by the status quo and thus in need of a particular voice that seek a party of their own. So the parties linked with a particular group are a good indication of those groups that at some time felt disadvantaged by the political system.

Much of the early study of voting behaviour linked people to a party on one of these socio-economic factors (Franklin *et al.* 1992; Rose 1974). In Britain and most west European countries the key cleavage was class with an expectation that working-class people voted for socialist and communist parties while middle-class people voted for the centre-Right parties. In countries where class was not the prominent cleavage there was still an expectation of group-based voting. In France and the Netherlands religiosity is an important influence on the vote while region has an impact in Canada and Italy. There was a strong idea in the voting behaviour literature that people habitually voted for the party that spoke for 'people like them' and that this habit created a party identification. The classic works on voting behaviour written in the 1960s and 1970s all follow this line, the Michigan model. Those who voted for the 'other' class were seen as an anomaly to be explained and a series of books in the 1960s studied 'cross-class' voters in Britain (McKenzie and Silver 1968; Nordlinger 1967). Some of these explanations were based on other cleavages such as religion or region. More recently the differences between those who work in the public and private sector were used to explain cross-class voting (Dunleavy and Husbands 1985). However, some 'cross-group' voting is totally unrelated to group identity because other forms of representation are present. Likewise some from the group may vote for that party because they agreed with the issues or ideology, not because of the group link, but socio-economic factors affect policy views, so there is an intricate mix of representation types. In some cases the old links between group identity and party have been eroded but the parties remain. Parties may outlive the cleavage that led to their creation by building a new bloc of voters. A rural party may survive long after the urban–rural divide fades as a major cleavage because they gain new groups of voters based on their ideology or success in government. Established parties evolve to fit the changing situation but at the same time their continued success in elections makes it hard for new parties to enter the political contest (Kitschelt 1997). Parties representing new ideologies or cleavages find it harder to enter the legislature, so more recently politically conscious groups are likely to seek to make links with an existing party or to work across all parties. Again, the way that the electoral and party systems interact plays a major role in representation in a country.

Groups that do not create a distinct party are no less important as a source of political identity. For instance Iceland is one of the few places with a women's party, but many women feel that their political concerns are shaped by their gender. Likewise there are countries where ethnicity is important in political views but is not reflected in political parties, for instance the USA and Britain. Members of these groups nevertheless want a political voice. In many cases the group is associated with one party: most black people in the USA vote for the Democrats and Labour wins most of the afro-Caribbean votes in Britain. Members of the group may also prefer a candidate from the group, either within their preferred party or regardless of party, depending on the relative strength of identity. So I choose a person who shares my views by selecting a candidate who is also of my group and I expect that the decisions that person makes will be the ones I would make because we have a shared group consciousness. This form of representation is also important for bodies outside of mainstream politics where there are no political parties. So in choosing members of a committee, in the absence of organised groups and no clear policy divide I may decide that a person like me will make the type of decisions I will like.

The electoral system has a major impact on the ability to choose a representative like yourself in that it structures the type of choices that are made. In an open list a working-class woman may vote for the socialist party and then give preferences to the women candidates. Using the STV, people can also choose between candidates from the same party but can cast their votes across party lines. The same working-class woman might vote for all the socialist candidates, women then men, and then do the same for the other parties, or she might vote for all the socialist women then the women from other parties, then the socialist men then the other men. The way in which she gave her preferences would indicate whether her political identity is primarily based on gender or class. In the single-member systems voters, in theory, choose a candidate but in most places party is the strongest motivation. In the USA, where party allegiance is weaker than in Europe, there have been occasions when normally Republican women voters have voted for a Democrat woman (Rinehart 1992: 171).

Gaining a representative who shares your issue stance, ideology or background is easier in a multi- than a single-member system. In a single-member district there is one representative for all in the area who is deemed to speak for the geographically based collectivity even though those people hold a wide range of views. In a multi-member district, each area has a number of MPs, from the range of parties that receive votes in the area. So those with a common view can share an MP even though they do not live in one neighbourhood and the representative's constituency is a community of interest rather than a geographic area. In single-member systems a group can only gain a representative if they are the largest group within the electoral district. So if a group is to be given the ability to elect the representative of their choice then the authorities must create districts where that group dominates. This can be done by creating separate electoral rolls (see below) or drawing district boundaries with an eye to socio-economic composition. Districts where a minority group dominates can happen naturally, for instance with a regionally based group such as the Welsh speakers in North Wales, or French-speaking Canadians in Quebec. In South Africa, the concentration of Inkatha members in the Kwazulu-Natal area was important for the success of Chief Buthelezi's party. In India, federal boundaries are drawn on linguistic lines but only 50 of the 24 main languages (there are over 200 dialects) are recognised.

In the USA there are few natural districts where African-Americans or Hispanics are the majority even when there are large ethnic communities in a geographic area. However, under Supreme Court interpretations of the Voting Rights Act in the 1990s minority-majority districts were created. Until 1994 only six blacks had won a congressional race in a district with an Anglo majority. In 1994 the two black Republican representatives were from white areas but the remaining 36 blacks and the 17 Hispanics were from minority-majority seats (Peterson 1995: 113). The underlying theory, derived from the doctrine of an equal vote, is that a group must have a realistic opportunity to choose their own representative (Peterson 1995: 113; Phillips 1995: 85). If a group is geographically compact and politically cohesive (i.e., votes the same way) then it should not be stopped from choosing its own representative. If boundaries are drawn so that a minority group is divided between several districts so that in each they are a minority, then this dilutes the power of their votes. Voting dilution is defined as a situation where rules or practices in the electoral process combined with a majority group voting as a bloc reduces the voting power of an identifiable minority group (Grofman and Davidson 1992: 24). Later Supreme Court rulings on boundary drawing now mean that vote-dilution must be avoided but race cannot be the prime reason for the boundaries and compactness must be a consideration. Other countries have not followed the 'minority-majority' practice.

Representatives chosen because the voter assumes common views and concerns are acting on behalf of the voters but not directly instructed by them. Voters make a selection based on their assessment of what the candidates will do if elected and may build in evidence on what the candidates have done in the past. Voters do not have any direct control over the representatives, unlike in the delegate model. However, a form of control is assumed under the responsible party model with the use of party discipline in parliament to keep MPs voting according to the party manifesto.

A body of decision makers

In contrast to the view of delegates is the idea of the representative as a trustee. Here the representatives make decisions as they see fit, for the good of the nation as a whole and removed from the pressures of voter demands. Some variants of the trustee model stress the making of good decisions while others put emphasis upon having the full range of views raised during the debate (see Table 5.3). As the assembly is a body of people making decisions based on the information they have and their own conscience, the role of elections is to confirm or reject the MPs based on their performance. In reaching decisions the representatives may be striving to discern the best solution or they may each be arguing in terms of their own views. The important distinction is that the MPs act as they think best and do not follow instructions from the voters. The independence of MPs is not meant to detract from the power of voters but rather to free representatives from being mere agents of local interests. MPs and the government still have to answer

Table 5.3 Ways of composing a body of decision makers

Role of the assembly	Composition of assembly	Type of representation
To make good decisions	Competent and conscientious people	Pure trustee
To hear the range of views	One person from each significant group	Virtual or symbolic
To take account of the size of each group	Replicates major divides in society	Proportionate presence, microcosmic

to the voters in periodic elections where they may be removed if their actions are deemed incorrect. Here voting is seen as entirely retrospective: a reaction to what has been done, not a choice of what is wanted as is the case with the ideas discussed above. If an existing MP was to be removed, a replacement should be selected on personal qualities such as good judgement and then allowed the life of the parliament to prove ability.

The idea of MP as trustee and parliament as a body striving for the good of the nation is associated with Edmund Burke, who, in 1774 in an address to the voters in his constituency, explained that rather than being a place where people representing different interests came together to fight for their cause, parliament was a place where decisions were taken for the good of the nation (Lively and Lively 1994: 93–94). Although elected by a local constituency Burke claimed that the MP then became a member of parliament whose job was to make good judgements and not to follow the orders of the voters (Lively and Lively 1994: 62–63). So there is the idea of parliament as an elite composed of educated politicians who have access to detailed information which they can understand and will use to make good decisions for the whole. Representatives are trustees acting in the interests of the people because they are better able than the general population to determine what is best for the nation. The utilitarian thinkers added to this idea the belief that it is possible to scientifically discover the best solution, based on the aim of increasing the sum total of human happiness (Birch 1971: 54). In part, the trustee model entails MPs making hard decisions and looking at the long-term situation not just short-term gains and losses. The government may have to make unpopular decisions if it is for the good of the country and the solution wanted by the people has undesirable consequences.

While this view of MP as trustee and parliament as an assembly for the nation was popular amongst British thinkers in the eighteenth and nineteenth centuries, it is not widely expressed in present political practice. However, some European constitutions follow this view. For instance Article 67 of the Italian constitution states that deputies represent the nation and carry out their duties 'without restraint of mandate' while Article 56 of the Danish constitution states that representatives 'shall be bound solely by their own conscience and not by any directions given by their electors'. The constitutions of both Belgium and the Netherlands specify that members of the legislature represent the nation as a whole. Some models of voting behaviour also concur with the idea of MP as trustee in that they stress the retrospective view. This model suggests that many voters see an election as a time to punish or reward the government for what they have done. So the voters' choice is based on a reaction to the results of government activity and not on any policy orientation, the people not the promised policy is the focus.

While there is little evidence of parliaments acting as a body of trustees making decisions for the good of all with no reference to what voters want, another aspect of the idea of representatives as a body of decision makers is evident in practice. While the utilitarians believed there was a discernible best solution they also recognised that most people seek to maximise their own happiness, and MPs are no different from all others. In reaching a decision there will be debate. So what is needed is a parliament that is made up of a range of people so that if each seeks what is good for themselves then all sections in society will have someone seeking what is good for them (Birch 1971: 54). As with the idea of shared interest, discussed above, this notion of representation assumes that there are group or sectional interests. Recently this idea has been evident in pressure for parliaments to represent their society in the way a portrait or mirror will represent a person.

In other words, each group within society that has distinct political views should be present in the decision-making body. If a group is left out then their concerns and views may not be heard, not necessarily through a desire to exclude but because no-one is present who knows of those concerns. Such a situation can be seen as akin to adults making decisions for children who have not gained the ability to decide for themselves. Feelings of exclusion from the system are at the base of many claims for group representation. Contrary to the liberal view that to gain equality all should be treated in the same way, so all are 'blind' to differences, there are claims that group identity is important to individuals as part of who they are and also that groups are treated differently by the system so this must be recognised and discrimination rectified (Taylor 1994: 37–44). The clash between ideas of achieving equality and the desirability of recognising differences gives rise to much debate and is at the base of much of the controversy surrounding claims for particular groups to be ensured a representative in the decision-making body. Note that these ideas differ from those discussed above. Here the emphasis is on the need for each group to have a voice, whereas the arguments above relate to a voter wishing to choose a representative based on shared group membership.

Not all groups who claim to be under-represented seek the same level of involvement in the legislature. In some instances the excluded group wants a voice while for others the presence in the elected body should be the same size as their presence in the community. As with earlier discussions of group representation there is the question of which groups should be given a representative. Obviously it is not possible for all groupings within society to have a member in parliament but again the argument relates to those groups who feel that they have a different political viewpoint, particularly if it is not being expressed by those who have been elected. At the turn of the century, trade unions were in the forefront of pressing for the representation of working people in parliament. In recent decades arguments about the need for elected members from key groups have concentrated on personal characteristics such as race, gender and religion. Not all of these factors matter in all countries but they become an issue if there is some feeling that a group is being discriminated against. People tend to care that there is under-representation when the group in question has a political aspect (Rule and Zimmerman 1994: 235–36).

Some groups seeking representation emphasise the desire for a voice, not its size, as they want recognition rather than equity. For those groups that suffer systemic discrimination there needs to be a way to give them access to the policy-making process. So gaining one representative is a major achievement. The inclusion of a representative from a previously excluded group has great political impact as an official recognition of the importance of the group, regardless of whether or not the new representative makes any obvious impact on the actions of government (Phillips 1995: 40). Often gaining a voice is the first step towards reaching proportionate presence and so can be seen as 'threshold representation': the important action of crossing the first hurdle. Such representation is often called symbolic because the presence of the one representative is taken as symbolising the fact that the political system recognises the validity of that group's voice. Detractors call the same situation 'tokenism' because there is a feeling that those in power have allowed an excluded group one representative to recognise their position but in the knowledge that a lone voice can have little impact.

The nineteenth-century concept of 'virtual representation' is like symbolic representation in that the concern was to ensure that each sectional interest had a voice. Ideas of virtual representation assume that a country is divided into a finite number of interests and so parliament needs a member from each interest regardless of its size (Birch 1971: 51–52; Pitkin 1967: 173–76). Interests are economically defined and relate to a locality such as a mining town or seaport or agricultural area. As the aim is a decision-making body where the concerns of each group are raised, it is not necessary for all those people deemed to be connected to the interest to have a part in electing the representative. Before 1832 Manchester and Glasgow did not have an MP but this was not deemed a problem because other industrialised port towns such as Liverpool did elect an MP who spoke of those interests. This Whig view made a clear distinction between the idea of promoting and raising interests: they favoured the latter. The member for Liverpool would be aware of the concerns of an industrial town with a busy port and so would raise them in relevant debates and thus Glasgow did not need a voice of its own. The role of the virtual representative is to voice the concerns of a particular group so that all in parliament are aware of the views of particular interests when reaching decisions. One person can express the concerns of a group so there is no need for larger groups to have more representatives. Only if the representatives are expected to argue in favour of those interests does the size of the group representing each interest matter.

When the representatives are expected to argue for the interest of their groups then the argument is one of size and relates to the other aspect of descriptive representation: the idea that the elected body should mirror the population. So women's groups across Western democracies agitate to increase the number of women in their legislatures because although women are over half the population in each country, nowhere are half the legislators women. In 1997, 14 parliaments had over a quarter of female MPs, the largest proportion being in Sweden with 40 per cent. Likewise ethnic groups complain of under-representation when the proportion of MPs of their ethnicity is lower than their proportion in society. For the elected body to claim to talk for the people it is felt that the body should mirror society in important ways. Such arguments are controversial and less widely accepted than arguments for symbolic representatives. Some ethnic minorities, especially indigenous ones, argue that proportionate presence is not enough as they will still be in a minority and to gain some real power in government they need a larger say or some other form of institutional arrangement to give self-determination.

Whether following the symbolic or descriptive arguments, there are instances where political bodies have accepted arguments that a particular group must have representation and so have adopted specific measures to ensure this. Political groups other than parliaments are particularly likely to have made arrangements for key groups to have a place on the decision-making body. Again, there is a debate over the form of representation. For example, is it important to have a black MP or to have an MP elected by black voters? Is the symbolic representation of a group based on the presence of someone who shares their characteristics or someone whom they elected and who also is a member of their group? When looking at proportionate presence the emphasis tends to be on having the people there rather than who chose them. However, sometimes the easiest way to gain a proportionate presence is to allow key groups to elect a certain number of people: if you want 10 per cent of the MPs to be from the ethnic minority then allow voters from the ethnic group to elect 10 per cent of the MPs. This process is distinct from those related to representation based on voters choosing a candidate who shares their identity (discussed above) because here it is the government rather than voters who are deciding that there should be MPs from certain groups. When the government does want to ensure a specific group has seats there are a variety of methods available. Voters of one group can be separated so that they elect their own representative, thus giving the group control and presence. Alternatively, all voters can be instructed to choose candidates from specific groups so that the presence is guaranteed but the representatives are not accountable just to voters from their group. The third common practice is for places to be reserved for key groups with a variety of methods used for their selection, some based on the group selecting those people, others with all voters making the selection.

Ensuring a minority presence by creating a distinct electorate happens in a handful of countries. In New Zealand and Fiji voters are registered on separate rolls according to their ethnic group (Grofman and Lijphart 1986: ch. 6). The indigenous Maori in New Zealand can choose to be on a separate roll and the country is divided geographically into overlapping Maori and general seats. Fiji also has overlapping seats but voters must be on one of four ethnic rolls: Fijian, Indian, Rotuman and 'other'. It is not always ethnicity that determines the construction of separate electoral rolls: in the Republic of Ireland, six Senators are elected by graduates of Irish universities; in Morocco professional bodies and employees' organisations elect 42 members; in Gambia and Zimbabwe traditional chiefs elect some MPs; in Bhutan ecclesiastical bodies elect 10 MPs; and the 'untouchables' in Bombay used to be on a separate electoral roll.

Another process to ensure a specified ratio of MPs from each group is to instruct all voters to select a slate of candidates that fits the desired profile. In Lebanon, before warfare stopped elections in 1975, allocation of seats was carefully organised to ensure that there were six Christians to every five Muslims (Grofman and Lijphart 1986: ch. 6). However, different Christian and Muslim groups were also balanced within that ratio, reflecting the results of a 1932 census. In electoral areas that contained a mix of religious groups, it was specified what number of each group were to be elected. For example, a five-member seat may require two Sunni Muslims, two Druses and one Greek Orthodox representative and people must cast their five votes in that pattern. In Singapore, the ethnic background of candidates is also regulated: electoral areas are grouped into threes, each contested by a team of three, one of whom must be of non-Chinese origin. In Egypt, half the MPs must be labourers or farmers so in each of the two-member districts each voter must select one candidate from this category and one other candidate. Smaller organisations may also use this method. For instance, British Labour MPs, when voting for the members of the shadow cabinet, have had to vote for at least four women.

The third method of ensuring representation for key groups is to have reserved places. Seats are reserved for members of a particular group in other ways. In Bangladesh, 30 women are brought into parliament, elected by the legislators; Tanzania does the same for 15 women. Several international organisations also ensure that specific groups of countries have members on the executive committee. For instance, the International Fund for Agricultural Development divides places between Organisation for Economic Co-operation and Development (OECD), Organisation of Petroleum Exporting Countries (OPEC) and 'other' countries while the International Maritime Organisation uses three categories related to types of maritime involvement. The European Federation of Green Parties specifies a minimum level of women in the delegations from each country to their Council and Congress.

Political parties may also affect the type of people in parliament due to their role as gatekeepers on candidates. Where a party selects a slate of candidates then it is easy to aim for some kind of quota or balance. If the major parties have a high proportion of women in the higher places on their lists then this will increase the number of women in parliament. In 1995, of the 14 democracies where over a quarter of MPs are women, 12 use a party-list system, seven of them a closed list. Parties of the Left in the Scandinavian countries led the way in instituting a minimum quota for women on their list of candidates. The Norwegian Liberal and Socialist Left parties had adopted a gender quota for their lists in 1975 (Rule and Zimmerman 1994: 61). Such a policy has been adopted across much of Europe and in new democracies such as the ANC in South Africa. Parties in plurality electoral systems are less able to specify a quota for women candidates as the party is not creating a list but rather each local group chooses one candidate. The British Labour Party had a policy of all-women shortlists in half the target seats but this policy was challenged as employment discrimination.

When MPs are deemed to create a body of decision makers who will look at the evidence and then reach their decision a very different form of representation is provided from the delegate and party roles discussed previously. Voters are being asked to choose a person who will be a good decision maker and then trust them with that job. Arguments about the composition of parliament relate to the need for certain viewpoints to be heard or for certain groups to have sufficient MPs to argue their corner and influence votes. As with participatory democracy, hearing a range of views and taking part in discussion is a vital part of the parliamentary process, so under this model of representative it is crucial that voters do not bind MPs to a particular course of action. In this case, accountability is retrospective at the next election when voters can show disapproval of the way the MP made decisions.

Bringing together ideas on representation

Different forms of representation have been considered separately, but in reality voters and representatives combine these forms. Models of voting behaviour now tend to mix aspects of group membership and political attitudes while most MPs will perform several of the representative roles depending upon the specific issue. In seeking representation, previously excluded groups want their voice to be heard in a number of ways. For instance during debates on extending the vote to women in Britain a number of arguments were used: so that women representatives could campaign for legislation beneficial to women; so that women could elect women MPs; so that parliament would more closely resemble the population; to symbolise the equity of men and women in society; to increase the pool of people available for political appointments (Birch 1971: 70). In similar vein, the New Zealand Royal Commission on the Electoral System summarised the different types of representation when it considered what was needed to ensure that Maori voters were served by the system (Royal Commission on the Electoral System 1986: ch. 3). It concluded that five principles were important. First that Maori MPs are in parliament to raise the Maori viewpoint, second that all political parties should compete for Maori votes, third that all MPs are accountable to Maori voters, fourth that Maori MPs are accountable to Maori voters and fifth that the process of candidate selection in each party should enable Maori members to have some say in the choice (ibid.: 88). So ensuring fair representation for Maori needs a multiple approach. For full representation we need to consider what people think and who they are and so combine a variety of forms of representation. Ideas of representation are discussed in discrete terms but real representatives perform most of the roles some of the time.

   Although representation is the central component of democracy as practised in national government, there is no common approach in the academic literature. Rather the different parts of the process (candidates, voters, electoral system and parliament) have been studied separately and the theoretical literature also remains largely separate. The way that elections and government are organised and the behaviour of voters indicates that political parties are the central players, but theorists writing on representation rarely mention parties. Political parties campaign for votes by stressing their policy and ideology, but models of voting behaviour suggest that for many voters socio-economic cleavages are more, or equally, important. Individual candidates may stress their personal qualities and record of making decisions but voters may not be primarily concerned with trustee forms of representation. PR electoral systems assume votes are cast for parties and thus tend away from forms of representation based upon the personality of the candidate. Single-district electoral systems are designed to allow a choice between candidates but most voting is on party lines. In the voting-behaviour literature, representation is mostly of the 'share my views' type, be it based on issue, ideology or common group membership. Models of voting behaviour, whether they look at one key determinant or the interplay of many, tend to assume voters are choosing a candidate or party that shares their views, a party whose policy they support (Catt 1996b: ch. 2). One exception is the retro-spective voting school that fits the trustee model of representation with the idea that voters punish or reward the incumbent.

Mixed with the literature on voting and representation are assessments of the capability of the mass public. Early studies of voting behaviour sought to look at the information that voters used in making their decision but instead found most voters had little interest in or knowledge of politics and relied on an emotional link with one party (Lazarsfeld *et al.* 1948). Such findings added weight to growing ideas on democratic elitism, a strand of thought that saw the need for political experts to run government with elections acting as a periodic check on their power and a forum for competition (Held 1996: ch. 5).

Central to ideas of representative democracy is the idea that people have power because they choose representatives and those representatives are regularly accountable to the voters for the decisions that they make for the collectivity. Representatives are meant to make decisions for the population, either as dele-gates with instructions or as trustees relied upon to listen to the arguments and to make good decisions. People have power to the extent that they have a choice between candidates and can periodically make the choice anew, thus keeping the MPs accountable for the decisions that are made.

6   Elected bodies

The central idea of representative democracy is that the people rule because they elect individuals to make decisions for them. Chapter 5 described the different ideas related to the choice of a representative and this chapter considers the ways in which an elected body makes decisions. Throughout this chapter the focus is on the extent to which the people, whether directly or through those they elected, make the decisions. Most studies of elected bodies concentrate upon national legislatures but the same arguments hold for other elected bodies where people are periodically chosen to make decisions on behalf of the wider population and are held accountable for those decisions.

In each British university the students elect an executive to run the students' union and also have the ability to make decisions at regular general meetings that all can attend. The officers are elected to specific posts: usually a president and treasurer as full-time posts and a number of others such as officers for the student newspaper, women, graduates and so on. These people make the daily decisions on running the students' union and may sit on university committees to represent the student body. On matters of policy such as opening times for the café or participating in a political protest, decisions may be made by the executive or at a general meeting. In politically active universities, regular meetings for the whole student body are well attended and they do vote on policy. However, at many universities there is rarely enough interest for a meeting to reach quorum and so the elected officials take all of the decisions. The elected officials are expected to report to a general meeting on what they have been doing and they may be challenged. With due notice a vote of no confidence can be called on an office-holder, which if they lose means that another election will be held for that post. So there is a mix of the elected officers making decisions and the wider population passing policy and keeping the officers accountable. How well it works depends upon the level of interest amongst the student body both in terms of them attending general meetings to make policy and in calling for a vote of no confidence.

For a national pressure group there is likely to be again a mix of elections and meetings. Annual elections will be used to choose a president, treasurer and other members of the committee who will make the decisions about how to run the political campaign, raise and spend money, react to changes in the political world and make public statements. At an annual general meeting all members are invited to attend and they will receive reports from the elected office holders and vote on any policy that has been tabled for the meeting. Again under normal standing orders there is a mechanism for members to call for an extraordinary general meeting to censure the actions of an elected officer or the executive as a whole. During the year local groups will also meet but this will be to organise campaigning and fund-raising activities rather than to make policy decisions. Again there is a mix of direct involvement by members and allowing the elected officers to make decisions.

The management board of a self-governing school in Britain is made up of parent members who are elected by the parents, staff members who are elected by the staff plus some appointed members from the community with numbers such that the parents are always in the majority. The management board has responsibility for curriculum development, budgeting and staff appointments. Members must report annually to the parents about their activities but are also expected to ascertain the views of parents on matters of concern throughout the year. No specific mechanism for achieving this consultation is mentioned but there is an assumption that parents will have a say because the parent members are the majority and were elected by the parents. Also the board is seen as having a duty to promote contact with parents and thus discuss matters in light of the views of the parents. As a last resort, parents can demand a special meeting to consider their views if sufficient parents' signatures are collected. This is a classic example of representative democracy, with members elected from the two key groups of interested adults and then able to make decisions with accountability attained through annual reporting and the ability for a petition to call for a consultative meeting.

These examples of representative democracy in a small organisation show the ways in which the elected representatives make decisions and the people can both keep them accountable and have some direct input. Accountability depends on regular reporting and interested voters. However, as representative democracy is also central to national government it is vital to look at how that works in more detail and in particular the way in which new laws and regulations are passed. As well as the elected MPs and government ministers, influence can be exerted by those who are not elected, in particular bureaucrats, pressure groups, political parties and the media. Institutional structures are the other key components that cause variation in relative power over policy. The next section will briefly outline the pertinent institutional differences and describe the key actors and the following section looks at who has influence over each part of the policy-making process.

Several institutional structures have a significant impact on the way in which decisions are made and the relative influence of actors. The clearest distinction is between those countries where the head of government is directly elected by the people and those where the assembly chooses the head of government. This is broadly the distinction between Westminster and Madisonian systems, of which Britain and the USA are the prime examples respectively. Another way to categorise countries is using Lijphart's (1984: ch. 3) majoritarian-versus-consensus model that again uses Britain as the example of one extreme but here the alternative is exemplified by Belgium. While the USA is placed by Lijphart midway between the consensus and majoritarian ends of the continuum, there are important differences between the Madisonian model and both other models, giving three distinct categories (see Table 6.1). The Westminster model is based on the idea of parliamentary sovereignty meaning that no other body can overturn the decisions of parliament and government power derives from the assembly. Power is normally concentrated in a one-party government based on the idea that the majority view should prevail. In comparison, the Madisonian model is based on the separation of power with checks and balances provided by a written constitution, a directly elected executive and the assembly. Clearly lines of power and influence differ in the two and this will become apparent throughout the discussion. The consensus model is another form of parliamentary government but is based on the idea that policy should be acceptable to as many people as possible, so government will be by coalition of a wide range of parties, there will be a role for an upper house representing minorities and referenda may be used. The views of the range of people are also expressed through a federal structure and protected in a

Table 6.1 Institutional differences across democracies

	Westminster/ majoritarian	*Consensus*	*Madisonian*
Whose view is followed	Majority	As wide a group as possible	Bargain between separate interests
How head of government chosen	By majority in parliament	Agreement between parties	Presidential – elected by people (through a college)
Executive power	Concentration, one-party cabinet	Power-sharing coalition	Concentration
Relation between executive and legislature	Fusion – based on party discipline	Separation	Separation of powers
Division of power	Unitary	Federal	Federal
Upper house	Less power	Equal and looks to minorities	Equal and looks to states
Party system	Two-party; unit-dimensional	Multi-party; multi-dimensional	Weak parties
Electoral system	Plurality	Proportional representation	Plurality
Constitution	Unwritten; parliamentary sovereignty	Written	Written and judicial review

Sources: Adapted from Lijphart 1984 ch. 3

written constitution. These different institutional structures impact on the relative influence of political actors in policy decision making.

The actors

Regardless of the institutional structure, the same key actors are present within the political decision-making process. From our focus the first group of interest are the elected representatives who make up the assembly in the lower house (the backbenchers); elected upper house members; and the executive. Then there are the key groups that are not elected. Most important are the bureaucrats who staff the government ministries. Then there are the pressure or interest groups, the media and the political parties who all seek to have their views heard. Finally, judges interpret the law and so play a part in implementation. Before looking at the relative power of the key actors within the policy process, each will be briefly described in terms of what they do, their relationship with other actors and democratic contact with the people.

There is a clear distinction between what an individual MP may be able to do and what the assembly as a collective can achieve. In many parliaments it is hard for a single MP to make an impact as they have few opportunities to speak in the chamber, to ask questions of ministers or to introduce new legislation. Mostly MPs have strength in groups, either in committees or as part of a party voting bloc. Policy work by the assembly is primarily done in two forums: as the whole voting to pass legislation; and in committees looking at the details. Therefore it is these roles that need to be examined as part of an appraisal of MPs' influence.

Much of the work of MPs is done in committees, mostly as part of efficiency drives to allow a division of labour and specialisation in distinct policy areas as the work of parliament is too large for all to be involved in everything. Also, as discussed in Chapter 3, discussion is easier with a small group. Although committees carry out much of the important work, each is created by and answerable to the assembly and so is an extension of the assembly as a whole and not a substitute. In many multi-party assemblies, places on committees are allocated to parties in the same proportions as their size in the house, for instance Denmark, Ireland and Spain. In the Scandinavian countries the MPs elect committee members, while in Australia and Italy the party leaders nominate members and Canada and Ireland use a special committee to assign places. In general there are two kinds of committees: permanent and ad hoc. The terms 'standing committee' and 'select committee' are widely used but have different meanings in different assemblies and so can be misleading as categorical labels.

A permanent committee will be created for the life of the parliament with an expectation of continuing after the election. Usually they specialise in a particular policy area such as finance, health or agriculture and will look at all bills in that area as well as scrutinise the activities of the relevant ministry. Canada, Spain, Japan and the USA are examples of the countries where the division of issues between committees mirrors the divides between ministries, but in Israel, Ireland and Italy the division into subjects does not correspond with ministerial areas.

Permanent committees, due to their stable membership and concentration upon one policy area, can build up immense expertise in the field. Often there is a limitation on the number of committees one MP is allowed to attend, thus increasing the idea of policy specialisation. The recent growth in the number of these functional committees is part of the professionalisation of assemblies. Ad hoc committees are created for a specified purpose and time span. In Britain the detailed work on a bill is done by an ad hoc committee rather than the relevant policy committee, as in most other democracies. In other countries a special committee may be created to inquire into a particular issue that does not fall under the jurisdiction of an existing committee, for instance constitutional reform or corruption. Most committees can call on experts and documents to help in their deliberations. The key components for a strong committee are expertise in the policy area and funding or staff support. The expertise tends to come from having a stable membership and this can also help foster another useful attribute: a unified identity that does not always split on party lines.

MPs generally do more of their work in committee than in the assembly chamber but it is the latter that is shown in the media and thus is seen by the public as the key arena. The visible part of an assembly is when all members are in the house debating, questioning the government or passing legislation. In contrast to committee work, these activities are more formally constrained by procedural rules. Voting is usually on strict party lines so party discipline or cohesion within the party becomes an important component. Strong discipline means you can predict the behaviour of members whereas weak means they may act along party lines or they may not. Where party discipline is strong, MPs who vote against the party will be sanctioned in some way, ranging from assignment to unpopular committees, withholding leave to be absent from a vote and no promotion to expulsion from the party. Except in the USA parties are the organising unit within the assembly and therefore much of the representative role played by an MP relates to their membership of a party and abiding by party discipline. Parliament is the arena for the contest between parties and teams of leaders that is central to modern democracies. The interplay between strong parties and democracy will be discussed in more depth at the end of the chapter.

Within a Madisonian presidential system the people elect the head of government. Just over 20 democracies have a directly elected executive officer, mostly in Latin America plus the prime example, the USA. Many are large countries and/ or federal. As presidents are elected directly by the people for a fixed term they have a personal mandate for their policies and are not dependent upon the assembly for their position. This security of tenure allows a president to make unpopular decisions for the good of the country without fear of being immediately removed from office. However, independence from the assembly is also one of the major problems for presidents, as their actions can be blocked. The USA Congress can refuse to pass a bill that the President wants and the President can veto Congressional legislation. But the President can also make changes using executive decrees and Congress can overturn a Presidential veto. So the two bodies are balanced in their ability to frustrate the will of the other. The President of the USA has to rely on the ability to persuade Congress and will be able to achieve little if opposed by Congressional committees. Gridlock, when the President's party does not control Congress or Senate as was the case when Presidents Reagan and Bush faced a Democratic controlled Congress, is a problem in USA, but Carter and Clinton also faced opposition when Democrats controlled Congress.

In about two-thirds of democracies the people do not elect the head of government, instead the executive is created by the assembly. In a parliamentary system a major function of the assembly is to choose the executive: the German Basic Law sees the assembly's main function as the choosing of the leader. In a number of countries where coalitions are the norm, for instance Austria, Belgium, Israel, Italy and Spain, the government must receive a vote of confidence from the assembly before taking over power. In Germany the assembly votes for the Chancellor. In Britain and many Commonwealth democracies there is no requirement for a formal vote of confidence. Whatever the procedure, the Prime Minister has the job because of the backing of the majority of the MPs and so the assembly creates the head of government.

Within parliamentary systems there is an important distinction between single-party and coalition governments which relates to Lijphart's Westminster and Consensus models. In situations where one party covers the majority of MPs then the Prime Minister is simply the leader of that party. However, in most countries, primarily because they use systems of proportional representation, no one party has half the MPs and so a coalition between parties is needed. Generally the largest party in parliament will be part of the coalition but this is not always the case. In creating a coalition the parties will discuss the policy programme and the make-up of the executive. The leader of the largest party will usually be the prime minister but that position is dependent upon the continued support of all coalition partners. Exceptions occur when coalition agreements give leadership to another party leader, as in the case of Turkey after the 1995 election where the party leaders agreed to each have a year at the helm. Once the majority of seats are won in an election or the coalition make-up is agreed then the Prime Minister has potential for a great deal of control. With a coalition there is the constant tension between coalition partners to keep the deal together and to reach agreement on new issues. However, single-party governments are not immune from these problems but instead have to deal with internal factional tensions. Whether head of a single-party or coalition government, the Prime Minister holds the job only as long as the majority of MPs want it that way, and as that is based primarily on party strength, power depends upon keeping the parliamentary party happy. It was the Conservative party MPs, in particular ministers, who ended Margaret Thatcher's reign, not the opposition MPs or the voters.

But as assemblies make governments they can also unmake them. Most European constitutions specify that the parliament can pass a vote of censure or no confidence in the government. This is hardest in Germany where a 'positive vote of confidence' is needed which means that the Chancellor can only be removed if over half of the deputies vote for an alternative. This has happened once when the FDP left the coalition with the SDP and joined the CDP, voting for Kohl against Schmidt in 1982. While most assemblies can bring down the government with a vote of no confidence, most Prime Ministers can dissolve parliament. Thus, there is a balance of destructive power. So the power of the Prime Minister comes from the strength of the party they lead and once a majority is established, assuming party discipline, that majority will only be lost by a change in composition of the assembly. Such a change in party size may be caused by replacement of MPs, or when MPs change allegiance. In countries with PR elections the latter is the most likely while the former is the most common cause of change in plurality systems, with opposition parties often winning in by-elections to replace MPs who have died or retired. The President depends on powers defined in the constitution and in the personal mandate from the vote while a Prime Minister relies upon support from the majority of MPs voting on party lines. A Prime Minister has more power while in the job but less security of tenure.

To assist the head of government a cabinet, with each member responsible for a specific policy area, is created. The way in which cabinets function also differs between Westminster and Madisonian countries. In the USA, secretaries of state are there to advise the President who then makes the decisions about policy direction and the overall government programme. In the USA, Brazil and Venezuela, these people are not taken from the elected assembly but are chosen by the President for their political or policy expertise. Although the President of the USA is the only directly elected member of the cabinet, nominees for departmental heads have to be ratified by Senate and this is not just a rubber-stamp operation. Cabinet ministers are accountable only to the President because their role is to advise the President, in contrast to parliamentary ministers who are answerable to the assembly because MPs are the source of sovereignty. In Westminster systems, the Prime Minister is generally responsible for choosing the members of the cabinet, although there are some limitations on who they can choose. Generally ministers must be members of the assembly, however in Norway, Sweden, the Netherlands and France the opposite is true. In Japan and Britain some members of the cabinet may come from the upper house; note that in the latter case this means people who were not elected. Within a coalition the Prime Minister may only be able to choose the ministers from their own party as the other party leaders will nominate the people to fill positions assigned to their party. Some coalition deals place emphasis upon the allocation of specific ministerial positions while others look to the number of ministers in each party and allow the Prime Minister to decide which person has which portfolio.

In the parliamentary system, as well as running a department, ministers collectively decide government policy and this allows dialogue between the parts of government and means that all work together rather than in public opposition. However, in most cabinets there is no time for all decisions to be fully debated by all members and thus many decisions are ratified by cabinet after they are taken by the relevant minister or sub-committee. In these cases the cabinet can become more hierarchical than collegial. However, the principle of 'collective responsibility' plays an important part. This operational norm means that, regardless of the extent of debate and even if there were deep disagreements, once a decision has been made then all will back it and will not discuss the cabinet debate. Thus cabinet can be seen as an entity, more than the sum of its parts. But not all cabinets work in a collective manner and it can be particularly hard with a coalition, especially if disagreement was along party lines.

The high-ranking bureaucrats within each government ministry are the most influential of the non-elected actors, along with those pressure groups with insider access. All states have a bureaucracy, not just democracies, because any government needs people to put the decisions into practice and provide other routine administrative services. Within each government department there is the political leader plus the chief civil servants who together run the department. A bureaucrat is likely to be in a ministry for longer than a minster, and to be on a more secure career path. Also, as they are graduates with good degrees, in most cases they are better educated than the ministers. The longer tenure of top-ranking bureaucrats means that they both build up a great expertise in the specific policy area and know more about the process than the ministers.

Pressure or interest groups (the two terms are used interchangeably here) are organised groups with an interest in a specific policy area and which aim to influence government policy in that area. The group may be concerned with an issue, for instance Greenpeace, or with the position of their members, for instance a trade union. Of particular importance in many countries are the 'peak' organisations representing business and trade union interests: for instance the British Trade Union Congress has as its members most of the individual trade unions and so is a collective voice. Some pressure groups have insider status in that they are routinely consulted by bureaucrats and ministers from the relevant party: in most countries farmers' groups have a close working relationship with the ministry of agriculture. Many outsider groups want to be insiders but either are unsuccessful or are rejected by government departments because of their views, for instance neo-Nazi groups. However, some groups choose to remain outside the government system so that they feel able to criticise government actions publicly, for instance groups campaigning for the rights of the homeless. Obviously the influence of insider and outsider groups differs.

Although the key actors can be seen as separate groups with distinct roles and aims, it is also common to find them working together within a policy area. In the USA and Japan there are strong connections between the bureaucrats, pressure groups and assembly committees within each area, commonly known as 'iron triangles'. Even when the connections are not so strong there is likely to be a network amongst those involved in the same policy area if for no other reason than that they will meet each other in doing their work on that issue. There is a clear power distinction between an advocacy coalition where all agree on the way in which an issue should be addressed and a policy community that just denotes that all have a common interest in the issue.

The policy process

Having described the main political actors and explored the institutional structures that affect their exercise of power, it is now time to look at the process of creating new laws, otherwise known as the policy process. In the literature on policy there are four main stages in the policy process: agenda setting; policy creation; implementation; and evaluation. The first two cover the three parts of a decision discussed in earlier chapters: what is an issue, what are the possible solutions and which solution to follow. The third is needed by government so that the decisions are put into practice and the fourth takes the process full circle in that the debate on existing policy is part of the process of deciding which issues need to be addressed. In assessing the relative influence of MPs and others, it is useful to look at the policy process in two distinct sections. First the creation of policy and then the creation of law. In the policy creation phase an issue is identified as needing attention, possible solutions are canvassed and one is chosen as the policy direction to follow. This part is not necessarily done in this neat three-stage process, as the proposal of a solution is often part of the initial presentation of the problem. The law-making stage is much more public and formalised. In terms of looking at decision making it is useful to split this stage into two parts. First the new policy, in the form of a bill, passes through the legislative process in the assembly and then the law is implemented through administrative changes or through the justice system. In the long term, part of the implementation of a law comes through its interpretation in the courts. As the focus here is on the democratic element of government decisions it is important to look at the influence that the elected actors have as compared to the non-elected (see Table 6.2).

Within the study of public policy there are a number of different models that are used to explain the process and determine who has the greatest influence (Howlett and Ramesh 1995: ch. 2). In particular there are those models that concentrate upon the role of organised groups, such as pluralism and Marxism, then there are those such as rational choice that are interested in the behaviour of individuals. Rationalist models assume that decisions are made after the alternatives have been assessed and thus the best option identified, while instrumentalist models assume that decisions are the results of bargains between different groups acting in their own self-interests. Shunning these ideas of an ordered and rational process the 'garbage can' model suggests that many policy decisions are taken in an ad hoc manner. There are also arguments about the extent to which the institutional arrangements play a role in constraining the activities of the key actors. Common to authors from the different models is agreement that the actors are interested in what is good for themselves rather than for the country as a whole and so any policy making amounts to a contest between the self-interests of various groups or individuals. This fits with the main liberal democracy theorists of this century: competitive elitism, pluralism and legal democracy (Held 1987: 184, 204, 251). These ideas relate to the arguments about representation discussed in the previous chapter, in particular that the MP talks for a group or that an MP makes decisions based on their own views and thus will probably do what

Table 6.2 The influence of key actors throughout the policy process

	Executive	Parliament	Bureaucrats	Pressure Groups	Other
Agenda – what are the issues that need action?	May have ideas of own, either as minister in relation to the department or the cabinet collectively	May initiate bill or suggest ideas through party	May make suggestions related to their department	Put pressure on ministers and to a lesser extent bureaucrats Stimulate public debate	Party policy at conference Media may highlight a problem or cause
Possible solutions to the problem	Will set context of which solutions are acceptable Ministers may have ideas	May debate the issues generally May create the context of acceptable policies	Provide the options that ministers see	Will try to pressure bureaucrats or ministers	Party may have proposals Research units may have ideas Media may highlight possible solutions
Choose one of the solutions to create policy	Exclusively – in departments or collectively	Government party may lobby	May overtly lobby	Will lobby	Media may exert pressure
Write legislation	Play a part within each department	No role	Provide expertise and do most of the drafting	May provide expert knowledge May be consulted on the draft	Party advisors and research units may provide expertise May be consultation of the draft
Make a new law	Play a part in terms of blocking amendments, how it is voted on and exerting whip	Do it all – legislative process may include major redrafting and amendments	May give evidence to committee	May lobby for changes May give evidence to committee	May be consultation and public or media debate
Implement the new law			Make the administrative decisions		May be judicial review Courts interpret as cases are brought

those from a similar background want. These views on policy making do not fit with the idea of the MP as a trustee looking out for the good of the country.

Agenda setting involves a wide range of actors including pressure groups, public opinion, the media, political parties, MPs and bureaucrats. This is especially the case in a pluralistic society with freedom of press and expression and a politically active media and populace. Policy networks are important when they have access to the government, and particularly if bureaucrats are part of the network. There are a large number of issues which concern people, but only a few are considered by the government for action so the decision of which issues to look at can be crucial. Ministers tend to have a large role in agenda setting in that they decide which issues are to receive money and what new legislation is passed. Often they reach these decisions in reaction to pressure from other groups but ministers are usually pivotal in the final decision. A newly elected government is likely to have a list of urgent issues that they want to deal with and which they highlighted in the election campaign. A party that has been in power for a long time is likely to have dealt with all of its pressing concerns and so may be more open to pressure from other groups. At any time a new issue may emerge through the work of pressure groups and the use of the media to highlight a particular situation.

Once an issue is on the government agenda then the next step is to assess the possible solutions. This part of the process happens primarily within the government departments, although party policy committees may play a large role if the policy was constructed while the party was in opposition (as was the case for much of the early legislation of the Blair Government in Britain). The departmental bureaucrats provide the basic information about possible alternatives, how feasible they are and their probable impact. In some places independent or party policy advisors may also produce a range of alternative solutions. The range of solutions that is offered will be constrained by what is deemed to be acceptable policy. In some places certain options are not acceptable because they would breech the constitution or go against the political culture and norms. Others will have undesirable side-effects necessitating further government action. If the government has a particular strongly held ideological position then the bureaucrats are unlikely to present solutions that do not fit with that world view. In preparing this information the bureaucrats may call upon pressure groups and academic research units as well as looking at what governments in other countries have done. If a problem is portrayed as technical then it tends to be dominated by experts but if it seen as social then there will be a wider range of actors involved (Howlett and Ramesh 1995: 112). On some issues the media discusses possible solutions, looks to experience overseas and suggests alternatives, sometimes those proposed by pressure groups.

Choosing the best solution, and working out the details, are also done by insiders. The executive will make the decision on which option to follow and the bureaucrats write the new legislation or administrative regulations. Pressure groups, party members, the media and MPs may lobby the bureaucrats over details of the legislation, but much of the debate surrounds the stage when possible solutions are formulated rather than the actual decision. In some countries relevant pressure groups will be formally consulted at the drafting stage. In Austria it is expected that the peak organisations for employers and workers will be consulted over draft legislation. In the British-influenced countries, a draft of the legislation, the White Paper, is published to allow consultation before the final bill is written. This process was once common in Britain; however, under the Thatcher Government the use of White Papers was severely cut.

On most issues that make it onto the government agenda, a new law or amendment will be introduced, although for some an executive decree or change in regulations is all that is needed and for other issues the government needs to take action on the international stage. New legislation is the clearest sign of those issues that have made it onto the agenda. It is the government that initiates the majority of successful legislation. The number of bills that are introduced in a country can range widely, from several thousand in the USA to under a hundred in Ireland. In some countries regulations are used for many needed changes, instead of legislation, and some places favour large omnibus bills rather than a series of more specific ones. Not all bills that are introduced are expected to become laws; in some places the opposition introduces bills to make a point or start a debate. One sign of countries with a strong parliament is the extent to which MPs can initiate legislation. In both Italy and Sweden many successful bills are introduced by MPs rather than the government. At the other extreme, in Australia non-government bills are a rarity. Again backbench MPs will often use the introduction of a bill as a way to raise an issue with no expectation that a new law will be created. There are often restrictions on what the assembly can do; for instance, in France the legislature cannot propose an increase in expenditure or a decrease in revenue. In many countries MPs cannot initiate a bill that has financial implications and in others such a bill is only admissible if backed by the government. Another problem for MPs in introducing legislation is the lack of assistance and expertise in the drafting of legislation as they do not have access to the bureaucrats who draft government legislation. The reverse pattern holds in the USA as only members of Congress can initiate legislation so the President needs a sponsor, but still over 80 per cent of proposed bills emanate from the President because there is a convention that the chair of the relevant committee will sponsor the bill.

In making policy decisions the people and their representatives have a small part to play. The executive, which is either directly or indirectly elected, makes the final choice but details of the possible solutions are provided by the bureaucrats. In all stages of the process the ministers will be lobbied by pressure groups and the media may play a part if there is public debate. It is at this stage that pressure groups that have good access to those inside the system are at an advantage: they can lobby the bureaucrats and so help to shape the initial legislation. In a few cases an MP can put an issue on the agenda, and in those cases pressure groups and the public may have had a greater influence and bureaucrats will not have played a role.

Once a piece of legislation has been decided upon then it has to go through the legislative process. In creating a new law, the parliament will accept the general principle, give detailed scrutiny of the clauses of the bill and vote to accept the entire thing. Correspondingly, many places have three readings, for instance Britain, USA, Denmark, Germany, Israel. The first is for consideration of the general principle. The legislation then goes to a committee for clause-by-clause consideration. The second reading is a detailed examination of clauses, the third is a final consideration of the principle and the vote makes it law. Another pattern is to have just one reading of a piece of legislation, after a committee has seen it and made amendments. In countries with an upper house, legislation will go through the same process in that house as well. If the upper house amends the legislation then such changes must be accepted by the lower house, so a contentious piece of legislation can go through each house a number of times. A second chamber is seen as serving one of two main functions: to represent states within a federal system; and to provide a 'sober second thought'. Some upper houses can only delay the passing of a bill, or there is an understanding that they will not defeat certain items, for instance in Britain those contained in the election manifesto. The Japanese lower house can overturn a Senate defeat with a two-thirds vote. In some countries the houses are equal, for instance in the USA no bill can be passed if the Senate does not approve. In Germany the upper house, whose members are chosen by *Länder* governments, has a veto over all legislation that affects the *Länder*. In most countries the two houses are elected in different ways so it is common for the political make-up of the two houses to differ and this means that the government cannot expect the same party-based backing that it has in the lower house. For instance, in Australia the lower house is elected using the preferential vote and one party can control government but the Senate is elected using STV (see Chapter 2) which means that a wider number of parties gain Senators and no single party can dominate. This situation has meant that recent governments have faced their greatest opposition from the Senate rather than within the lower house. Even when the party balance is the same, the upper house may feel less inclined towards party discipline as it is one step removed from the government. It is often easier for the upper house to criticise the government and to amend legislation because of the weaker party discipline and the different balance of power.

Whether there are three or one readings of a bill in the assembly, the detailed work is done in a committee, so again this is the basis of MPs' influence. When a bill is debated in parliament and a vote taken on the principle before it goes to the committee stage for detailed scrutiny there is a limit to the extent that the committee can make amendments. As parliament has already accepted the basic principle the committee cannot make radical changes to the proposed legislation. However, when the committee sees the draft legislation before it goes to the assembly, they may make major changes. For instance, in the USA a committee looks in detail at the bill before it goes to Congress and thus the committee may redraft whole sections of the legislation. The Dutch assembly also redrafts much of the legislation that is presented. Generally committees can call on experts to assist in their scrutiny of the bill. The Swedish norm is for consultation over the details of any new laws. In New Zealand the committee calls for public comment on the new legislation and hears submissions from individuals and organised groups. Other countries tend to have less widespread input with committees able to call on bureaucrats or ministers to answer their questions. Again it is the specialist knowledge built up by committee that is used to scrutinise the suggestions made by the executive. However, any committee will have a smaller membership than the ministry, smaller secretariat and less money, so it is never possible to keep abreast of developments and decisions in the ministry being scrutinised. Much of the information the committee needs must be supplied by the ministry, so the bureaucrats have some control. The main alternative sources of information are pressure groups who will lobby the MPs on a committee with details of the changes they would like. If there is an iron triangle between bureaucrats, committee MPs and key pressure groups, then there are unlikely to be conflicts as the legislation is scrutinised. But if there is major disagreement between bureaucrats and pressure groups then the committee members may be squeezed between two groups claiming to be experts.

Once a law is passed it has to be implemented and non-elected actors are central in this last part of the process. Much of the administrative detail is undertaken by the bureaucrats and some legislation only lays down the general principle, leaving it to administrators to fill in the detail. In France a new law will be followed by numerous decrees from the bureaucrats explaining the intent of the new law, providing new regulations and setting out administrative procedures. The other major players in the implementation of new laws are the judiciary. Although a vital part of liberal democracy is the idea of the rule of law and an independent judiciary, this does not mean that judges do not play a political role. Judges are meant to be above politics so cannot show bias and cannot be sacked by politicians because of the decisions they make. But there are two ways in which the judiciary can play a role in the policy process: interpretation of law and judicial review. The role of the judiciary in the political process tends to vary across countries to a greater degree than the role of the other actors considered here.

In countries based on Roman law, such as France, the written law is all, judges interpret the law and may use as evidence of intent the debates in the assembly when the legislation was passed. In common-law countries, such as England, case law is vital so judges are basing decisions on what previous judges decided and therefore judges play a larger role in the process. However, if the government or assembly does not like the interpretation, a new law may be passed to change the interpretation of a law that has been established by the judges. In the USA, the Supreme Court, through interpretation of the constitution and other laws, plays an important part in making changes to national policy. The early stages of the civil rights movement came about through decisions of the Supreme Court, such as Brown versus Board of Education, which rejected school segregation in 1954. Only later did the government pass civil-rights legislation. Likewise, much of the debate on the creation of voting districts, discussed in the previous chapter, is based on judicial interpretation of the Voting Rights Act, not legislative action.

Judicial review refers to the power of determining if legislation is allowable. In those countries that have a constitution the government and assembly may pass laws that contravene the constitution and so somebody must adjudicate, the US Supreme Court being the best-known example. In Canada, Finland and Denmark the constitutional validity of a proposed piece of legislation may be determined before it is introduced. However, many other countries have judicial review, such as Ireland, Australia, Norway, Brazil and Japan. In Germany the constitution court is the watchdog of the Basic Law and mostly deals with demarcation disputes between parts of government. In most cases the government still has the final say in that there are ways to change the constitution. So in the USA the constitution was amended to allow federal taxation after such taxes were ruled as unconstitutional. Also the constitutional court has no means of enforcing its decisions, so the Supreme Court decision against segregated schools in the USA had to be enforced by the National Guard who were sent in to Little Rock, Arkansas, by President Eisenhower two years after the Supreme Court decision. Where there is no constitution then a law cannot be struck down by the judiciary because the assembly has the final say. In Britain the laws of parliament are sovereign. However, judges can (and have) told ministers that they are acting outside their executive powers on some changes made by executive decision rather than the passing of legislation. For instance, in 1995 Douglas Hurd, then British Foreign Minister, was censured in court for using overseas aid money to help with the construction of the Pergau Dam in Malaysia. The role of judicial review of a constitution raises an interesting question about types of democracy. The Canadian judiciary does not rule on the constitutionality of new legislation, arguing that it is upholding the actions of the democratically elected assembly. In contrast, the USA Supreme Court argues that it must uphold the constitution against the wishes of elected assemblies because the constitution embodies the democratic rights of the people. Especially when a constitution has been endorsed through a referendum, it is not clear which has the democratic high ground, legislation passed by the assembly or the constitution.

Throughout the policy process, the institutional arrangements impact on the relative influence of the actors, sometimes because of the formal division of power but sometimes because institutional configurations embody the norms and ideas about how politics works, and thus will shape perceptions. In Westminster systems there is a concentration of power with the executive but the role of the party is vital as a leader has power through controlling the majority in the assembly. In the consensual systems there is an assumption of consultation and seeking a solution that is acceptable across a range of groups. Therefore pressure groups play a greater role, especially peak organisations, and the second chamber, as protector of minorities, will also be important. In Madisonian systems there is a diffusion of power between the assembly, executive and the courts that uphold the constitution, so decisions are a balance between these groups. This spread of power points means both that pressure groups have more targets and also that their success in one place may be overturned in another. In assessing the influence of MPs it is vital to know: the power relationship between the assembly and executive; if the norm is majority rule or acceptance by most people; and whether the constitution or parliament is sovereign.

Assessing the power of the people and those they elect

Most constitutions say the legislature is sovereign: the Japanese Diet is the 'highest organ of state power' and the German Bundestag is the centre of legislative activity. But in reality, although it provides government with legitimacy, the assembly is not the source of power over policy and legislation. Instead it is the government that makes decisions, although academics argue about how much ministers are swayed by their bureaucrats and how much they are able to impose their own will on their department. There are also competing views on how successful certain pressure groups are at influencing the government and bureaucrats to follow their preferred line. Individual MPs who are not part of the executive play only a small part in creating legislation, and much of what they do is controlled by party discipline. On the face of it there seems to be little popular control of policy because the cabinet and bureaucrats are the central players with successful pressure groups able to influence some decisions. However, one important role for the MPs is to scrutinise the government, to make them accountable for what is done by them and their bureaucrats.

In parliamentary systems the key role of MPs is to keep the government accountable to the people by scrutinising their actions. In presidential systems the assembly also has a scrutiny role as part of the checks and balances integral to the Madisonian model. A common and public form of scrutiny occurs when MPs ask ministers questions in the assembly. The role of the opposition is to make the government answer for its actions, and in parliaments with party discipline it is the opposition that does most of the questioning. In this way the government is made accountable to the voters and the voters are shown an alternative set of political leaders in action. The less public scrutiny of the government is generally carried out by functional committees which monitor the actions of a particular ministry. Only by questioning the bureaucrats and ministers on the reasons for their policy choices, and the outcomes they expected, can the MPs keep the policy-making process accountable to the people. As well as ensuring that the government is called to account, MPs can question the wider workings of departments. Under the doctrine of ministerial responsibility, a minister is answerable for all that happens inside the department, even if done by bureaucrats and without the knowledge of the minister. Thus, in theory, the non-elected but influential bureaucrats are kept accountable to the people through the MPs. Scrutiny can only be effective if the committees have resources to rival the bureaucracy: they need alternative information on the specialist area so that they know what to probe and where choices were made. The job of scrutiny is easier where there is a Freedom of Information Act, like in Australia, the Netherlands and the USA, and much harder in places like Britain where the government can withhold information.

Scrutiny is the strength of assemblies, and in a parliamentary system it is what keeps the executive accountable to the people. Ministers are appraised not in terms of the legality of their action but how it is seen by the MPs, usually in relation to how it fits with their views and ideologies. On paper MPs are usually given the power to make laws and change governments, but what they actually do is scrutinise legislation and question the government. Of course MPs have roles over and above ruling on behalf of the people, but it is that aspect of their job that is the focus of interest here. Most parliaments are reactive as they can do little but react to what the government is doing. So a key democratic role is to try to keep the executive accountable to the voters, if only by ensuring that the details of government decisions are made public.

Pressure groups can play a large part in both policy creation and law making due to their reservoir of relevant expertise and their ability to make contact with the different players in the system. As unelected groups pushing the interests of one part of the population, pressure groups are usually seen as undemocratic. Thinkers of the new Right see pressure groups as vested interests out to capture government money and policies for the benefit of their own members. But another interpretation, the approach of pluralism, is that pressure groups add to democracy. As it is unlikely that MPs will represent the full range of opinions in a country, pressure groups are needed to fill the gap, and also to provide a voice for those whose own MP takes the opposite view to theirs on a particular issue. Groups defend individuals from the government and they also aid democratic responsiveness by applying pressure to MPs. Decisions are the result of bargaining between different interests and so a wide range of views will be taken into account. Pluralist theorists see pressure groups as representing the views of the people and, thus, a crucial part of democracy. However, these representatives of the people have not been elected in any way so it is a different sort of representation than that provided by MPs. In pluralist thinking each person will join those pressure groups that espouse her or his own interests, because politics is about the safeguarding of personal interests.

The relative influence of actors has been examined in the creation of new laws, as this is a visible part of government actions. However, to concentrate on legislation is to look at just one group of policy decisions that are made. Many executives can make changes without going through parliament: the Presidents of France and the USA, and UK ministers, can use executive decrees. In these cases the elected representatives must rely on their ability to question government ministers and the accountability that the assembly can demand from the government. There has also been an increase in the number of decisions that are taken outside the governmental sphere, with two trends applying across Western democracies: globalisation and contracting out. As part of moves to decrease the size of government and to improve efficiency of provisions, many functions previously undertaken by bureaucrats have been contracted out to independent agencies. So there has been a rise in the number of quangos and other agencies that implement or regulate government policy. Such agencies are created by government and receive money from them, but are separate entities and thus are not directly accountable to MPs via the ministers. These organisations are expected to meet demands of efficiency and cost effectiveness rather than accountability to the elected politicians and thus the growth in the use of quangos has led many commentators to talk of a growing democratic deficit (Weir 1996: 25–27). Globalisation refers to decisions moving in another direction, beyond the state boundary.

There are a number of strands to this concept: that economies are interdependent and so cannot be controlled by one government; that more decisions are made between states as they sign international agreements; or that there is greater knowledge about what happens elsewhere and less tolerance for breaches of agreed norms of behaviour, such as protecting human rights and stopping racial discrimination. As more political decisions are made in places other than government and parliament, the already weak influence of MPs is further reduced.

Having looked at the extent to which the MPs make decisions, it is important to tie in these ideas with those relating to representation. In particular, expectations as to how an MP will make decisions: based on the interests of those in the electorate; based on interests that are shared with the voters such as issue stance, ideology or socio-economic group membership; or based on personal consideration of the evidence and what is best for the country. In other words clientelism, responsible party and trustee. An important distinction is between those where the representatives follow the wishes of voters and those where representatives use their own judgement.

When looking at changes in parliament, the role of committees, the work of cabinet, the job of the bureaucrats and the influence of pressure groups, a common theme is the ever-increasing complexity of government life. Bureaucrats have a large impact on the creation of policy because they provide technical information for the ministers; pressure groups also have the greatest impact when they are accepted as sources of expert knowledge and committees are strong when they build up expertise. The view is that government has to deal with a growing number of issues, that these issues are more technical than they used to be and that decisions are needed fast and efficiently. Thus it is that decisions and detail move from the amateur politician to the trained expert. As government became involved in managing the economy, providing education and health services, and negotiating with other states, then a more specialist knowledge was needed. Therefore MPs have to be trusted to look at the evidence provided by experts and make a decision, rather than follow the views of the uninformed public. As a corollary the more technical government becomes, the harder it is for the voters to follow and to pass judgement on what has occurred. In some technical areas such as finance or the environment there is a growing debate as to whether ministers have the capability to understand the issues and to question the advice offered by bureaucrats and pressure groups. Increasingly party policy advisors are being used as a buffer between the minister and the bureaucrats, to provide an alternative source of expertise that is attuned to the party view. As the technicality of government decisions is stressed, so there is a move towards the MP as trustee, making decisions on behalf of the people and seeking their blessing at the next election. The responsible party model may also tie in here, in that MPs are chosen to make decisions based on their basic worldview as expressed in their party's aims and objectives.

Political parties play a central role in modern government, but interpretation of, and reaction to, this dominant role varies widely. On the one hand countries that are deemed to have a strong assembly are those with an absence of large, strong parties. On the other hand, the model of 'responsible party government' is seen as the basis of modern liberal democracy, except for in the USA. In other words a strong parliament is one where the MPs are autonomous from the parties and thus a government may have its legislation defeated by members of its own party or parties. But responsible party government assumes that the voters delivered the government with a mandate to implement its manifesto or worldview and so the government MPs should be voting with their leaders to deliver promises to the voters. The same arguments rage in relation to committees. The composition of committees usually reflects the relative size of the parties in the assembly and positions are assigned in consultation with the party leadership. With positions assigned to maintain relative party strength there is an assumption that members will express their party's view on the committee. But if each committee divides on party lines then it will not question the actions or proposed legislation from the government and the government will have a majority on the committee. Again are the MPs there as party members or experts on the issue? This argument is another manifestation of the 'trustee versus delegate' debate found in studies of representation. Another aspect of committee work that relates to representation is when an MP is seen as part of a key group, such as women or an ethnic minority. In this case, does the MP have an added role of scrutinising the legislation or government actions in relation to their impact on that group? The USA Black Congressional Caucus aims to have a member on each important committee so that all key legislation has been seen by a black representative.

Whether strong or weak, parties play a central role in the organisation of assemblies. The link between the party and the actions of MPs is central to responsible party government ideas of democracy, but it is simplistic to assume the direction of influence as being top-down from leader to cabinet, then MPs, and finally the party at large. Within a party there are the members, the leaders of the party outside the assembly, the MPs and other elected people such as senators or local government members and the leader of the party in parliament. At different times talk of 'party' can refer to various of these groupings. The relationships between the MPs and the party outside parliament differ but so do relations between the leadership in the assembly and the leadership outside; between the leadership in the assembly and the other MPs. When MPs are said to follow the party line on a vote are they complying with the wishes of the party leader, with a collective leadership wish, with policy created by the party at large, or with a decision reached collectively by all of the MPs? In other words it is not at all clear who makes decisions for the party and this will vary across countries, parties, and policy issues, and will alter when a party is part of the government as opposed to in opposition. Such questions impact on the type of representation that is provided by MPs.

The role of party discipline in the scrutiny of party legislation relates to the arguments about discipline in relation to representation. If the representative is chosen because of their party line then the voters may have an expectation that they follow the party thinking in all matters and all roles and therefore, on a committee, will refrain from disagreeing with the party. However, if the representative was chosen as a person with a particular set of interests, as a person who could be trusted to make good decisions, or as one who is expected to argue for the interests of their electorate, then there is an expectation that they will act according to those interests or their conscience and not according to the party doctrine when they scrutinise the government and legislation. Keeping MPs accountable is also affected by the extent of party discipline. It is easy to follow the work of MPs when it is all associated with the line of the party as these broad activities are recorded in the media. Following the actions of an individual MP is harder. Lists of who voted on which side of an issue are published but it is harder to gain evidence of the work an MP has done on a committee, or in questioning government, even though these are vital parts of their democratic role. So the ability of voters to scrutinise the work of their representatives is also affected by the way in which that parliament works.

Summary

To make government democratic the people choose representatives, those representatives make the decisions and are then accountable to the voters. The first and third parts happen through elections but the weak link is the second. While elected representatives are not the central players in policy creation, let alone executive and administrative decrees, they do have a role in scrutinising those who do make decisions. Individuals also have other means of trying to influence government decisions through membership of political parties and pressure groups and through public debate. Nevertheless, liberal democracy is premised on elected representatives making decisions and this is clearly not how policy in modern democracies is made. In the light of this deficiency there has been a growth of interest in ways of assessing the extent of democracy within those countries that are generally considered to be democratic, and this is covered in the next chapter.

7 Assessing the practice of democracy

Previous chapters have demonstrated the diversity of democratic practice, both between the participatory, direct and representative models and within each. All allow the people as a group to make decisions and, thus, at the most fundamental level are democratic. But spanning the practices within three models there is a wide range of procedures. Therefore it is pertinent to ask if we can assess different systems in terms of the extent to which they provide power to the people. Obviously, as there is no agreement on the exact meaning of 'power to the people' there is no agreed way to measure the extent to which a given set of procedures provides democracy. One problem is that of determining a threshold: those procedures and behaviours that are the bare minimum for democracy. Having determined which examples are democratic, there is then the question of distinguishing between them or putting them in rank order. Taking this line of thought to the extreme would lead to specification of the ideal democratic situation or the best that is achievable.

As with the rest of this book, the material covered here relates to actual attempts to assess the extent of democracy rather than a theoretical discussion of normative values. Despite disagreement about interpretations of democracy, a number of academics have created schema to measure the level of democracy in a country. Some, such as Dahl, attempt to specify the minimum requirements. The largest group seeks to put countries in rank order according to how much democracy they have, usually so that a democracy index can be used in statistical analysis linking democracy to economic development or human rights. A third approach is to examine details of democracy in one country and compare them to some standard of democratic practice. All groups are looking for the essence of representative democracy in terms of particular types of institutional arrangements or forms of behaviour. This chapter will consider various schema that have been used to measure democracy and look at their theoretical underpinnings and the measures they use. The whole idea of measuring democracy will also be discussed, as will the possibility of creating a measure that covers participatory and direct as well as representative democracy.

Threshold of democracy

The earliest study to attempt analysis of the link between economic conditions and democracy was by Lipset, who studied the countries of Latin America and of Europe (Lipset 1960). To do this, he categorised the countries within each geographic region. He divided European countries into 'stable democracies' and 'unstable democracies and dictatorships' while the Latin American countries were divided between 'democracies and unstable dictatorships', and 'stable dictatorships'. In assigning countries to a category he specified that, in a democracy, the government can regularly be changed through constitutional means and that most people can have an influence on major decisions by choosing between competing teams of political leaders (ibid.: 45). He specified three conditions that are needed for this to occur: a set of beliefs about what is legitimate; one set of political leaders; and a political opposition. Drawing from these descriptions, a democracy needs regular election of political leaders, with competition and a wide franchise plus norms of civil and political rights, and the absence of any of these will render a country undemocratic.

While Lipset's set of criteria was created so that he could use democracy as a variable in analysis, Downs and Dahl were interested in specifying the requirements for democracy as an exercise in itself. Identifying the threshold for democracy requires a listing of all components that are needed, so that once a country meets all of these requirements it is a democracy and if any one of them is missing then it is not. Downs set out eight conditions for a democratic political system based on government formed through periodic competitive elections with full franchise and equal voting: a single party or coalition elected to run government; periodic elections; franchise for all permanent residents; one person one vote; the party or coalition with a majority of votes can be government until the next election; losing parties do not try to take over; government does not restrict activities of opposition; and at least two parties compete in elections (Downs 1957: 23–24). These are similar to those specified by Lipset except that there is more detail on the way elections are to be conducted.

Dahl lists five democratic criteria: voting equality; effective participation; enlightened understanding; control of the agenda; and inclusion. So polyarchy, the closest he says that a country can practically get to democracy, is distinguished by the fact that the citizens have the right to replace those who govern them and that few are excluded from citizenship, thus covering ideas of sovereignty and participation. To meet these key aspects there are seven necessary institutions for a polyarchy: officials are elected, through free and fair elections with an inclusive suffrage and the right to run for office. Individuals also have the right to freedom of expression, a range of information sources and associational autonomy (Dahl 1989: 220–22). In each case it is the right to do something rather than it happening that is specified. However, Dahl says that in assessing whether or not a country is a polyarchy it is important to look at the actual rather than the written rights of the citizens. Using these seven criteria, a country or regime can be classed as a polyarchy or not: if they meet all seven then they are, but failure on any one of them denotes a non-polyarchy. The additional components that Dahl introduces are specifications of civil and political rights such as information and association and thus consideration of society and not just government.

Downs and Dahl specify that all components are needed for a country to be a democracy (or polyarchy) and failure on any one takes the country into the non-democratic category. By specifying a dichotomy the categories on either side become very wide: non-democracies range from those who are nearly democratic to those with none of the necessary components, that is from a country with multi-party elections but restrictions on the franchise to military dictatorship with no human rights. Providing a threshold also says nothing about the extent of democracy within those countries that meet the minimum requirements. If democracy is seen as a continuum then it is also important to be able to distinguish between countries that are deemed to be democratic. Dichotomies are unsatisfactory if used alone because there is a vast range of procedures included on either side of the divide and because the middle group are of interest when considering questions of democratisation.

If we are interested in the process of democratisation or specific components such as elections or party competition, then specification of a middle area with those almost over the line and just over the line would be useful. In assigning countries Lipset found several problematic cases, for instance Mexico, a country which has freedom of press, information and political opposition but where widespread electoral fraud is suspected. On a strict reading of the definition Mexico should be in the undemocratic category but Lipset counts it as 'democratic' because the people have some influence over government (Lipset 1960: 48). Many of the older democracies had an evolutionary path to democracy with a slow widening of the franchise, increase in the number of parties, decrease in corruption and widening of information. Many emerging democracies in Africa have also moved slowly from elections with one party to multi-party elections and freedom of expression and information. Is it possible to say that there is an exact point when they move from non-democratic to democratic or are they just becoming more and more democratic from the time they hold some form of election for government? Measures need to accommodate changing ideas about democracy. At the turn of the century a full franchise in most places meant all men, whereas now it means all adults, but there is still debate as to when one becomes an adult. Ideas about the desirable level of other components may also change over time. As the specified democratic threshold relates to behaviour or the institutions then norms may change, suggesting that as ideas of democracy change then so will the threshold.

The other questionable component of these sets of minimum criteria is the 'all or nothing' approach. Is democracy a package, so that all things must be present, or can doing well in one area make up for deficiencies in another? If some of these components are more important than others, as Lipset seems to imply in his placement of Mexico, then these schema do not really provide a definitive list of the necessary components of democracy. On Lipset's example, the existence of competitive elections is the vital component and the others make the democracy better, again suggesting the need for a third category in the middle. Discussion of the specification of a threshold mainly raises ideas related to democracy as a continuum with states moving towards a basic democracy and also able to improve the level of democracy within that category. So the view is that countries can be ranked in terms of the extent to which they have a democracy.

Ranking the extent of democracy

During the 1960s and early 1970s, statistical political science was applied to ideas of democratisation, democratic stability and the impact of democracy upon equality (Banks 1972; Bollen 1979; Cutright 1963; Jackman 1974; Neubauer 1967; Olsen 1968; and Smith 1969). There has been a resurgence of interest in the measurement of democracy in the 1990s with the tide of new democracies and renewed interest in questions of democratic stability (Arat 1991; Vanhanen 1997). Such studies depended upon having a numerical measure of democracy for each country under consideration and each author tended to create their own measure. The fact that there are as many measures as there are studies underlines the problem of agreeing upon a measurement of democracy. Disagreements between authors are based primarily on which concepts need to be covered and how to operationalise them. Due to a lack of accurate information, sometimes it is not possible to acquire a value for the desired measure and so a substitute that is available must be used. Despite the differences between the criteria that are used there are commonalties in terms of the components of democracy they seek to tap and in the type of institutions and behaviour that are covered, and all include the need for elections.

When creating a measure of democracy, the authors seek to isolate the key components and then identify ways in which these can be measured. In this way their measures are based upon ideas about the core theoretical aspects of democracy. So Cutright, the first to create a numeric scale of democratic stability, bases his ideas heavily on the role of parties, following Weberian ideas, and also rewards stability (Cutright 1963: 255). Bollen sees democracy as meaning that the elite are accountable to the non-elite and so focuses upon popular sovereignty and political liberty tempered with the need to find data (Bollen 1980: 372). Vanhanen, the most recent exponent in this field, concentrates upon ideas of competition and the extent of popular participation (Vanhanen 1997: 34). All numeric measurements are based upon the use of elections and common underpinnings are participation, competition, absence of coercion, popular sovereignty and access to information. Several writers also base their scales upon the writings of Dahl and Downs discussed in the previous section.

Each measurement of democracy has more than one component with the norm being four. For instance Flanigan and Fogelman (1971) used electoral succession, competition, participation and absence of suppression while Arat (1991) used participation, inclusiveness, competition and absence of coercion. Both the first schema and the most recent one rely upon two measures: Cutright (1963) creates a cumulative score based on the existence each year of a competitively elected legislature and an elected executive; Vanhanen (1997) uses party competition and voter turnout. At the other end of the spectrum, Smith (1969) used 20 measures taken from scales published by Banks and Textor (1963). Researchers use a mix of numeric and categoric data. Some of these measures are real numbers, such as the percentage of the vote received by the largest party or the percentage of the population who voted. Other measures, indeed the majority, are categoric, so that countries are assigned a score because they meet certain criteria (see Table 7.1) and thus the numbering is based upon the judgements of the researcher(s). Authors differ as to whether or not they consider institutional provisions, like the right to compete in an election, or behaviour, for instance the number of parties that compete. Cutright and Vanhanen concentrate upon the

Table 7.1 Different measures of party competition

ARAT – COMPETITIVENESS – COUNTRY ACCUMULATES POINTS AS FOLLOWS

0	No political parties or just one political party
1	Parties allowed but there are significant exclusions
2	Only extremist parties excluded
3	No exclusion of parties
2	Largest party has less than 70 per cent of vote
1	no election or largest party over 70 per cent of vote

BANKS AND TEXTOR – PARTY SYSTEM: QUANTITATIVE

One-party	All other parties non-existent, banned, non-participant
One party dominant	Opposition but numerically ineffective at national level
One-and-a-half-party	Opposition significant but unable to win majority
Two-party	Reasonable expectation of party rotation
Multi-party	Coalition or minority party government

FLANIGAN AND FOGELMAN – POLITICAL COMPETITION

0	Presence of legal opposition parties and opposition in regular, important elected legislature
1	Presence of either legal opposition parties or opposition in regular, important elected legislature
2	Presence of neither feature

JACKMAN – POLITICAL COMPETITION

0	No voting
1	Plebiscite voting with a single party and no effective primary
2	Single party but may be effective primaries
3	Multi-party system with a ban on extremist parties
4	Multi-party system with no bans

NEUBAUER – COMPETITION – NUMERIC SCORE IN TWO PARTS

Alternation	Per cent of time period in which dominant party held office
Closeness	Mean per cent of the vote received by the winning party

VANHANEN – COMPETITION

	Per cent vote gained by all parties other than the largest party

---

Sources: Arat 1991: 25; Banks and Textor 1963: 97; Flanigan and Fogelman 1971: 451; Jackman 1974: 37; Neubauer 1967: 1006; Vanhanen 1997: 34

institutional rights while Gastil advocates a concentration on the way in which rights are used and so looks at political behaviour (Gastil 1985: 161).

Where institutional measures are used the most common are that: the government is elected; there is a wide franchise; the constitution includes civil rights and a free press. Definitions of an elected government are broad and tend to mean that the legislature and head of government are directly or indirectly elected in fair elections thus allowing for presidential and parliamentary systems plus use of an electoral college. Most specify that the elected body must be effective and not just a rubber stamp for the decisions of non-elected people. Banks' (1972) scale of legislature effectiveness is used by a number of authors and has four categories: no effective legislature, parliament as a rubber stamp, some powers, legislature can override executive veto and raise tax. When behavioural aspects are used common measures cover participation; party competition; associationalism; critical and free press; effective and constitutional government and parliament; lack of government oppression. Participation levels generally apply to elections looking at suffrage (Flanigan and Fogelman 1971; Lenski 1966; Muller 1988; Neubauer 1967) or turnout as either a percentage of the population (Vanhanen 1997) or adults (Jackman 1974). Arat (1991) looks at who is allowed to stand as a candidate. The existence of political competition and freedom to form groups is a common component but measured in a wide variety of ways (see Table 7.1). Within competition different studies look at the existence of opposition parties, their chances of being in government and the size of their collective vote. Measures of oppression or public sanctions consider the extent to which government restricts the press, opposition groups and public debate and demonstrations (Arat 1991; Bollen 1980; Flanigan and Fogelman 1971). Press freedom is often included as a separate item and looks at the extent of official interference with the media (Bollen 1980) or the ability to criticise the government (Jackman 1974). Neubauer (1967) takes a different approach and looks at the number of separately owned newspapers in the capital city as a measure of access to diverse information sources. Again these measures cover the numeric and the categoric.

These different schema are not attempting to specify all necessary components of democracy but rather to identify salient aspects that show the extent of democracy and that can be measured on available information. Therefore, the criteria that are chosen show those aspects of representative democracy that can vary across countries and that indicate increasing levels of democracy. So the percentage of the population which is allowed to vote is both easy to count and also indicates a progression in ideas about inclusiveness and a widening of citizenship from an elite to all adults. Likewise the extent of party competition rewards countries that have moved from a one-party state, to having some opposition, to those with a multi-party system. Party competition is the tip of the iceberg of general political debate, freedom of expression and organisation and a state that allows political opposition. So in measuring the extent of party competition a whole raft of conditions are taken to exist behind this measure. Concentration on the freedom of the press rather than wider rights of expression and debate has mainly practical justifications but also works as a wider measure. It is easier to obtain factual information about the number of newspapers, government restrictions and the extent of opposition that is allowed than it is to measure the extent to which people feel free to discuss political matters including criticism of the government. But the two are also related, so that a state with restrictions on debate in the press will also be restricting public debate and vice versa.

While the authors mentioned above in discussion of numerical matters created a measure of democracy for a particular statistical exercise, there are organisations that collect and collate information on all countries and publish lists to be used by others. In the 1960s *The World Handbook of Political and Social Indicators* (Russett *et al.* 1964) and *A Cross Polity Survey* (Banks and Textor 1963) each provided information on states across a range of political indicators. The handbook mainly provides numeric data such as daily newspaper circulation, turnout levels, and deaths from domestic group violence. Later editions in the 1980s added measures of political and civil rights, levels of political and economic discrimination and party fractionalization (Taylor and Jodice 1983). *A Cross Polity Survey* contained mostly categoric variables such as freedom of group opposition, party system, vertical power distribution and character of bureaucracy. In each case the authors described the core elements of each category (for example on party competition see Table 7.1, Banks and Textor entry) and assessed the appropriate category for each country, so the scores are based on their judgements.

The annual survey in *Freedom in the World* (Gastil 1994), assigns each country a score on political rights and civil liberties and creates tabulated ratings ranging from one to seven that are then grouped as 'free', 'partly free' and 'not free'. The category of 'free' is equated with democracy because political freedom means that people have a proven right to change their government through elections and to organise and spread information in trying to achieve a change (Gastil 1985: 162), in other words what would be recognised as representative democracy. The nine questions in the political rights checklists are similar to those used in other schemata (Gastil 1994: 672–73). Items one to four deal with the use of free and fair elections to create an effective executive and legislature. Party competition and opposition are covered in the next two items. The last three items cover areas not included in the other schemata: self-determination for the country; self-determination for minority groups within the country; and decentralised elected bodies. The civil liberties checklist has 13 items, six of which relate to ideas of associationalism. Other items cover: freedom of the media, debate and assembly; equality under the law; absence of coercion; and social and economic equity. This schema is used to place countries into categories rather than give each a discrete score for democracy, although the categories are used by others in statistical analysis as a measure of the level of democracy.

Quite apart from debates about which measures are used, these rank-order or numeric schema raise questions about the whole idea of assigning a score for democracy. Giving a score with a decimal point provides an aura of pinpoint accuracy that may be neither justifiable nor necessary. While a dichotomy seems too restrictive, categories may be more useful than a score. If more detail is needed then putting countries in order is more important than the actual score (see Tables 7.2 and 7.3). Then there are questions relating to the multi-dimensionality of measures. Given general agreement that there are a number of theoretical components of democracy, should these then be amalgamated into a single measure or would they better be kept separate: do we want to look at how a country scores on average across a number of criteria or to look at their relative place on each individual one? If the values are to be combined then there are a number of arithmetical ways of achieving this, each of which has its impact on the final values. These questions of measurement are at the heart of political science.

While some variables, like voter turnout, are readily available in numeric form, it is still a point of debate as to whether it is more useful to know exactly what percentage of adults voted or to know if that country has high, medium or low turnout compared to other countries. In other words do we want to know about groups of countries that share certain attributes and could be said to have a similar level of democracy even if they differ in some details, or do we want to put all countries in order? Sometimes when a measure is countable, such as newspaper circulation, this value has no meaning unless we also know about the literacy rate and economic situation: if a quarter of the population buys a daily paper in a country where few can read and a newspaper represents a significant part of the daily wage this is much more impressive in terms of the spread of political information than if a quarter of people buy a newspaper in a country where all can read and afford a newspaper. It would also be relevant to have information about the availability of news via radio and television. So if we expect a measure to be affected by other circumstances in the country should this be taken into consideration? For instance Arat, when measuring coerciveness, looks at the extent to which a country differs from the level that would be expected when the extent of social unrest is taken into consideration (Arat 1991: 26).

In choosing between measures the relative merits are that numbers provide precision, rank order gives relativity and categories are easier to work out, but the real question is over the amount of differentiation and detail that is wanted. Table 7.2 gives the values for 16 countries across a range of measures, showing both numeric scores and categories. Faced with this basic information the categories are easier to make sense of, but the scores could be used in statistical analysis. To make some sense of the numeric scores, the 14 countries that are included in all of the analysis of the 1960s are put in rank order for each schema (see Table 7.3). It is easier to gain an overall picture from knowing that Belgium is usually more democratic than the USA than it is to compare the raw values. Putting the same group of countries in rank order for a number of measures covering the same time period also shows up differences in the results. Comparing the best and worst scores reveals a wide range, for instance France is second for Neubauer but eleventh for Smith, Bollen and Vanhanen. The smallest range is Mexico, which is always near the bottom. The variation amongst countries that are seen as democratic again reveals the problems in looking at the extent of democracy rather than a dichotomy. In nine cases, one of the extreme values comes from Vanhanen

Table 7.2 Democratic scores for 16 countries

	Neubauer 1967	Smith 1964–66	Arat 1967	Bollen 1960	Bollen 1965	Vanhanen 1960s	Vanhanen 1970s	Dahl* 1968	Lipset* 1958
Belgium	214.9	127.9	99	99.9	99.7	34.2	38.0	Yes	Yes
Canada	196.8	125.3	100	99.5	99.9	22.9	24.4	Yes	Yes
Chile	184.6	119.5	97	97.0	99.7	13.2	1.9	Near	Yes
Finland	229.2	125.3	100	97.3	97.3	28.6	19.4	Yes	No
France	231.4	115.5	101	90.8	89.7	17.1	33.4	Yes	No
India	172.7	107.3	97	91.2	93.6	14.7	16.1	Yes	–
Italy	198.6	123.0	99	96.8	97.0	36.5	38.4	Yes	No
Japan	212.7	116.8	101	99.8	99.3	20.2	26.5	Yes	–
Mexico	121.6	106.4	80	74.5	80.1	2.4	3.4	No	Yes
NZ	209.4	137.7	101	100.0	100.0	25.5	27.5	Yes	–
S Africa	–	114.3	69	58.9	64.7	2.9	2.5	No	–
Turkey	–	110.7	94	76.4	59.1	14.8	18.1	Near	–
UK	236.3	131.6	98	99.1	99.3	26.9	30.0	Yes	Yes
USA	190.9	127.9	103	92.4	94.6	17.5	17.6	Yes	Yes
Venezuela	188.3	109.8	88	73.4	72.5	25.1	22.2	Near	No
(West) Germany	199.4	117.4	92	88.6	88.0	30.7	32.8	Yes	No

Sources: Neubauer 1967: 107; Smith 1969: 104–05; Arat 1991: 136–67; Bollen 1979: 387–88; Vanhanen 1997: 251–73; Dahl 1971: 248–49; Lipset 1960: 49
Notes: For Dahl, the question is if it is a polyarchy?; for Lipset, if it is in the democratic category for that region (for Latin America this includes unstable dictatorships)

Table 7.3 Rank order within each schema for 14 countries in the 1960s

	Neubauer	Smith	Arat	Bollen 1960	Bollen 1965	Vanhanen 1960s	Best	Worst
Belgium	4	3 =	7 =	2	3 =	2	2	7
Canada	9	5 =	5 =	4	2	8	2	9
Chile	12	8	10 =	7	3 =	13	3	13
Finland	3	5 =	5 =	6	7	4	3	7
France	2	11	2 =	11	11	11	2	11
India	13	13	10 =	10	10	12	10	13
Italy	8	7	7 =	8	8	1	1	8
Japan	5	10	2 =	3	5 =	9	2	10
Mexico	14	14	14	13	13	14	13	14
NZ	6	1	2 =	1	1	6	1	6
UK	1	2	9	5	5 =	5	1	9
USA	10	3 =	1	9	9	10	1	10
Venezuela	11	12	13	14	14	7	7	14
(West) Germany	7	9	12	12	12	3	3	12

Notes: Using values from Table 7.1 above

(1997), which suggests that he is tapping different components of democracy from the other schema.

All of the indexes of democracy specify that, for theoretical reasons, a number of different concepts must be measured but this raises the questions of if and how to amalgamate these scores. If these measures are indeed tapping distinct components of democracy then it would make analytical sense to use them separately for statistical analysis. However, when Olsen compared correlation of measures of economic development with the five components of democracy and with an amalgamated index he found very little difference in results (Olsen 1968: 707). While there are theoretical arguments for considering distinct aspects of democracy, the separate measures seem to be sufficiently statistically inter-correlated to allow for the use of an index. However, we may wish to know on which component a country is failing or doing well and to judge that accordingly. Elklit, in a comparison of five countries (Bulgaria, Kenya, Latvia, Mongolia, Nepal) across Dahl's seven institutions of polyarchy, shows that their rank order varies across the indicators and thus it is hard to determine which is the most democratic. For instance, Latvia is first or equal first on four criteria but last on the measure of an inclusive suffrage (due to exclusion of Russians) whereas Bulgaria is never below third but only equal first in the right to run for office and availability of alternative information (Elklit 1994: 105). It is a matter of judgement as to which country has the greater level of democracy. Elklit shows the details of the seven indicators to illustrate the problems of amalgamating different measures but in the numeric schema, when country details are given, often only the final score is recorded. This problem relates back to the question raised in discussion of thresholds: can doing well in one area compensate for weakness in another?

If a number of measures are to be added the question is then how this is to be done. Few of the authors make explicit the way in which they merge their component measures into an index. The easiest method, particularly when using categoric measures, is to add the scores together. This means that a country that scores 20 on three criteria and 80 on three would gain a score of 300 that could also be obtained by a country scoring 50 on all six components. The question is then if we think those two countries are equally democratic. Again this relates back to ideas of a threshold for democracy that hold on each of a number of criteria. To preserve the idea that the specified components are necessary for democracy, Vanhanen multiplies his two measures then divides by 100, meaning that if either measure is zero, then the final measure is also zero (Vanhanen 1997: 35). This thinking is followed by Flanigan and Fogelman, who specify the combination of answers to their four components of democracy that are needed for each category of democratisation: the category of highest democracy specifies a top score in each of the component parts (Flanigan and Fogelman 1971: 455–57). When using a number of components, if it cannot be assumed that each has the same weight, then all that can be done is to rank each country on each separate measure and allow others to make their own judgement as to which combination is the most democratic.

Identifying weakness

To avoid the compression of information on a number of components a detailed study of the situation in each country is needed so that specific strengths and weaknesses can be identified. The Democratic Audit of the UK provides this third approach to the idea of measuring the extent of democracy. This study aims to examine in detail the level of democracy within one democratic country. Unlike Dahl and Downs it is not aiming to specify the necessary conditions of democracy and unlike the numeric schema, the Democratic Audit does not seek to rank countries in terms of their democracy. Rather the aim is to examine the detailed workings of democracy within a country that is accepted as being a democracy: it is about extent not existence of democracy. As the first stage, the team created a list of 30 criteria to guide the task of an audit. The aim is to publish a series of studies each of which examines the situation in Britain for one area raised in the Democratic Audit (Beetham 1993a: 3–4).

The indices are based on two basic principles that are necessary for democracy: popular control and political equality. In other words, that the people have control over communal decisions or over the decision makers and that all citizens are equal in the exercise of that control. In assessing the extent to which these two ideals are met investigation needs to cover: government institutions including local government, the judiciary and non-elected bodies; the behaviour of voters and the political elite; and provision and exercise of civil rights. The Democratic Audit's 30 questions are organised under the headings 'elections', 'government institutions', 'the territorial dimension', 'citizenship rights' and 'a democratic society' (Beetham 1993a: 13–17; Beetham 1994: 36–39). They consider that society, not just the government, can and should be examined when looking at levels of democracy. For these reasons the 30 criteria are more wide ranging than the lists of indices used by the other studies examined above.

As well as having a different objective from the other works that measure democracy, the Democratic Audit asks to what extent something happens rather then setting a level that should be met. So the question that looks at the extent of party competition asks the extent to which the electoral and party systems allow voters a choice in elections and how easy it is for a candidate or party to contest an election and how easy and equitable access to the media is for those contesting an election (Beetham 1993a: 14; Beetham 1994: 36). This approach to party competition differs markedly from those given in Table 7.1, in part due to the assumption that there is party competition, because their project aims to investigate the level of democracy within existing democracies. The question does not imply what level is desirable, which means that a report based upon the Democratic Audit would provide information which others could use to determine whether or not this was an acceptable level for democracy. Also, the questions ask to what extent something happens, rather than asking about the existence of specified institutions, and so consider outcomes. So for each component of democracy the extent to which the outcomes meet ideas of political equity and popular control are considered.

Detailed study of one country, looking at the extent to which something happens, raises another set of problems. If these descriptions are to be more than descriptive, then there needs to be some benchmark to measure the country against. Given that democracy is a continuum, there need to be agreed points on that continuum that equate with the threshold of democracy and an ideal endpoint to be able to make sense of details on 'how much' of something a country has. So if I find that political parties in New Zealand are given access to the media during the election campaign in accordance with their success at the last election and current opinion poll ratings, how do I know if this is an indication of good practice or a weakness? In seeking to specify the threshold for democracy arguments fall back on the writings of Dahl and Downs, discussed earlier. However, their criteria do not cover the range of questions asked of the Democratic Audit and so in some areas the debate continues. At the other end of the spectrum, Dahl argued that no country could reach a pure democratic state and critics of the numeric scales question the idea of a country receiving the perfect score (Smith 1969). But this still leaves the problem of knowing how close a country is to perfection.

There are three feasible means of answering this question of the endpoint but all are based on comparing the described situation with something else: everything is relative. The three forms of comparison are with an ideal, with similar countries, and with the best practice. So, if looking at the correlation between the proportion of votes cast for a party and the proportion of MPs they have, then we could count any deviation from strict proportionality as a problem or we could look at the normal level of proportionality achieved by other countries with the same electoral and party systems or we could look at the highest level of proportionality achieved in any country. On a commonly used measure of proportionality (Loosemore–Harby) the UK scores 12.9 but this could be compared to the unattainable perfect score of 0 or the lowest that has been achieved which is 0.4 in Malta or the lowest for a country using plurality elections, which is 5.9 in the USA or the lowest for a country with plurality elections and a multi-party system which is 12.4 in New Zealand (Lijphart 1994: 60, 160–62). For some aspects of democracy such as how to run an election or basic components of the rule of law, there are internationally agreed ideals as expressed in the Inter Parliamentary Union's criteria for free and fair elections (Goodwin-Gill 1994) and in the UN Declaration on Human Rights. The importance of being able to identify the endpoint is to show how far from it a country is rather than to say it has been reached. But, in practical terms of wanting to suggest how the level of democracy in one country could be improved, finding the best practice elsewhere probably has more merit as it shows what is achievable. The danger of looking at best practice is to equate a particular institutional arrangement with delivery of some component of democracy: a Bill of Rights may be seen as the only way to deliver human and political rights. There may also be a danger of giving the impression that the country with best practice has no room for improvement.

In looking at the extent of democracy it is more important to look at how institutions work than which institutions exist (Beetham 1994: 31–32; Weir 1994:

114). In comparing levels of political rights it is important to identify the ways in which they are guaranteed in each country and compare the effectiveness of these measures rather than looking to see if each country has a Bill of Rights. So another problem is in interpreting the situation. If a country has no legal constraints on people forming a party and contesting the election, but it takes a lot of money to buy the advertising that is needed to stage a successful media campaign, then what does this say about the extent of democracy? Or to take the question of central government control over local government, there are political debates as to whether local voters should be allowed to vote for variations in certain laws, such as having prayers in schools, or whether such decisions should be made by the entire population. Both are democratic decisions based on elections or referenda, the question is about which people should decide. So central government interference in insisting that schools say prayers could be interpreted as highly democratic or not democratic depending upon your interpretation of democracy. In assessing the extent of democracy it is vital to define what is meant by democracy and to determine whether it is conceptual outcomes, rights, institutions or behaviour that make democracy, as discussed in Chapter 1.

Problems with measuring democracy

These different approaches to assessing the extent of democracy within a country raise a number of interesting points about the way in which democracy is viewed. One of the areas of debate concerns the need to look for legal provisions, or the way in which they are used, or the behaviour of the political actors. Related to this is the question of how far into the workings of the system one needs to delve. Continuing with the idea of the extent of detail needed, to what extent are the workings of the system to be addressed. For instance is it sufficient that democracies have regular elections with an inclusive franchise and one person, one vote, or is there room to compare the different electoral systems, boundary-drawing rules and methods of compiling the register and assisting those who have difficulty getting to a polling booth? The impact of different election rules are discussed in Chapter 2 and the effect of boundaries in Chapter 5.

Most of the measures of democracy are based on specified aspects of democracy, such as competition, participation, accountability and political equality. But most then specify the institutions that are needed to obtain these goals and so look for the existence of elections or a free press or an opposition party. Dahl and Downs specified why such institutions are necessary to provide key aspects of democracy, but in concentrating upon the institutions the focus of measuring democracy shifted. In Britain in the mid-1980s there were opposition parties, but with the plurality electoral system there was no real chance for an alternation of power so the extent of democracy at that time needs to be questioned. While there were alternative parties there was no alternative team of leaders with a real chance of electoral success because other aspects of the system (for instance the electoral system) were not working towards a fully democratic outcome. By concentrating on the existence of key institutions or players the link to how these things provide democracy is not considered. In general it is the existence of elections or the right to vote or opposition parties that are examined rather than the extent to which these institutions deliver. Some of the numeric assessments of democracy do include aspects of the extent to which the parliament actually makes decisions but they do not address the full range of issues about MP input into policy making that were considered in Chapter 6. Likewise, while there are criteria that ask about the lack of constraint upon the media and the existence of freedom of expression, they do not consider the extent to which issues are debated although this is seen as a vital component of democratic decision making amongst those backing participatory democracy (see Chapter 3). At the centre of this question are ideas about democracy as a set of institutions or procedures or behaviours or some combination of the three.

One important consideration for those attempting to compare all countries is the accessibility of information. There are differing views on how much detail is needed about the countries that are being assessed. Many measures use official data and so are accepting the government's position on what is happening and how closely regulations are followed. Elklit, who gathered his data while working as an official observer of elections, provides examples where there are important differences between the legal position and the practice during the election. For instance in Kenya the electoral law spells out the qualifications needed to be a candidate but only observers would be aware that the time within which candidates could register was limited to five hours (Elklit 1994: 100). In terms of an inclusive suffrage there are vast differences between those countries that allow all to vote and put money and energy into ensuring that all do and those countries where all have the right but it is also their responsibility to use that right. The former would seem to illustrate a greater adherence to democratic ideas. So if institutions are to be considered it is important to know how they work in practice, which means that detailed information is needed from those who have experienced the institutions at work. On the one hand collection of such information provides a more realistic picture of the situation in a country but it is not possible to obtain such information from all places to conduct a comparative study. The choice comes down to the balance between accessible data and data that mean something.

When considering the working of democratic institutions there is the question of which details to look at. Is specifying the use of elections enough or should the different systems be assessed for the way in which they deliver on important components such as popular sovereignty or political equality. Different interpretations of key ideas such as votes of equal weight or levels of participation can substantially alter the assessment of the level of democracy in a country (Catt 1997). This position relates to the classic liberal arguments about equality of rights being about the opportunity to do something not the ability to make use of that opportunity. Traditionally, voters are seen as equal if each vote is counted as one vote so that no one person has a greater or lesser say. However, there are more stringent interpretations of the idea of votes of equal value. In the USA and Canada the 'one person one vote' doctrine has been central in rules about the creation of districts, and in particular the need for equal population in each constituency (see Chapter 5). Votes of equal weight could also be interpreted as relating to how proportional the results are at each election (Lijphart 1994). Another component of the argument relates to the working of the electoral system and the extent to which each voter has a chance of influencing the result. As discussed in Chapter 2, there are a number of different approaches to aggregating the views of the voters and they use different types of information. So electoral systems could be assessed to see how many voters expressed a preference for the winners or the extent to which voters have a choice between people as well as parties. These are hard questions because they could result in saying that the USA and the UK, the oldest democracies, are not as democratic as other countries. On the other side of the argument over electoral systems is the question of accountability and ideas that it is better to have a one-party than a coalition government so that the voters know who to blame. In this case most of Europe would be seen as having weak democracy.

Another important aspect of interpretation is the unit of measure that is used (Dunleavy and Margetts 1994). For instance, New Zealand scores highly on most measures of democracy (see Table 7.3) but inside New Zealand the indigenous Maori people are calling for major political changes and greater self-determination and thus would not see the country as highly democratic. Using existing measures and looking at the turnout for New Zealand as a whole it is one of the highest for a country without compulsory voting, but if the figures are divided into ethnic groups it is clear that turnout and registration amongst the Maori population is very low, which raises questions about the inclusivity of the political system (Catt 1997: 170). This situation challenges ideas of the nation state as the unit for democracy and introduces arguments about group politics and internal conflict. Similarly, Dunleavy and Margetts show that using a series of regional values, rather than one national value, to measure deviation from proportionality gives a different picture of the situation in a country (Dunleavy and Margetts 1994: 162–65). Again, although the measure for the entire country may be good this could be masking regional differences which in reality mean that some of the people in the country are not experiencing democracy to the same extent as others. So in looking at the extent of democracy in one country it is important to know if the measures apply to all or if there are major differences based on social group or location. This question seems to be fundamental to ideas of political equality given when it is equality of use not opportunity that is being considered. Taking a measure for the whole country and looking only at legal restriction means that equality is only superficially considered. Again the question is the extent to which practice meets an ideal.

If investigation into the extent of democracy is based upon meeting fundamental ideas such as political equality, and no assumptions are made about the institutional methods needed to achieve these aims, then it may be possible to widen these models to encompass models of democracy other than representative democracy. At an early stage in the evolution of his list of institutions needed for a polyarchy, Dahl specified some looser steps that related to behaviour (Dahl 1956:

84). These may be more widely applicable to other models of democracy. Dahl determined that it was important to look at the point of decision making, by which he meant elections, and at the way decisions were made between elections. Further, he divided the decision-making process into three parts: pre-voting, voting and post-voting. In the pre-voting stage the two crucial aspects are that every person can have an alternative option added to the list that is under consideration and that all members have equal information about the options. At the voting stage every person should vote or in some other way show a preference and all of these votes are treated equally and the option that receives the most votes wins. After the election those who won must be obeyed and not obstructed by those who lost, even if they had previously been in power. Between elections decisions must either follow the above process allowing all MPs to have an equal vote or decisions taken at the election must be followed, or a combination of both. Hence, although the first criteria are taken as primarily applying to elections, Dahl himself also suggests that they should be followed when decisions are made over policy alternatives.

So can these criteria usefully be applied to the different models of democracy and the range of ways in which they are used? There is common ground with the three parts of the decision process talked of in earlier chapters: what is the problem, what are possible solutions, which solution to follow. Adding to this the need for debate, that decisions are followed and that this procedure is used for all collective decisions gives six crucial criteria for a democratic process (see Table 7.4). These criteria could be applied to participatory democracy, referenda, the election of MPs and decision making within a parliament. Looking at the theoretical ideas of each model, in all cases everyone can raise an issue for the agenda, have an informed debate, decide on the options and see the decision followed through and the process used on each option. The only weakness is for referenda, where there is not the possibility of proposing alternative solutions because dichotomised questions are central to referenda. All that this exercise does is reinforce the idea that each is a model of democracy because they cross the basic threshold. Therefore, to distinguish between the models, it is necessary to ask to what extent each is present. Again there is the problem of deciding whether to look at who has the right to do something and who actually does it. For instance, in most parliaments all MPs can suggest an alternative solution to a recognised problem but in practice only the views of government MPs have any chance of

Table 7.4 Questions for a democratic group

Who can put an issue on the agenda?
Who can suggest alternatives? (Dahl 4)
Is there informed debate on the issues? (Dahl 5)
Who decides on the option? (Dahl 1–3)
Are the decisions that are made followed? (Dahl 6–7)
Are all collective decisions made in this way (Dahl 8)

Note: Dahl 1956: 84

becoming law. Similarly, in countries where there are citizen-initiated referenda, any citizen can trigger the process but in reality only those with time, money and campaigning experience do so successfully.

This approach to assessing the extent of democracy moves away from the insistence on a particular set of institutions but is still procedure based. Moving to an even wider definition, May suggests a definition based upon the extent to which the actions taken by government match the wishes of the people (May 1978: 3) which can be applied to any group regardless of size or type. The emphasis is upon the governmental acts, not the ways in which the people involved in decision making are picked, or the procedures that are used to reach the decisions. So democracy depends upon the final decisions regardless of how that objective was achieved. This is in stark contrast to the work of Dahl, who looks at how the decisions were made rather than what the outcome is. Given the differences in decision-making procedures that are all accepted as giving each person an equal vote (Chapter 2), then a decision could be democratic in Dahl's criteria but not May's. If plurality rules are used, all have an equal vote, and the winner is liked by the largest group, then it meets Dahl's specifications that the option gaining the most votes wins (Dahl 1956: 84). However, if those backing the winner made up a third of the group, because views were split across a range of options, then the result is not the same as the desires of the governed if we take this to mean the view of the majority. Again there is the question of how far differences in voting procedures and interpretations of key aspects of democracy need to be taken.

Also related to earlier arguments, May stresses the need for a separation between an essential definition of democracy and a description of those pro-cedures or institutions that often coincide with what is seen as a democratic regime. There are a number of procedures that ensure that each person's prefer-ence is given the same weight as the preferences of all other people and so produce a close correspondence between the governmental acts and popular preferences and therefore no one model of democracy can be prescribed as the way to obtain democracy. Specifying particular procedures or institutions mixes one means of achieving the objective of democracy with that objective. If May's definition is to be used to assess the extent of democracy within any group then the various procedures have to be assessed as they are used on a case-by-case basis. Further, the assessment is of the way that the procedures deliver, rather than of the procedures themselves. Therefore, it could be that one group using partici-patory democracy is more democratic than one country using representative democracy, which is itself more democratic than another group using participa-tory democracy. To apply May's definition, or any definition based solely on an outcome such as equality or sovereignty, there are still problems of knowing when a threshold has been passed and how one group's practice relates to another's.

In all this discussion, procedures or countries have been assessed just for the extent to which they have democracy (although some measures widen this to cover human and civil rights). But, in practice, when a group is choosing the procedures it will use they have other considerations in mind. Time, legitimacy and feeling comfortable with the process are some of the other components that may influence the decision. This point reinforces the comments made in Chapters 3–6 about putting the models into practice. With each form of democracy there are attendant conditions that assist in the use of that model. So for participatory democracy it is vital that people believe in the system and so will spend time discussing an option to reach a decision. For direct democracy to work well there is need for a homogeneous society or for mechanisms that ensure minorities do not feel excluded or cannot be oppressed by the majority. For representative democracy the existence of parties and an energetic media are important. Specific examples of democratic procedures can be put into rank order according to the extent to which they meet various criteria but a group or country may be content with a lower score because they included some other consideration when designing the decision-making process. Using an adaptation of Dahl's criteria (Table 7.4) any procedure can be assessed in terms of the basic requirements, and May's definition helps to clarify the key aspects of the democratic situation. Other judgements about which model, country or group is more democratic depend upon which components of the democratic ideal are seen as more important and the extent to which other considerations, such as efficiency or time, have some bearing on the situation.

8 What future for democracy?

Descriptions of democratic practice in previous chapters illustrate not only the desire for democratic decisions by a wide range of groups but also practical problems for each model when put into practice. With changes in society, such as developments in telecommunications and the subsequent increase in information, some of these problems may now be solvable. The other major area of change is in the location of political decision making with the growth in global and local political units. Just at the time when more countries are moving towards democratic government many decisions are moving away from the scope of national bodies. Taken together, such changes suggest that the practice of democracy will continue to evolve over the coming decades as new political units are formed and different methods are used for discussion and decision making. One question that is central to ideas about the future of democracy is that of which people should be included in the group making a decision. A number of current views on this subject are considered in the first section of this chapter. The second section examines the main factors that impede the members of a group from having full control of decisions and some of the new methods that are being used to extend popular control.

Who should make decisions?

In the past two decades there have been significant changes in thinking about relations between individuals and the state, often focused on economic matters but with relevance for democracy. On one hand are forces that reduce the extent to which democracy is used to make the main decisions affecting people's lives, such as globalisation and monetarist economics. On the other hand are ideas stressing the role of the people and moving the focus of decision making below the national government to regional and local groups. Subsidiarity in the European Union (EU) and the impact of Agenda 21 are the most prominent examples of this ideal but increasing pressures for regional devolution also fall within this camp. All of these have implications for the locus of decisions, the way in which the people are viewed and what role they are deemed to play in the wider political community. Therefore these trends are important in current arguments about the desired reach of democracy and which people should be consulted on specific decisions.

During the 1980s, monetarist economic policies were followed in many Western democracies with wide-ranging expansion of the role of the market and a reduction in the areas seen as the responsibility of the government. With the stress on market individualism there was a move away from the 'nanny state' which intervened in people's lives to a minimal state that allowed people to live their lives as they wanted. Drawing strongly on liberal theories, the state was seen as having a constitutionally restricted role with the market as the preferred mechanism for directing policy. The voters gained accountability through periodic elections and that was sufficient. Much of the thinking was the result of a perception that government was too big because voters' expectations were too high, due largely to politicians making promises of low taxes and high spending in a bid for election. The suggestion was that most voters did not understand the complexities of government finance and thus did not realise that the demands they were making were unrealistic: that the level of welfare provision that was being demanded could not be provided. Instead of leaving policy to the dictates of voters and pressure groups, it was better to use appointed experts and stress efficiency. Therefore many functions were moved from government departments to quangos or other independent appointed bodies with no direct accountability to parliament. 'Administrative modernism' insists that decisions are so complex that they must be left to the people who are able to deal with such issues, the bureaucrats and those appointed for their managerial skills (Weir 1996: 21). Another important strand was the centrality of the individual rather than any idea of a collectivity, in Thatcher's infamous phrase 'there is no such thing as society, only individuals and their families'. Taken together, the new Right thinking led to a minimisation of the role of voters and pressure groups plus the movement of many decisions away from scrutiny by elected representatives. The accompanying view of people was of individual self reliance and a downplaying of any ideas of society as a collectivity. Behind much of the thinking on the new Right is the need for greater efficiency in decision making, by which is usually meant quick decisions that allow the organisation to carry on with its primary goal. The contracting out of areas of government actions to bodies composed of experts underlies the belief that there is an objective truth and that this must be found without the distraction of the demands of different groups within society. Generally efficiency is used as an argument against the use of democratic processes.

Globalisation of the economy and the growing tendency for states to come together as economic or political blocs have had similar impacts on the democratic situation in most democracies. As more of the matters with which governments deal are interconnected, then the extent to which one government can control what happens in that country diminishes. This interconnectedness is most noticeable in the economy but also plays a large part in thinking about the environment. An outside event may radically change the range of options open to government, for instance worries about unemployment levels in Germany impacting upon the stockmarkets around the globe, weak economies in Asia impacting on other economies and on trade, and Indonesia's forest fires which affected the environment of many other countries. Another part of globalisation is the idea that decisions in one area may impact on another. This refers to decisions taken by international organisations such as the UN but also decisions taken in other countries. For instance EU specifications of what constitutes chocolate impact on the confectionery industry in other countries that export to EU countries, and in countries that grow cacao, and so the decisions of a large political organisation affect people in non-member countries. International treaties can also supersede the decisions of national governments: global agreements on air pollution impact on domestic policies for transport, manufacturing and power generation; the adoption of UN declarations on human rights set an international norm of behaviour that presses governments to conform or face trade embargoes. In some instances the government is part of international negotiations that impact on the internal politics of the country but the assembly usually has little chance to influence the decision. However, some international agreements need domestic legislation to be passed to make the agreement a reality. For instance the international treaty banning landmines must have legislation passed within each country before the treaty can be ratified. The decisions of people in one country can also affect large regions. For instance when Swiss voters decided to limit heavy lorries on alpine passes then this impacted on the transportation of goods across Europe. So part of the process of globalisation is the increase in decisions that are taken outside of the national government but nevertheless impact on the people within that country. Not only are decisions being made elsewhere but the actions of those in other states can have a major impact on the policy context for a national government. The elected government cannot control many decisions that affect the lives of the people who elected them.

Globalisation also incorporates a recognition of locality, of political units smaller than the national state. The increasing number of regional and ethnic groups demanding some level of self-determination is one indicator of the growth in group identity as separate from national identity, and thus different ideas of community. Scotland and Wales have separate elected bodies to oversee certain issues, and similarly asymmetrical devolution in Spain means that areas such as Catalonia which want some autonomy are allowed it, while other areas retain their traditional areas of jurisdiction. The creation of the new province of Nunavut in Canada was mostly a reaction to Inuit demands for autonomy in an area where they make up the majority of the stable population. However, not all moves to increase political power at the sub-national level are related to separate group identity. As more people feel alienated from national government, because of a perception that they have little control over major decisions and so can do little about their quality of life, then there is a move to involvement in localised activities where people feel that they can have an impact. As political communities within a nation are recognised then the idea of society comprising a number of groups with distinct views and needs becomes an important part of democratic debate.

Subsidiarity is acknowledged in the Treaty on European Union (Maastricht Treaty) as the basic principle to be used to assign jurisdiction between the different levels of government. The principle, at its simplest, is that issues are best dealt with where they are relevant to the people directly involved. As a consequence, decisions are taken at the lowest level unless it can be shown that decisions cannot effectively be taken at that level. Only when the lower level shows an incapacity to deal with the matter may the higher level assume responsibility. Historically, the idea of subsidiarity is associated with the Catholic Church, based on the assumption of individual self-reliance and a preference for small units to carry out needed work. The underlying thinking is that decisions should be made by those who know the most about how the issue will impact on people. There is also an assumption that the people in the relevant localities are capable of making these decisions and have the information to do so.

In the context of the EU, subsidiarity is used to determine whether it is local, regional, national or European-level bodies that have the authority. On any given issue there may be layers of decisions taken at different levels. The EU may agree a policy on workers' rights to a minimum number of holidays but each state will decide which national holidays are a statutory right, and in some cases there will be more localised variation within a country so that regional festivals can be recognised. The principle of subsidiarity can be used in other contexts, and is indeed the basic principle within federation in Germany as the central government has only those powers which are specified, all others residing with the *Länder*. Changes in the balance have come about slowly as efficiency necessitated centralised action. Subsidiarity fits closely with ideas of federalism but the two can each work independently in that some federal states do not assume decisions reside at the lowest level and subsidiarity can work in a unitary state with local government rather than federal states.

In terms of the use of democracy and which people should be making decisions, the idea of subsidiarity makes some interesting assumptions. For subsidiarity to work in its fullest sense then decisions will be taken by local groups and thus there is the assumption that people in the locality have the information and capability to make decisions. This position contrasts with the belief that most political decisions are so complex that they can only be taken by experts. In asserting the rights of those in the locality to make those decisions which they can show they are capable of making then the claim is that having a decision impact upon your life gives you the necessary expertise to make a decision. In a practical sense there is also an assumption that people are organised into groups who can make decisions and thus subsidiarity is at odds with the concentration on the individual as the basic unit of politics. While in the EU context the lowest level is likely to be that of existing local government, the ideal allows for more localised groups to be involved when appropriate. The other clear implication of both the ideal of subsidiarity and the way in which it is being used in the EU is the recognition of differences in identities within the member states: both differences between nations and also between areas within a nation. If groups do not have different views then there is no need to let them each make a separate decision.

Within the arguments over European union, those who wish to maintain national sovereignty and avoid a federal structure view subsidiarity as a guarantee of the powers of national government as the EU is restricted to those matters that cannot be effectively achieved by the member states. Those pushing for regional devolution or more localised decision making see subsidiarity as a means of moving decisions away from national government to lower levels within the nation state. Thus subsidiarity can be seen as fitting with arguments of the new Left which call for wider political participation, arguing that if it keeps decisions local and near the people then the people will feel that they are part of the decisions. However, these decisions do not fall foul of calls for efficiency in the way that the push for participatory democracy in the workplace does (see Chapter 3). In the way the EU uses subsidiarity the higher level can only take a decision if it can do so more efficiently than lower levels acting separately. So efficiency is a vital part of decisions about who has jurisdiction. As yet the way in which efficiency is determined has not been shown, but subsidiarity is being pushed as a way to allow local autonomy while maintaining efficiency.

'Agenda 21' is used as shorthand for the agreement issued after the UN conference on Environment and Development, commonly called the Rio Earth Summit. Although ostensibly about sustainable development, this document also looks at the way in which the new policies are to be created. In particular it has a strong commitment to broad public participation, by which is meant that individuals and groups should play a part in the decisions that affect them at work or at home (UN 1992: 8.3, 23.2). There is a crucial role for local authorities because the issues and projects involved in the plans for sustainable development are of a local nature. Local government was seen as playing a vital role in the realisation of the objectives, in particular it has a role in educating the public and building interest in sustainable development and in responding to the people's views on specific projects (ibid.: 28.1). Each local authority is charged with the creation of a local policy on achieving sustainable development. In creating the policy they must involve those in the locality both as individuals and organisations so as to inform the public on the issues but also to ensure the formulation of the best strategies (ibid.: 28.3). Agenda 21 explicitly recognises the importance of social groups and specifies that decision-making bodies must work to ensure the input of women, children and youth, and indigenous people as well as more organised groups such as non-governmental organisations, trade unions, and farmers (ibid.: section III). They also stress that good decisions must be based on relevant and reliable information that is available to all involved in the decision making, so countries need to set up mechanisms to allow people to access information and provide the skills needed to use that information (ibid.: 40.11). Throughout, there is an emphasis upon providing people with the necessary information as well as involving them in planning.

As with subsidiarity, there is an emphasis upon local decision making because that is where the impact of problems and solutions will be felt. The thinking in Agenda 21 can be closely tied to post-materialist ideas with its emphasis on environmental concerns and on the push for greater democratic decision making and the widening of political rights so that all groups participate in the decisions. It also echoes moves in other areas of UN activity which encourage greater involvement by women and indigenous peoples in decision making. In seeking to implement Agenda 21 a number of local authorities have turned to new methods of public consultation such as citizens' juries (see below). The recognition of local groups as well as individuals also has important implications for the development of democracy.

Tony Blair, the current British Prime Minister, has talked much of the 'stakeholder' society as a new principle for government in Britain. Although most of the discussion has been of the stakeholder economy and company there are also implications for the political system and decision-making processes. Central to the stakeholder idea is that policy and planning should take account of the needs of stakeholders, that is any person or group who may be affected. In terms of the company, stakeholders are employees, suppliers, local communities and banks as well as the traditional shareholders. When transferred to the running of the welfare state or society more widely, the stakeholder idea emphasises the range of people who are affected by decisions and the importance of considering their views when reaching decisions. Social cohesion is integral to the stakeholder society and this means that people must feel involved in society, care about other people and feel that they matter: people must feel they have a stake in their society. So stakeholder politics must be a politics of power-sharing, negotiation and mutual education based on participation and a devolution of decisions to a local level. The stakeholder society would enable people to have a say in how they are governed. In practical terms this means more power to local government, a reassessment of the electoral system and composition of the House of Lords, and elections for many of the boards that run public institutions such as the BBC or the health service. The whole debate of the stakeholder society has emphasised the wide range of people who are affected by any given policy and the idea that they have a right to some influence over the decisions that affect their lives. This debate also highlights the idea of individuals as members of specific groups and stresses that it is the voice of each group that must be heard rather than each individual. In part an echo of the idea of parliament as a place where each perspective on an issue can be heard (see Chapter 5).

Related in some ways to ideas of the stakeholder society is the idea of communitarianism. This strand of thought stresses that a strong community is a vital part of a healthy society and so people must think of their duty and responsibilities as well as their rights. A part of caring for the community is the idea that people feel they are part of the collectivity and thus must take a part in decisions that affect it and care about what happens to those around them. While sharing certain ideas with those found in the idea of the stakeholder society, communitarianism tends to be used by politicians on the right who want to strengthen traditional ideas of community based on family values and a respect for authority. Proponents tend to be wary of accepting the differences inherent in a multicultural society that entail accepting the varied views of a range of self-identifying groups. More generally there have been many calls for an increase in civil society or a civic culture (Barber 1996; Putnam 1994). In stark contrast to the idea of individuals but no society, this trend stresses the need for a community feeling. A strong civic culture means that individuals want to give time to activities for the good of all and are concerned about those around them and think that their lives are interconnected with others. So there is a desire to increase the number of people participating in political groups or in local decision-making bodies like school boards or in voluntary work. The focus of community can vary from a neighbourhood to a workplace to an organised group or a shared facility (Wright 1996: 15). The important common theme across communitariansim, stakeholder and civil society is the idea that for democracy to work there needs to be some idea of a community, and that means individuals who care about what happens to others and will give time and energy to help create shared facilities.

In terms of where decisions are made there are pressures within the UN for a localisation of decisions, exemplified by the Agenda 21 statements on educating and informing those who will be affected by a decision so that they can participate in the decision. The same forces can be seen within the EU's adoption of subsidiarity and also in the number of regional and ethnic groups that are pressing for, or who have won, some measure of local devolution. On the other hand, the new Right policy of minimising the role of the state has moved many areas outside the democratic arena while others are removed from voter accountability through the globalising impact of an interconnected economy. There are also contrasts in views on the role of the individual. New Right politicians concentrate on the individual and the family and see individuals as responsible for themselves with rights to autonomy and minimal interference from the state. In a stakeholder society individuals should feel part of the collectivity and have a responsibility to care about society and thus participate in decision making. Agenda 21 and the myriad groups pressing for devolution stress the importance of groups within the nation state and want decisions to be taken by those most immediately affected by the problem or solution. At one extreme the post-materialist concentration upon civil and political rights calls for greater participation and group recognition while at the other extreme market individualism stresses the autonomy of the individual. Within these current debates there is a wide range of ideas about the proper domain of democracy.

New solutions for the problems of democracy

In the chapters looking at the three models of democracy, five factors were mentioned repeatedly as affecting the way in which democracy worked: composition of the group; size of the group; the complexity of issues in relation to the ability of the people; the accessibility of information; the need for speed and efficiency (see Table 8.1). The five can be grouped as those concerned with questions about 'the people' or the political unit that is making decisions and those which deal with the process of deciding on an issue. The final impediment, the need for efficiency, falls into the group of arguments about whether or not democracy should be used, discussed above. This section will consider arguments relating to the make-up of 'the people' and to the problems of complexity and information and will cover both perceived problems and proposed solutions. These arguments assume

Table 8.1 Impediments to widespread democracy

Composition of the group	Is a collectivity recognised; is the group homogeneous; are groups recognised and guaranteed a voice?
Size of group	Can the group meet in one place; do people know others in the group, are there feelings of common cause?
Complexity of the issue relative to the ability of the people	Can the people understand the issue; how interconnected are issues; how important are experts?
Availability of information	Is the relevant information readily available; do people have the relevant skills to use the information?
Need for speed and efficiency	How fast do decisions need to be made; how are decisions evaluated; is efficiency the prime consideration?

a wish to extend the use of democracy, as shown in Agenda 21, and pressure for subsidiarity.

As democracy is only relevant when a group of people want to make decisions collectively for the group, the existence of a group is vital, but issues of its size and composition can raise problems for the success of democracy. Relations within the group are important. When the group is seen as a collective, as a cohesive whole, then decision making will be different from cases where the group is seen as an aggregation of individuals. Hence the new-Right argument that individuals and families are the only political units pushes democratic decisions down a certain path. In contrast ideas of subsidiarity assume a local community that should be consulted when decisions are made. Another crucial aspect of group composition is the way in which divisions are perceived and dealt with. Size interacts with composition because the larger the group the greater the likelihood of division and also because methods of communication will differ and thus the ability to build consensus. Size also impacts on the kind of decisions that can be made, remembering that it is the size of the whole group that is important rather than the number of people actually making a decision: the size of the electorate not the executive. Finally there are arguments about which people form a relevant political unit, that is, which groups will make decisions for themselves and which form part of a larger decision-making group.

As underlined in the ideas of a stakeholder society and communitarianism, cohesion or a feeling of belonging are being stressed as important for future democracy. Underpinning the growth of democratic bodies is the need for people to feel that they are part of a community and want to take part in decision making for the group rather than attending to their individual needs. Democratic decisions using majority rule, where the final outcome may be contrary to what a large number of people wanted, must be based on trust and so the feeling of belonging to a group is important. Barber argues that communities need to be created and people to learn to be citizens who care about others in their society

(1996: 146–47). The nation state is still a common rallying point for feelings of community togetherness and many local government areas are created on the basis of local community and so have legitimacy with the voters. However, the EU suffers from the fact that few people feel a European identity and so the creation of a feeling of community is an important part of spreading democracy into European-wide decisions. The extent of group feeling is an important component of discussion of the appropriate political unit.

Feelings of oneness are not vital if there is agreement on the need to reach a decision for the group despite differences in opinion and approach. Those who prefer participatory democracy stress the need for discussion so that each member of the group can become aware of the views of others and so all will strive for a solution that is acceptable to the whole group. The trustee model of representation where MPs are expected to come together to hear the different arguments, and then reach a decision for the good of all, is based on the same idea of a collectivity and not an aggregation of individuals. When the group is homogeneous then discussion of the issue is likely to take less time and be easier as there will be few fundamental disagreements. A homogeneous group will also tend to make people feel comfortable about taking part. While working at cohesion, the group has to be able to deal with conflict and so again the importance of procedures to determine the final choice are underscored. A direct vote is safe in a unified group as there is no minority to be oppressed. If there are irreconcilable cleavages in the group then participatory democracy will not work, but when there are minor differences on specific issues then the process works to ensure a continuity of group cohesion. A central component of maintaining the group is the idea of equal respect and trust, that each member will work for the good of the whole. In this case homogeneity does not mean that all agree on everything but that there is enough common ground and mutual respect for all to aim at the solution that is best for the whole group and at the same time no one individual feels that they are sacrificing their own wants for those of the collectivity. So the group may accept difference but strive for cohesion by ensuring that decisions are acceptable to all and that all were able to express their views.

When there is no strong feeling of cohesion that subsumes division or when there are clearly identifiable sub-groups then different procedures are needed. If there are divides then all parts of the process will be harder because there are deeply held opposing views to reconcile. In participatory democracy and the model of representative democracy that sees MPs as a group of decision makers, the discussion of the issue is important as a time for each member to hear the views of others and to strive for a solution acceptable to all. The greater the range of sub-groups with distinct views, the more important it is to have time for all views to be heard and indeed to ensure that each group has a voice in the discussion. If the divides shift from issue to issue then the main needs of the process are that all feel they can have a say and all accept the procedure used for the final choice. However, if the divides are permanent, so that there are clearly defined groups, then procedural details matter even more. Some of the biggest problem areas in the spread of democracy across nation states are in places with strong divides such as Nigeria, Fiji and parts of the former Yugoslavia. Of the three parts of the decision, it is the way in which the choice is made that is the most important for divided groups (see Chapter 2) and thus arguments about electoral systems and the creation of local government boundaries and jurisdictions often take centre stage. When divides are permanent then there may be arguments for the creation of new political units, at least for some decisions. When groups are divided on the basis of religion or language then there may be agreement on separate jurisdiction for education and cultural matters.

The size of the group is seen as a problem primarily in participatory democracy but this does have relevance for other models and for the spread of participation. The size of the group has a major impact on the agenda-setting and debate parts of the process but little on the act of choosing because there are a range of voting procedures that can aggregate the views of many people. Where group members need to be able to discuss the issues at length and to understand the views of others then a small group is needed. This is most apparent in participatory democracy, but the use of committees within legislatures for most of the detailed decision making is another example of the importance of size. If the group is to understand the views of others then it is vital that each member can see the reactions of others and being physically close increases empathy and concern for others. In practical terms size has a great impact: large populations cannot gather together to make decisions, so direct or representative democracy is needed.

The main movements to increase democracy have an element of localism with decisions taken to smaller groups of people with a common identity and close to the issue. While subsidiarity seeks to blend local decisions with international ones there is still the problem of allowing small groups to make large decisions. With the spread of decisions to the local community then there is a dilution of the types of decisions that can be made. Problems are broken into a number of local reactions rather than a national approach. So there is a tension between the desire for small community groups and the desire to make decisions for the whole state. This distinction also marks the difference between solutions based on the local structure and solutions that attempt to impact on the total infrastructure of the nation. For instance, the difference between creating local bicycle and bus lanes and the introduction of a tax on private cars and subsidies for public transport. Agenda 21 faces the same problems as it sets up a global desire for sustainable development and recognises that problems cross national boundaries, but also stresses that solutions are not only in the hands of national governments but must also involve local groups. It also recognises that there will be different local responses to the commonly agreed problems. An international problem but many solutions based on a mix of very localised projects, national schemes and international agreements.

Although there has been a concentration upon increased local government input, 'local' is still not small in the sense used for participatory democracy. In general 'local' means the area covered by local government and thus could be a city. So members of these small local groups could not all come together in one place for debate but they are deemed to have a common link. The idea of localism is based on an assumption of community feeling, with those in a locality having common concerns, and being likely to know many others in the area and to care about what happens to the people in that community. Of course many cities and communities contain major divides based on class, religion or ethnicity and in these cases arguments for localism need to think carefully about how they define the group at the base of the decision pyramid. Many cities are also very large: London has more than three times the population of the whole of New Zealand. Again this raises the question of the composition and size of the most appropriate political unit.

The growth in group-consciousness, based primarily on class, ethnicity, religion, locality and gender, has changed the ways in which democracy works. In the early decades of the twentieth century there was a strong pressure to consolidate national identity as new states were created through the federation of regions, the break-up of empires and in the aftermath of war. While such countries recognised internal divides there was a premium placed upon creating a sense of oneness and so national cohesion and solutions for the good of all were stressed. However, as more groups are recognised as having a distinct political voice then this has changed the way in which decisions are made. As discussed in Chapter 5, there are ever-growing demands for representation to reflect the key groups through a variety of procedures. Growing recognition of identities within the state are also fuelling moves towards devolved decision making and other plans to allow distinct groups a voice. Geographically based devolution of decisions is still the norm, for instance Nunavut, the recently created province in northern Canada and the regional devolution in Spain and for Scotland and Wales. Such movement of jurisdiction is easy as there are distinct geographic boundaries around 'the people'. Workers' co-operatives can be seen as having a distinct boundary within the workplace and so fit with this pattern. What is harder to imagine is for groups that co-exist in the same space to have separate decision-making bodies. Such overlapping jurisdictions do happen in some places. Those who belong to the Islamic or Jewish faiths follow a distinct set of rules in their conduct of family life and morality, alongside the laws of the country. In New Zealand, Maori systems of justice are used in some cases of domestic violence and sexual abuse of children. Schools operate different sets of rules concerning discipline, uniforms and so on and parents can decide which they prefer. In Brussels people register as being in the French or Flemish community and thus are under differing community boards (Budge 1996: 167). In each case people choose to be associated with a particular community and follow its rules in certain areas. Would it be possible for people to opt into one of a number of decision-making bodies for other issues such as welfare provision or economic regulation? A number of writers forcibly argue that to allow for people to participate, and for minorities to have some respect, then society needs to be recognised as pluralistic with different groups given specific powers over decisions that affect them (Budge 1996: 168; Wright 1996: 15). Hirst, in particular, argues for a greater array of groups involved in decision making, which he calls 'associational democracy' (Hirst 1996;

1994). In particular he suggests that consumers of health and education be involved in decisions about the way such services are run. Workers also should have a say in how their workplace is run and thus the arguments are akin to those described as relating to the 'stakeholder society' above. These arguments stress the role of groups and thus differ from those seeking greater participation for individuals.

Similar concerns about group identity are expressed at the international level with the feeling that the state is not necessarily the most appropriate unit for democratic decision making as the world is made up of layers of political communities, some within nation states and some crossing national boundaries (Budge 1996: 169; Held 1993: 43). As decisions move to a global and a continent-based level there is a need to recreate the boundaries around the groups making decisions so that elected bodies are again accountable for the actions that impact upon the people rather than being able to blame them on other bodies which are not accountable, such as the government of another country. Taking the ideas inherent in subsidiarity, that those who are most directly affected by a decision should make the decisions, then new areas of jurisdiction can be created for different groups of issues. Such political units would range from a local community to regions within a country, existing nation states, groups of nations and the global community. Such bodies will, of course, overlap, but areas of common concern can be dealt with collectively and areas of difference left to smaller units (Budge 1996: 169). The three bodies outlined in the Northern Ireland Peace Deal of Easter 1998 illustrate the layering of government bodies. Northern Ireland has an elected assembly which will deal with policy and will be able to pass new laws in those areas devolved to it from the British government in London. Then there is the North–South Council to cover areas where co-operation across Ireland is of mutual benefit, such as transport and the environment. Taking the membership wider is the Council of the Isles, where members of the Northern Ireland assembly meet with members of the devolved bodies for Wales, Scotland, the Isle of Man and the Channel Islands along with MPs from the British and Irish parliaments. This forum will also discuss areas of mutual interest such as health and transport links. By setting up cross-border bodies the new structure shows recognition of the interdependency of geographical units and the benefits of mixing local decisions with mutual co-operation.

Another area of interest in the literature suggesting a spread of democracy is the use of information technology and telecommunications networks to assist in the political process. In terms of problems associated with the creation of 'the people' the argument is that electronic media can facilitate a group which is geographically spread and also allow people to participate from home. Electronic town meetings seek to use a range of information technology, such as television and telephones, to allow a large number of people to participate in a decision without the need to bring them together in one place. For an electronic town meeting there must be presentation of information, deliberation and voting. Information technology may be used for any or all of the three vital components. There has been a great deal of interest in this in the USA, but practical exercises show variation, with some closer to ideas of participatory democracy than are others which tend towards electronic referenda. One crucial difference is who suggests solutions to the problem. If those taking part in the deliberation determine the possible answers to the question then it is participatory democracy but if they are asked to choose between pre-determined solutions then, however much deliberation there has been, this moves into the direct democracy category. The Houston Electronic Town Meeting in 1994 is on the participatory democracy end of the continuum. Citizens, in groups, formulated possible goals for the future of Houston. Then television was used for a studio debate linking five local meetings and a panel of experts and members in each location were able to ask questions 'on-air'. After the debate the people at each local meeting discussed and ranked the 50 goals which had been created by the earlier citizen groups. This process combines local, face-to-face discussion, with wider debate and input from experts. Discussion is in local communities but they combine for a discussion concerning the larger city area.

One question about electronic debate relates to the importance that those using participatory democracy place upon non-verbal communication and the need to meet together to have discussion and reach a solution acceptable for all. Discussion via electronic means is different from a face-to-face meeting but not necessarily so different that this form of discussion is not useful (Budge 1996: 30). When the people involved already know each other then discussion in a telephone conference may work just as well because the bonds of friendship are already established and people are used to understanding the meaning of changes in tone and volume of each person. However, for a group where members do not know each other then debate via electronic means may have a very different feel to one conducted in the same room. Again the composition of the group and the propensity to act as a collectivity is important.

In parallel with arguments about the growing size of political units is the argument that most political issues are complex and that the general population does not understand them and thus decisions must be left to experts. The need to use experts is a central part of arguments for a reduction in the use of democracy. One key question is then what constitutes an expert. Another is the role of the expert: decision maker or provider of information for the decision makers? Third, what type of information is needed to fully participate in the decisions and to understand the issues? A number of elected bodies, especially local governments, have been trying new methods of informing the public and listening to their views and academics have suggested other methods. A range of approaches to making the people experts is discussed at the end of this section.

Who is an expert on a particular issue, the people with specialist knowledge and lots of information, the informed elected representatives or those who will be most closely affected by the decision? Elite thinkers stress the need for education and training in the subject, while populist groups emphasise that local knowledge is what is needed when reaching decisions. Arguments against direct democracy raise the point that many who vote on the issue do not understand it and that a complex issue must be compressed into a question for the vote. Likewise, those electing representatives are often assumed to have little understanding of the issues and thus should allow those who are elected to make the decisions. To what extent are elected representatives experts? As they are increasingly becoming specialists in one area then they are not experts on all matters presented to them. When each MP is putting energy into one specialist area, then when they must vote on another issue they may defer to their colleagues on the committee concerned with that issue. In the past the point was made that parliament was an assembly of able people who would deliberate and make decisions for the good of all. There is still an assumption that the very fact of being elected and allowed to take part in the debate on issues gives people expertise on those issues. However, as the number of issues which government has to deal with has increased and the technical complexity of each issue risen then the capability of MPs to make good decisions with no specialist knowledge is being questioned. On the one hand is the idea that anyone with the time to look at the information and hear the debate is qualified to make a decision. On the other hand is the idea of specialist knowledge on each issue and a need to concentrate on one area.

Another key element to this argument concerns the personal qualities needed to be an expert. Either anyone can learn about an issue or there is a need for intelligence, education and training in the making of an expert. If the latter is the case then it follows that only certain people should be making the decisions, which means that in a representative democracy either decisions should be left to bureaucrats or only the intelligent and educated should be elected. Those on the new Right also argue that there are objective truths with can be ascertained by those with the proper training and expertise and thus they should make decisions rather than those who claim expertise on an issue based upon their involvement with the area, such as pressure groups. So a strong strand in arguments that decrease the number of people who are involved in a decision is based on the premise that most issues are too complex to be understood by most people. As well as the power of the bureaucrats, the growing use of non-government bodies to run organisations leaves decisions to those deemed to be experts. In the past 15 years, the necessary expertise has often been seen as being in the field of management rather than in the specific service such as health, education or water supply. In pushing for greater participation in decision making the opposite argument is used when suggesting that those people who are closest to an issue and solution are, by definition, the experts. On the one hand expertise is based upon knowledge and objective facts, while on the other, first-hand experience of a situation gives expertise. Pushes for localised difference also suggest that there are a range of solutions to a problem rather than one solution for the country. As regional differences are stressed then it is harder for those in the centre to be aware of the variety of local situations or reactions to a specific issue. Again there is the idea of accepting difference.

When elected representatives or the people are seen as the experts then it is their ability to understand how an issue will impact that is prized and so there is still some need for technical or specialist information on the particular issue. Here the testimony of experts is contestable and is used by decision makers. Even when experts are used to assist with decision making there may be arguments about the weight that is given to their reports. On those issues where the experts agree, the political decision concerns what to do in the light of this information. But in areas where the experts disagree, for instance on the best education methods, then the decision makers need to look at the contrasting expert advice. There may also be disagreement on what information is relevant for a decision: the cost of a proposed change or the impact on society. For instance, in debates over tertiary education there are arguments about the cost of university and there are arguments about society's need for people with a degree and the role universities play as a conscience and critic of society. The experts may see the problem in a different way from various sectors of society, and pressure groups may each have their own experts. So even when experts are used only to provide information it is not always clear which information is needed and how it should be used.

In all three models of democracy, being an expert in how the system works can be vital. In participatory democracy, groups seeking to maintain equality between members emphasise the need to instruct all new members in the way that the system works; in direct democracy groups already in the political system are the most likely to initiate and win a referendum; and much of the influence of bureaucrats and committees within representative democracies comes from their knowledge of how the system works. Within parliaments it is hard for backbench MPs to introduce legislation when they cannot call upon the procedural expertise of the bureaucrats. In consequence, the level of expertise that is needed to operate the system can be lowered through simplifying the process and providing information. The ability of voters to comprehend the issues and vote based on their own interests is aided by good question wording, quality information packaged for the mass audience and the availability of debate. So again the way in which decision making is organised and supported can impact on the extent to which people can participate (Budge 1996: 115–16).

There are also arguments about the extent to which the people need to have all of the relevant detailed information on an issue. If you hold to a particular worldview or ideology is it sufficient to know how this particular issue is seen by others with the same ideology? Or is it enough to hear the views of those who have seen all of the technical information and debated the issues? In other words to make widespread involvement in decision making workable the majority of people need to rely upon the advice of those who have had the time to look at an issue in detail. A number of methods for achieving this division of labour have been suggested. Budge's (1996) version of enhanced popular voting would work alongside representative democracy, as would suggestions by Fishkin (1991) for deliberative polls and Barber's idea of popular assemblies. In the same way citizens' juries and teledemocracy work to increase the extent of popular discussion that is used when decisions are made by an elected body. The popular discussion and debate is used to assist the elected representatives in setting the agenda, formulating solutions and making decisions.

Widespread participation is irrational, in an economic sense, as it works counter to the idea of division of labour and specialisation. Understanding issues and creating policy alternatives takes time and energy so why not have politicians (parties) concentrating on this. Budge advocates a role for political parties in a system of wider public participation, acting as bodies which provide information, take part in debate and rally interests. With parties to mediate debate then people can participate without giving vast amounts of time to finding out about the issues and hearing all of the arguments. The politically interested people in the parties would have an important role in setting the agenda and providing policy cohesion (Budge 1996: 17–18, 38–43, 117–18). Budge envisages elections fought by parties but in between elections the government would hold popular votes, or allow popular challenges to legislation, although those policies specified in the manifesto would be exempt for the first part of the government's term. Leading up to each vote there would be widespread media coverage of debates in parliament and committees plus interactive popular debate using a range of telecommunications systems plus the provision of relevant information. Political parties would be active players in the debates but such a programme of debate would be regulated to ensure different viewpoints were heard. Voters would then make policy decisions based on information from public debates.

Citizens' juries are being used by various local government bodies in Britain and by a range of organisations in the USA. 'Planning cells', as they are called in Germany, have been used for some time. Various local authorities or other bodies within local government can instigate a citizens' jury and they have been used on a specific decision, such as the redesign of Cologne's town hall, or to discuss future directions in a general policy area, such as west Germany's future energy policy. Much like a jury in a courtroom, the group are presented with detailed information then discuss the matter between themselves and deliver a verdict. In Germany the local authority agrees to follow the decision of the jury or, if it does not, to explain why (Stewart 1996: 33–34). This structure is now being tried in other places such as Britain as local councils try to shed their image of remote bureaucracies (Coote and Lenaghan 1997). The emphasis in Agenda 21 of the Rio Earth Summit on bottom-up decisions and consultation has also prompted many local authorities to look at means for increasing public involvement. The Jefferson Centre in Minneapolis has organised a number of citizens' juries on issues such as 'at-risk children', health care reform, organ transplants and agricultural impacts on water quality. They balance their jury on a number of variables including age, gender, education and race. After hearing and questioning experts over five days the group is asked to propose a solution to a set question and they can create their own answers, not just choose between those suggested by the experts. Here, those making the decision are fully informed, but it is a group drawn from the general public rather than a group of experts who make the final choice.

Fishkin's deliberative polls have some similarities to basic aspects of participatory democracy in that they stress deliberation. His ideas have been used by Channel 4 Television in Britain in 1996 and in the USA at the National Issues Convention at the start of the 1996 presidential election campaign. A random sample of people are brought together to hear evidence on and discuss specified issues. At the end of the process they are asked to fill in a questionnaire on the issues to produce an opinion poll that reflects informed rather than off-the-cuff views (Fishkin 1995). While these deliberative polls contain the crucial participatory democracy component of face-to-face discussion, the participants are not making a group decision, neither are they asked to create possible solutions to a problem. Rather the information on the views of the people who have heard the debate is used by MPs when they make decisions. Another set of ideas which aims to allow the public to assist MPs is that of a consultative assembly. For instance, rather than an elected upper house there would be a body made up of several hundred people chosen at random from the population. Each person would serve for a year and be paid to do so. Every six months, half of the members would be replaced to ensure a mix of those experienced in the system and those attuned to public views. Again this scheme would allow the views of the informed public to play a part in government decisions.

In each of these examples a small group of people are given all of the information so there is a division of labour that allows decisions to be made by the non-elected without necessitating a lot of time and effort from the whole population. However, there are another set of ideas which aim to inform everyone so that they can vote on issues. Again the electronic media is the basis for these schemes. With people connected via telecommunications networks then the size of the group and their ability to meet in one place no longer pose a problem (Budge 1996: 1). There are also implications for arguments about the level of interest and information that voters possess. If a range of electronic media is used for debate then information is more readily available for voters. In looking at the use of electronic debate it is important to assume a professional organisation to run such things. A secretariat and formal rules would be needed as they are for debates in parliament. In any form of debate oratory skills, shyness, interest and time play a part so a mediator is needed in electronic debate just as is the case for more traditional forms of discussion (Budge 1996: 27–28).

Summary

Two themes run through this book: the diversity of democratic practice; and a questioning of the extent to which the people have power over the decisions that affect their lives. The range of alternative suggestions for new methods of democratic decision making illustrates that this diversity will continue as people perceive different impediments and come up with solutions. Of particular note is that many of the new suggestions look at increasing public participation in the second part of the process, in suggesting alternative solutions. In particular, there seems to be a trend in increasing the extent to which an informed public takes part in the debate about solutions, rather than leaving this part of the process to the elected or bureaucratic experts. But, in seeking to increase debate on the alternatives, each scheme weighs other parts of the democratic processes differently. Budge seeks to increase the number of people who can gain information, debate an issue and vote but is willing to sacrifice face-to-face discussion in order to reach a large and geographically spread group through telecommunications devices. A citizens' jury is based on informed face-to-face discussion striving for a common view and sacrifices widespread involvement. Deliberative polls go for large numbers and good information with face-to-face discussion but demand much time from those involved. All want greater public involvement but demand time and interest from the people and so depend upon a politically motivated population.

In discussion of participatory democracy it was clear that for the system to work the people involved have to have a strong belief in the system (see Chapter 3) but the same is true for democracy in general. Only when people have some interest in the collective will they care about the way in which decisions are made. Calls for a restoration of civil society build on this idea that democracy is a way of behaving and a way of perceiving and not just participation in a set of procedures. As decisions move to the international arena then there is need for an international civil society before ideas of democratic input can take root (Barber 1996: 155). As discussed above, the way in which people in the group view the collective is vitally important for democracy and so changes in how people identify themselves also matter. Barber has argued that there are three big challenges for those wishing greater democracy: indigenous struggle, global capitalism, and the absence of civil society (ibid.: 144). All relate to where decisions are made and how people view the collective group.

As discussion of globalisation shows, the main worry for those wanting democratic decision making is the range of decisions where democracy is used, rather than the way in which democracy is implemented. Gamble argues that the biggest threat to autonomy and democracy is that the nation state can no longer control all within its boundaries because the global market can now be seen as the primary institution affecting national economies (Gamble 1996: 127). Bobbio suggests that, in seeking to discover the extent of democracy, the important question is not about who can participate but which types of decisions are taken democratically. He argues that democracy needs to spread from the political to the social sphere. In practice this would mean democratic decisions inside big business and service providers such as educational institutions, local groups and workplaces (Bobbio 1987: 32, 56–57). In terms of the table in Chapter 1, questions of how the people are to rule provide variants within the realms of democracy. It is the other set of questions, who are the people and which political decisions are covered by democracy, which provide a more fundamental answer on the extent to which the people have power over the decisions affecting their lives. The challenge for democracy in the twenty-first century is not so much how democracy is achieved but which decisions are taken democratically and which group of people participates. Choices of democratic procedure will follow from the composition of the group and the type of decisions that are made. No set of democratic procedures is perfect and concessions are made for practical reasons. Where democracy is totally lacking is in the growing number of decisions that are made by other means or by people who are not accountable to the elected representatives.

Glossary

Many terms used in talking of democracy and comparative politics have both wide and narrow meanings that can vary from country to country. This list explains the way in which certain terms are used here. Only terms that are used across a number of chapters are listed here as those terms used only in one chapter are explained in context.

Assembly   the body of people elected to represent the country and to pass laws; used interchangeably with legislature and parliament

Constituency   geographic unit used to organise the election of representatives; used interchangeably with electorate and district

Direct democracy   all vote for or against a set question

District   geographic unit used to organise the election of representatives; used interchangeably with constituency and electorate

Electorate   geographic unit used to organise the election of representatives; used interchangeably with constituency and district

Executive   the elected leaders plus political appointments; used interchangeably with government

Government   the elected leaders plus political appointments; used interchangeably with executive

Legislature   the body of people elected to represent the country and to pass laws; used interchangeably with parliament and assembly

Liberal democracy   a few are elected to make decisions for the group; used interchangeably with representative democracy

MP   member of parliament, used widely for any elected member of an assembly; used interchangeably with representative

Parliament   the body of people elected to represent the country and to pass laws; used interchangeably with assembly and legislature

Participatory democracy   all discuss every aspect of each decision and agree on a solution for the group

Proportional Representation   assigning MPs to parties in the same proportion as the vote they received, as distinct from the meaning in USA which refers to the ethnic composition of the elected body

Representative   elected member of a decision-making body; used interchangeably with MP

Representative democracy   a few are elected to make decisions for the group; used interchangeably with liberal democracy

Bibliography

Abramson, P. (1986) *Change and Continuity in the 1984 Elections*, Washington DC: CQ Press.

Arat, Z.F. (1991) *Democracy and Human Rights in Developing Countries*, London: Lynne Rienner Publishers.

Arblaster, A. (1987) *Democracy*, Milton Keynes: Open University Press.

Bachrach, P. and Botwinick, A. (1992) *Power and Empowerment: A radical theory of participatory democracy*, Philadelphia: Temple University Press.

Banks, A. (1972) 'Correlates of Democratic Performance', *Comparative Politics* 4: 217–30.

Banks, A. and Textor, R. (1963) *A Cross-Polity Survey*, Cambridge, MA: MIT Press.

Barber, B. (1984) *Strong Democracy*, London: University of California Press.

—— (1996) 'Three Challenges to Reinventing Democracy', in P. Hirst and S. Khilnani (eds) *Reinventing Democracy*, Oxford: Blackwell.

Beetham, D. (1993a) *The Democratic Audit of the United Kingdom*, London: Charter 88 Trust.

—— (1993b) 'Liberal Democracy and the Limits of Democratization', in D. Held, *Prospects for Democracy*, Cambridge: Polity Press.

—— (ed.) (1994) *Defining and Measuring Democracy*, London: Sage.

Berry, J.M., Portney, K.E. and Thomson, K. (1993) *The Rebirth of Urban Democracy*, Washington DC: The Brookings Institute.

Birch, A.H. (1971) *Representation*, London: Pall Mall.

Black, D. (1958) *The Theory of Committees and Elections*, Cambridge: Cambridge University Press.

Bobbio, N. (1987) *The Future of Democracy*, Cambridge: Polity Press.

Bogdanor, V. (ed.) (1985) *Representatives of the People?*, Cambridge: Gower.

—— (1994) 'Western Europe', in D. Butler and A. Ranney (eds) *Referendums Around the World*, London: Macmillan.

Bollen, K. (1979) 'Political Democracy and the Timing of Development', *American Sociological Review* 44: 572–87.

—— (1980) 'Issues in the Comparative Measurement of Political Democracy', *American Sociological Review* 45: 370–90.

Bowler, S. and Farrell, D.M. (1991) 'Voter Behaviour under STV–PR: Solving the puzzle of the Irish party system', *Political Behaviour* 13: 303–20.

Brady, H.E. and Kaplan, C.S. (1994) 'Eastern Europe and the Former Soviet Union', in D. Butler and A. Ranney (eds), *Referendums Around the World*, London: Macmillan.

Brams, S.J. and Nagel, J.H. (1991) 'Approval Voting in Practice', *Public Choice* 71: 1–17.

Budge, I. (1996) *The New Challenge of Direct Democracy*, Cambridge: Polity Press.

Butler, D. and Ranney, A. (eds) (1994) *Referendums Around the World*, London: Macmillan.

Catt, H. (1989) 'Tactical Voting in Britain', *Parliamentary Affairs* 42: 548–59.

—— (1996a) 'The Other Democratic Experiment: New Zealand's experience with citizens' initiated referendum', *Political Science* 48: 29–47.

—— (1996b) *Voting Behaviour: A radical critique*, London: Leicester University Press.

—— (1997) 'Can the Democratic Audit Detect Calls for a 'Politics of Presence'?', in G. Crowder, H. Manning, D.S. Mathieson, A. Parkin and L. Seabrooke (eds), *Australasian Political Studies 1997*, Adelaide: Department of Politics, Flinders University of South Australia.

Cook, T.E. and Morgan, P.M. (eds) (1971) *Participatory Democracy*, San Francisco: Canfield Press.

Coote, A. and Lenaghan, J. (1997) *Citizens' Juries*, London: IPPR.

Cornforth, C. (1995) 'Patterns of Cooperative Management: Beyond the degeneration thesis', *Economic and Industrial Democracy* 16: 487–523.

Cornforth, C., Thomas, A., Lewis, J. and Spear, R. (1988) *Developing Successful Worker Co-operatives*, London: Sage.

Crespi, I. (1988) *Pre-election Polling*, New York: Russell Sage Foundation.

Cronin, T.E. (1989) *Direct Democracy: The politics of initiative, referendum and recall*, London: Harvard University Press.

Curtice, J. and Steed, M. (1992) 'The Results Analysed', in D. Butler and D. Kavanagh (eds), *The British General Election of 1992*, London: Macmillan.

Cutright, P. (1963) 'National Political Development: Measurement and analysis', *American Sociological Review* 28: 253–64.

Dahl, R.A. (1956) *A Preface to Democratic Theory*, Chicago: University of Chicago Press.

—— (1971) *Polyarchy: Participation and opposition*, London: Yale University Press.

—— (1989) *Democracy and its Critics*, London: Yale University Press.

Davidson, R.H. (1994) 'Congress in Crisis . . . Once Again', in G. Peele, C.J. Bailey, B. Cain and G. Peters (eds), *Developments in American Politics 2*, London: Macmillan.

Downs, A. (1957) *An Economic Theory of Democracy*, New York: Harper Brothers.

Dunleavy, P. and Husbands, C. (1985) *British Democracy at the Crossroads*, London: Allen & Unwin.

Dunleavy, P. and Margetts, H. (1994) 'The Experiential Approach to Auditing Democracy', in D. Beetham, (ed.), *Defining and Measuring Democracy*, London: Sage.

Dunn, J. (1992) 'Conclusion', in J. Dunn (ed.), *Democracy*, Oxford: Oxford University Press.

Elklit, J. (1994) 'Is the Degree of Electoral Democracy Measurable?', in D. Beetham (ed.), *Defining and Measuring Democracy*, London: Sage.

Farrar, C. (1992) 'Ancient Greek Political Theory as a Response to Democracy', in J. Dunn (ed.), *Democracy*, Oxford: Oxford University Press.

Fenge, T. (1993) *Political Development and Environmental Management in Northern Canada*, Canberra: NARU.

Fisher, B.A. and Ellis, D.G. (1990) *Small Group Decision Making: Communication and the group process*, 3rd edn, New York: McGraw Hill.

Fishkin, J.S. (1991) *Democracy and Deliberation*, New Haven, CT: Yale University Press.

—— (1995) *The Voice of the People*, London: Yale University Press.

Flanigan, W. and Fogelman, E. (1971) 'Patterns of Political Development and Democratization: A quantitative analysis', in J. Gillespie and B. Nesvold (eds), *Macro-quantitative Analysis*, Beverly Hills: Sage.

Fontanna, B. (1992) 'Democracy and the French Revolution', in J. Dunn (ed.), *Democracy*, Oxford: Oxford University Press.

Franklin, M., Mackie, T., Valen, H. *et al.* (1992) *Electoral Change*, Cambridge: Cambridge University Press.

Freeman, J. (1973) 'The Tyranny of Structurelessness', in A. Koedt, E. Levine, and A. Rapone (eds), *Radical Feminism*, New York: Quadrangle Books.

Gallagher, M. (1991) 'Proportionality, Disproportionality and Electoral Systems', *Electoral Studies* 10: 33–51.

Gamble, A. (1996) 'The Limits of Democracy', in P. Hirst and S. Khilnani (eds), *Reinventing Democracy*, Oxford: Blackwell.

Gastil, R.D. (1985) 'The Past, Present and Future of Democracy', *Journal of International Affairs* 38: 161–79.

—— (ed.) (1994) *Freedom in the World*, New York: Freedom House.

Goodwin-Gill, G.S. (1994) *Free and Fair Elections: International law and practice*, Geneva: Inter-Parliamentary Union.

Grofman, B. and Davidson, C. (eds) (1992) *Controversies in Minority Voting*, Washington DC: The Brookings Institute.

Grofman, B. and Lijphart, A. (eds) (1986) *Electoral Laws and their Political Consequences*, New York: Agathon Press.

Harrison, R. (1993) *Democracy*, London: Routledge.

Hauss, C. (1994) *Comparative Politics*, New York: West Publishing Company.

Heath, A., Jowell, R., and Curtice, J. (1985) *How Britain Votes*, London: Pergamon Press.

Held, D. (1987) *Models of Democracy*, Cambridge: Polity Press.

—— (ed.) (1993) *Prospects for Democracy*, Cambridge: Polity Press.

—— (1996) *Models of Democracy* 2nd edn, Cambridge: Polity Press.

Himmelweit, H.T., Humphreys, P., and Jaeger, M. (1981) *How Voters Decide*, Milton Keynes: Open University Press.

Hirst, P. (1994) *Associative Democracy*, Cambridge: Polity Press.

—— (1996) 'Democracy and Civil Society', in P. Hirst and S. Khilnani (eds), *Reinventing Democracy*, Oxford: Blackwell.

Holmstrom, M. (1989) *Industrial Democracy in Italy*, Aldershot: Avebury.

Howlett, M. and Ramesh, M. (1995) *Studying Public Policy*, New York: Oxford University Press.

Hughes, C. (1994) 'Australia and New Zealand', in D. Butler and A. Ranney (eds), *Referendums Around the World*, London: Macmillan.

Inglehart, R. (1990) *Culture Shift in Advanced Industrial Society*, Princeton, NJ: Princeton University Press.

Jackman, R. (1974) 'Political Democracy and Social Equality: A comparative analysis', *American Sociological Review* 39: 29–45.

Kitschelt, H. (1997) 'European Party Systems', in M. Rhodes, P. Heywood, and V. Wright (eds), *Developments in West European Politics*, London: Macmillan.

Kobach, K. (1993) *The Referendum: Direct democracy in Switzerland*, Aldershot: Dartmouth.

—— (1994) 'Switzerland', in D. Butler and A. Ranney (eds), *Referendums Around the World*, London: Macmillan.

Koedt, A., Levine, E., and Rapone, A. (eds) (1973) *Radical Feminism*, New York: Quadrangle Books.

Landry, C., Morley, D., Southwood, R. and Wright, P. (1985) *What a Way to Run a Railroad*, London: Comedia Publishing Group.

Lazarsfeld, P.F., Berelson, B. and Gaudet, H. (1948) *The People's Choice*, 2nd edn, New York: Columbia University Press.

Lenski, G.E. (1966) *Power and Privilege: A theory of social stratification*, New York: McGraw-Hill.

Lijphart, A. (1984) *Democracies: Patterns of majoritarian and consensus government in twenty-one countries*, London: Yale University Press.

—— (1994) *Electoral Systems and Party Systems: A study of twenty-seven democracies, 1945–1990*, Oxford: Oxford University Press.

Linder, W. (1994) *Swiss Democracy: Possible solutions to conflict in multicultural societies*, New York: St Martin's Press.

Lipset, S.M. (1960) *Political Man*, London: Heinemann Educational.

Lipset, S.M. and Rokkan, S. (1967) 'Cleavage Structures, Party Systems and Voter Alignments', in S.M. Lipset and S. Rokkan (eds), *Party Systems and Voter Alignments: Cross-national perspectives*, New York: Free Press.

Lively, J. (1975) *Democracy*, Oxford: Basil Blackwell.

Lively, J. and Lively, A. (eds) (1994) *Democracy in Britain: A reader*, Oxford: Blackwell.

Magelby, D. (1994) 'Direct Legislation in the American States', in D. Butler and A. Ranney (eds), *Referendums Around the World*, London: Macmillan.

Manning, M. (1978) 'Ireland', in D. Butler and A. Ranney (eds), *Referendums*, Washington: American Enterprise Institute.

Mansbridge, J. (1980) *Beyond Adversary Democracy*, New York: Basic Books.

Mason, R. (1982) *Participatory and Workplace Democracy*, Carbondale: Southern Illinois University Press.

May, J.D. (1978) 'Defining Democracy', *Political Studies* 26: 1–14.

McKenzie, P.T. and Silver, A. (1968) *Angels in Marble*, London: Heinmann Educational.

McLean, I. (1987) *Public Choice*, Oxford: Blackwell.

—— (1989) *Democracy and New Technology*, London: Polity Press.

McLean, I. and Butler, D. (eds) (1996) *Fixing the Boundaries: Defining and redefining single-member electoral districts*, Aldershot: Dartmouth.

Mendus, S. (1992) 'Losing the Faith: Feminism and democracy', in J. Dunn (ed.), *Democracy*, Oxford: Oxford University Press.

Merrill, S. (1988) *Making Multicandidate Elections More Democratic*, Princeton, NJ: Princeton University Press.

Mill, J.S. (1859) *Thoughts on Parliamentary Reform*, London: J.W. Parker and Son.

Miller, D. (ed.) (1991) *Liberty*, Oxford: Oxford University Press.

Morgan, R. (ed.) (1970) *Sisterhood is Powerful*, New York: Random House.

Morgen, S. (1994) 'Personalizing Personnel Decisions in Feminist Organizational Theory and Practice', *Human Relations* 47: 665–84.

Muller, E. (1988) 'Democracy, Economic Development and Inequality', *American Sociological Review* 53: 50–68.

Neubauer, D. (1967) 'Some Conditions of Democracy', *The American Political Science Review* 61: 1002–09.

Nie, N.H., Verba, S. and Petrocik, J. (1976) *The Changing American Voter*, Cambridge, MA: Harvard University Press.

Nordlinger, E.A. (1967) *The Working Class Tories*, London: MacGibbon and Kee.

Norris, P. (ed.) (1997) *Passages to Power*, Cambridge: Cambridge University Press.

Olsen, M. (1968) 'Multivariate Analysis of National Political Development', *American Sociological Review* 33: 699–712.

Oppenhuis, E. (1995) *Voting Behaviour in Europe*, Amsterdam: Het Spinhuis.

Pateman, C. (1970) *Participation and Democratic Theory*, Cambridge: Cambridge University Press.

Peterson, P.E. (ed.) (1995) *Classifying by Race*, Princeton, NJ: Princeton University Press.

Phillips, A. (1995) *The Politics of Presence*, Oxford: Clarendon Press.

Pitkin, H.F. (1967) *The Concept of Representation*, Los Angeles: University of California Press.

Putnam, R. (1994) *Making Democracy Work*, Princeton, NJ: Princeton University Press.

Riger, S. (1994) 'Challenges of Success: Stages of growth in feminist organizations', *Feminist Studies* 20: 275–300.

Rinehart, S.T. (1992) *Gender Consciousness and Politics*, London: Routledge.

Rose, R. (1974) *The Problem of Party government*, London: Macmillan.

Rose, R. and McAllister, I. (1990) *The Loyalties of Voters*, London: Sage.

Rothschild, J. and Whitt, A. (1986) *The Cooperative Workplace: Potentials and dilemmas of organizational democracy and participation*, Cambridge: Cambridge University Press.

Rothschild-Whyte, J. (1979) 'The Collectivist Organisation', *American Sociological Review* 44: 509–27.

Royal Commission on the Electoral System (1986) *Towards a Better Democracy*, Wellington: NZ Government Publications.

Rule, W. and Zimmerman, J.F. (eds) (1994) *Electoral Systems in Comparative Perspective: Their impact on women and minorities*, London: Greenwood Press.

Russett, B.M., Deutsch, K.W. and Lasswell, H.D. (1964) *World Handbook of Political and Social Indicators*, New Haven, CT: Yale University Press.

Sarlvik, B. and Crewe, I. (1983) *Decade of Dealignment*, London: Cambridge University Press.

Scarbrough, E. (1984) *Political Ideology and Voting*, Oxford: Clarendon Press.

Schmidt, D.D. (1989) *Citizen Lawmakers: The ballot initiative revolution*, Philadelphia: Temple University Press.

Slaton, C.D. (1992) *Televote: Expanding citizen participation in the quantum age*, New York: Praeger.

Smith, A. (1969) 'Socio-Economic Development and Political Democracy: A causal analysis', *Midwest Journal of Political Science* 30: 95–125.

Stewart, J. (1996) 'Innovation in Democratic Practice in Local government', *Policy and Politics* 24: 29–41.

Taylor, C. (1994) 'The Politics of Recognition', in A. Gutmann (ed.), *Multiculturalism*, Princeton, NJ: Princeton University Press.

Taylor, C.L. and Jodice, D.A. (1983) *World Handbook of Political and Social Indicators*, 3rd edn, New Haven, CT: Yale University Press.

Tocqueville, A.D. (1948) *Democracy in America*, New York: Alfred A Knopp.

United Nations (UN) (1992) 'Rio Declaration on Environment and Development'.

Vanhanen, T. (1997) *Prospects of Democracy: A study of 172 countries*, London: Routledge.

Weir, S. (1994) 'Primary Control and Auxiliary Precautions', in D. Beetham (ed.), *Defining and Measuring Democracy*, London: Sage.

—— (1996) 'From Strong Government and Quasi-Government to Strong Democracy', in P. Hirst and S. Khilnani (eds), *Reinventing Democracy*, Oxford: Blackwell.

Welch, S. (1990) 'The Impact of At-Large Elections on the Representation of Blacks and Hispanics', *Journal of Politics* 52: 1050–76.

Whyte, W.F. (1995) 'Learning from the Mondragon Cooperative Experience', *Studies in Comparative International Development* 30: 58–67.

Whyte, W.F. and Whyte, K.K. (1991) *Making Mondragon*, Ithaca: ILR Press.

Wood, G.S. (1992) 'Democracy and the American Revolution', in J. Dunn (ed.), *Democracy*, Oxford: Oxford University Press.

Wootton, D. (1992) 'The Levellers', in J. Dunn (ed.), *Democracy*, Oxford: Oxford University Press.

Wright, T. (1996) 'Reinventing Democracy?', in P. Hirst and S. Khilnani (eds), *Reinventing Democracy*, Oxford: Blackwell.

Zimmerman, J.F. (1986) *Participatory Democracy: Populism revisited*, New York: Praeger.

Zuckerman, M. (1970) *Peaceable Kingdoms: New England towns in the eighteenth century*, New York: Alfred A. Knopf.

Internet sources

There are a number of useful sources on the world wide web giving details of democracy in practice. The main organisations with a website are listed below, with the address as of 1998. However, web addresses do change, in which case the easiest way to find the information is to search for the organisation. Many of these sites also have links to each other and to a range of other sites relevant to aspects of democracy in practice.

Participatory democracy

ICA – International Co-operatives Alliance – **http://www.coop.org/**
Information on workers' co-operatives and many links to related sites.

Hyde Park Co-operative – **http://www.igc.apc.org/hpcoop/**
A working co-operative that runs several shops. Contains information on how they operate and links to other sites.

Ontario Green Party – **http://www.greenparty.on.ca**
Details on how the Green Party uses participatory democracy.

Mondragon – **http://www.mondragon.mcc.es/menuing.html**
Full information on the Mondragon co-operatives.

http://www.coop.org/en/int_orgs.html
A list of international organisations on the web, with a co-operative leaning.

Direct democracy

Centre on Direct Democracy – **http://c2d.unige.ch/c2d/about/index_e.html**
Has details of all referenda – in French in 1998.

Organisations involved in electronic democracy and other innovative projects

IPPR – Institute for Public Policy Research – **http://www.ippr.org.uk/**
British organisation involved in citizens' juries.

Teledemocracy Action News + Network – **http://www.auburn.edu/tann/**
Based in the USA – the web site of the Global Democracy Movement.

Charter88 – **http://www.charter88.org.uk/home.html**
British organisation pushing for greater democracy, holds information on Democratic Audit.

http://www.igc.apc.org/habitat/agenda21/index.html
Has the full text of the Rio Declaration on Environment and Development from the 1992 United Nations Conference on Environment and Development.

Information on national elections

IPU – Inter-Parliamentary Union – **http://www.ipu.org/**
Collects details of national elections and has policy on the conduct of elections, the role of MPs etc. Has directory of national government web sites.

IDEA – International Institute for Democracy and Electoral Assistance **http://www.int-idea.se/**
Has links to many other sites plus its own work on furthering democratic elections around the world.

Elections around the world – **http://www.agora.stm.it/elections/election.htm**
Has information on all elections for President and legislature.

BBC, CNN and major newspapers in each country also have web pages and usually provide details on elections and referenda.

Index